HUMAN SEXUALITY

Contemporary Controversies

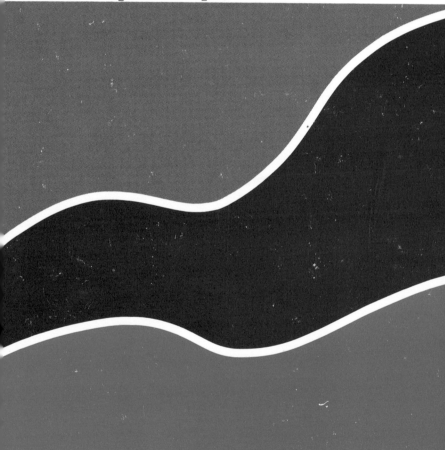

Edited by Harold Feldman
and Andrea Parrot

HUMAN SEXUALITY

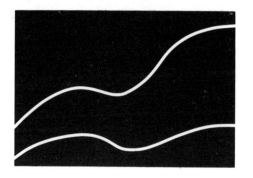

HUMAN SEXUALITY

Contemporary Controversies

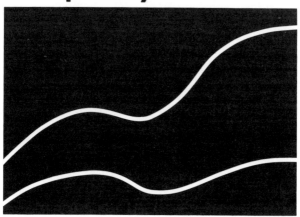

Edited by
Harold Feldman
and Andrea Parrot

SAGE PUBLICATIONS
Beverly Hills / London / New Delhi

Copyright © 1984 by Sage Publications, Inc.

For information address:

SAGE Publications, Inc.
275 South Beverly Drive
Beverly Hills, California 90212

SAGE Publications India Pvt. Ltd.
C-236 Defence Colony
New Delhi 110 024, India

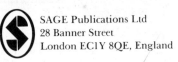

SAGE Publications Ltd
28 Banner Street
London EC1Y 8QE, England

Printed in the United States of America

Library of Congress Cataloging in Publication Data

Main entry under title:

Human sexuality.

    1. Sex--Addresses, essays, lectures. I. Feldman, Harold. II. Parrot, Andrea.
HQ21.H7385   1984   306.7   83-23072
ISBN 0-8039-2071-7
ISBN 0-8039-2072-5 (pbk.)

FIRST PRINTING

Contents

HUMAN SEXUALITY

TO OUR READERS

This book presents opposing arguments about a number of sensitive and hotly debated issues in the field of human sexuality. We deliberately chose this debate-like format because we believe that educated people are able to recognize some validity in other people's viewpoints. We think that it is possible, and preferable, to learn by studying contending ideas — not necessarily accepting them, but being open to them.

Much of what we call education (not only in the area of human sexuality) comes to us with value judgments deeply embedded in the "facts," and these value preferences are seldom questioned by either teachers or their students. We hope that this book will help you to examine ideas that are different from those you already hold, so that your intellectual journey through these pages will be an unusually profitable one. You may or may not be someone who is classified as a student, but this book is for people who want to be learners.

The issues covered here are divided, somewhat arbitrarily, under four headings: relationships, individual choices, social policies, and politics and legislation. Of course, some topics, such as birth control, may have important implications for social policy and relationships as well as for individual choice. We encourage you to keep this in mind and to look at the same issue from as many different perspectives as possible. We hope that the book will be useful to you if you are engaged or thinking about becoming engaged in sexual experiences; and we also hope that it will increase your awareness of the legal and policymaking issues involved in what was once the arena of personal, familial, or religious decision.

You will surely note that the contributing authors use widely different standards of evidence, authorities, and writing styles to make their points in the following pages. This, too, reflects a deliberate decision by the editors not to impose a common style throughout the book. We thought it would be more honest and much more interesting for you if we let the authors "speak" in the ways they find most compatible. Such questions as comparative

validity, and the possible connection between style and message, are ones we leave open for your own debate and decision-making.
   Bon voyage.

Ithaca, New York   —Harold Feldman
                                                    and Andrea Parrot

Relationships

This section deals with two issues — sex roles and modes of sexual expression. The first topic is a central issue in human sexuality — whether the persons involved in sexual relationships will follow traditional patterns of male-female behavior or adopt nontraditional sex roles. The second issue deals with the relationship itself. Will it be a conventional one or will it differ from what is socially expected? Is homosexuality or bisexuality more biologically natural than heterosexuality? The authors take clear and quite different positions on these issues, and the need for an open mind by advocates of both sides of these issues is important.

SEX ROLES AND SEXUALITY

I–A

Traditional Sex Roles Result in Healthier Sexual Relationships and Healthier, More Stable Family Life

W. PETER BLITCHINGTON

Sex roles, like other social patterns, have undergone apparently dramatic changes in the last few years. For most of human history, from what we can tell, our sexual roles have been somewhat rigid, sharply demarcated dichotomies of predictable masculine and feminine behavior. Men provided, explored, led, and dominated; women cared for the children, nurtured, stayed at home, and followed.

But today these distinctions seem to be on their way out. The current opinion seems to be that these patterns may have made sense at one time — based as they were upon the woman's capacity for childbearing — but were arbitrary to begin with. And in a modern, industrialized society, requiring flexible adaptations to rapidly changing circumstances, they are downright harmful. As a result, the new ideology of sexual equality predicts that we are now halfway through a journey that will ultimately carry us to a state of

12

unisexual roles and non-sex-typed behaviors. The only things that stand in our way today are outmoded laws and atavistic socialization patterns.

This journey toward sexual equality has been facilitated by three events. The first was a shift from a home-based system of production to an industrialized economy based upon factories and out-of-home manufacturing organizations. This change stripped the home of its production functions and carried husbands away from the family. But increasingly, with the inflationary world economy and the skyrocketing divorce rate, wives have also been thrust into the marketplace. As a result, the change in the economy has propelled married women toward the traditionally masculine function of providing for the family.

The second event was the breakdown in the family system, and especially the marital bond. As the divorce rate has climbed, increasing numbers of women have found themselves in the provider role; and not a few men have taken over traditionally female tasks. The traditional pattern of complementary contributions of husband and wife has been upset and the burden to fulfill both roles — and hence to adopt both sets of attributes, masculine and feminine — has fallen on women first and foremost.

The third and most recent event is a new ideology asserting that the movement toward sexual equality is psychologically advantageous. For years psychology followed the model proposed by Erik Erikson — that healthy adjustment results in part from a clear masculine or feminine identity. The goal was to acquire only those attributes associated with one's own sex.

But the new model of "androgyny" proposes that the healthiest personalities are those that possess a high degree of both masculine and feminine attributes. Proponents of androgyny assert that fully functioning men and women will possess *both* the masculine attributes of aggressiveness, initiative, and independence, *and* the feminine traits of caring, nurturance, and gentleness.

These three changes in our patterns of living and thinking have brought about changes in our sex roles. The rigid patterns of the past no longer suffice in the present. Today we need outlets for female energy and opportunities for women to develop their nondomestic talents. The divorce rate, the economy, and the declining number of births signal quite loudly the need for new arrangements.

It would be quite tempting, in the face of these changes, to advocate that we simply throw out the old roles and adopt a completely new pattern as our standard. But this would be a serious mistake. Evidence abounds that even with the changes in society mentioned above, the traditional pattern of sex roles is still our most reliable guide in the future. Indeed, it is our only tried and tested guide.

TRADITIONAL SEX ROLES

In an article designed to affirm the importance of the traditional sex roles, the first question that should be answered is "What are 'traditional sex roles'?" As used in this article, the traditional sex roles are defined as follows:

For men, the most important sex roles are

(1) *to assume major responsibility for providing for the family*;
(2) *to stimulate the children's development*: A wealth of studies have found that men contribute enormously to their children's development. Children without fathers in the home with whom they have a close relationship suffer in the areas of academics, work, emotional development, marriage, and family living (Lamb, 1976);
(3) *to provide effective leadership and authority in the home.*

For women the most important sexual roles are

(1) *to give a home its attractiveness*: In other words, women assume major responsibility for the running of the home and make the home attractive by linking their personalities and feminine natures to the home itself;
(2) *to assume major responsibility for the caretaking of children*;
(3) *To provide an atmosphere of love and support in which children can grow up with a sense of security and belonging.*

There are several outgrowths to the definition of traditional sex roles that I have offered above. One is that these definitions do not preclude one sex from taking over some of the functions that are most closely associated with the opposite sex. For example, the fact that husbands assume *major* responsibility for providing does not mean that wives should contribute nothing. But providing becomes a major role for the husband and a secondary role for the wife. (Of course, the situation changes quite a bit if the wife is the only parent in the home.) Another aspect of these definitions is that they do not dictate the specifics of how husbands and wives divide up the labor (e.g., who takes out the garbage, who mows the lawn). These questions are best left up to individual couples to work out in the general framework that the definition provides.

Neither does this position close its mind to the multitude of special circumstances that today's industrial society is creating. For example, the high divorce rate leaves many parents without partners. Those parents must then assume both sets of sex roles themselves. Also, quite a few couples are not deciding not to have children, and thus some of these different roles will not apply to them. (However, they will still operate best according to a division of labor by traditional sex roles, as I will demonstrate later.)

Finally, it should be emphasized that the traditional sex role framework is meant to be used as a guide, not as commandments that must be obeyed to the letter of the law.

With those qualifications, the next issue to cover is the question, "Do the traditional sex roles result in healthier sexual relationships and a healthier, more stable family life?" And the answer, from a variety of research findings, is a resounding "Yes!"

EVIDENCE THAT TRADITIONAL SEX ROLES WORK BEST

While special circumstances can always be identified where departures from traditional sex roles seem to benefit some couples, there can be no doubt that in general sex roles yield greater benefit to the family and to the individuals that make up the family unit. Social psychologist Carin Rubenstein (1982) recently reviewed some of the studies that investigated departures from the traditional sex roles. The following studies are taken from Dr. Rubenstein's review.

One departure from traditional sex roles would arise when women outearn their husbands. This situation places the *major* responsibility for providing on the woman's back. What happens in homes where the wife has the major responsibility for providing? According to Dr. Rubenstein's review, "evidence is emerging that this situation can be disastrous for marriages, and especially debilitating for men" (page 37). For example, studies show that when wives outearn their husbands, their sex lives suffer and their feelings of love diminish. The divorce rate increases; and the husbands *die prematurely from heart disease 11 times more often* than do husbands who outearn their wives.

Another study, carried out by sociologists William Philliber and Dana Hiller looked at wives who were in "traditional" occupations (teaching, nursing, secretarial) versus wives in nontraditional occupations (management, law, construction). The authors found that the rate of divorce for women in the nontraditional jobs was twice as high as those who held traditional jobs. This was true even when the husbands also held traditionally masculine jobs. Also, in these marriages where wives held nontraditional jobs, there was a much greater incidence of both physical and psychological abuse of the partner by *both* spouses.

The stunning results of these studies led Dr. Rubenstein and others to reevaluate the finding of a survey on attitudes about money reported in *Psychology Today* in December, 1980. They looked again at previous respondents who had reported that the wife outearned the husband with special attention to the effects this pattern had upon their love relationships. About one-third of the husbands who earned less than their wives said that their wives loved them less then they loved their wives (compared with only 15 percent of those who earned more). These men also reported that their sex lives were in jeopardy, that they had not had sexual relations at all for several months before filling out the survey, and that they were less happy with their marriages and less satisfied with their friends and family. They also had lower self-esteem than other husbands. Likewise, the wives who earned more than their husbands also felt that they didn't love their husbands as much as their husbands loved them. They reported unsatisfying sexual relationships, rampant arguments about money, and greater dissatisfaction with their mates than did wives whose husbands had the larger salary.

These studies would seem to verify the statement that homes operate best when the male sex role as primary and leader is fulfilled. What about the reverse? What about homes in which husbands and wives share the homemaking and child-care duties equally? The nontraditional view would be that those families would produce high satisfaction, at least among wives.

But investigations have revealed that these nontraditional homes create greater dissatisfaction among *both* husbands and wives. For example, Barbara Forisha (1978), a psychologist at the University of Michigan, reviewed the research on traditional versus egalitarian sex roles (Forisha, 1976). She concluded that the egalitarian family exists mainly in the minds of family sociologists and not in reality. One problem is that "there is substantial evidence that young egalitarian marriages become much more traditional in time. Couples who share the management of finances and household responsibility in their first years of marriage slowly slip into traditional sex-typed divisions of labor after five years of marriage. Joint decision-making policies often become male-denominated policies, and married women begin to define their husband's role as the 'breadwinner' and their own role as the 'mother and homemaker'" (p. 131). As a sidelight to that, in these homes where couples set out by equally dividing up responsibilities in a nontraditional manner, *the wives were actually the first to become dissatisfied with that arrangement* and to resist their husbands' efforts to take over responsibilities in the kitchen and in the home.

So, according to these studies, there can be little doubt that the traditional pattern produces the greatest amount of satisfaction within the home. However, the controversy is not so much over this fact as it is over the relative contribution of biology and environment to these sex role differences. If sex roles can be demonstrated to result from biological factors, then the traditional sex roles become inevitable.

EVIDENCE THAT BIOLOGY CREATES SEX ROLES

The idea that biological factors are strongly involved in sex differences now seems to be true beyond all reasonable doubt. A variety of studies combine to indicate that the traditional sex roles are based at least in part on biological differences between the sexes.

One evidence that biology creates sex role differences comes from anthropological and sociological studies. Sociologist Steven

Goldberg (1973), for example, reviewed a mass of studies on sex roles in other cultures. He found that in every society that has ever been studied, either directly or indirectly, males hold most of the leadership positions in the society and are seen as the primary leaders in the homes. And apparently women have had major responsibility for the children and the running of the home in all societies (though this statement is open to more controversy than the former). This is true even in cultures that have deliberately used the power of government to try to enforce equality of sexual roles.

Every now and then a culture turns up that is supposed to provide evidence against biological contributions to sex roles. But upon closer examination, these cultures generally follow the same pattern of sex role behaviors that all other cultures show.

Margaret Mead's report on three New Guinea cultures is probably the most often cited example of sex role reversals in other cultures. Mead (1949) found three cultural groups whose sex role patterns differed from the traditional. Arapesh men preferred to stay close to their wives in the home. Both husband and wife seemed to like the traditional female sex role. Mundugamor men and women were both aggressive and warlike. They apparently preferred the male role. And the Tchambuli appeared to have a true role reversal. The women were dominant and warlike, the men effeminate.

These three cultures show up often in the literature supporting environmental causes of sex differences. But in actuality they support the opposite view. In all three cultures the men were the leaders and the women took care of the children. Proponents of sexual equality usually overlook Margaret Mead's (1937) own assessment of the meaning of these three cultures: "Nowhere do I suggest that I have found any material which disproves the existence of sex differences" (p. 559). In fact, as George Gilder (1973) points out, if there is any lesson these three cultures teach us, it is that even minor departures from traditional sex roles create havoc for societies. All three of these cultures were rapidly approaching extinction; and their sex role patterns seemed to be contributing to their demise.

If the anthropological investigations are only suggestive, research from psychophysiology seems conclusive. Studies are rapidly accruing to suggest that the brains of males and females are constructed differently. A wealth of experimentation with mammals has already demonstrated that the male central nervous system is molded into the 'masculine' pattern by the presence of testosterone during the critical period of brain development (Hutt, 1973). While the research with animals was quite conclusive, until a few years ago nothing had been done with humans that could verify this process of sexual differentiation of the central nervous system.

However, beginning with John Money's studies of masculinized females in the 1960s, several studies have been done which extend the findings with animals to humans. The research indicates that pregnant females who are exposed to male hormones will produce female offspring who are more aggressive and assertive than females who are not exposed to male hormones in utero. Psychologists Anke Erhard and Susan Baker (1974), for example, studied mothers who had taken the drug progestin. These mothers had a tendency to miscarry, and progestin was commonly prescribed to combat the tendency to lose the unborn. Unfortunately, progestin contains a testosterone derivative; and these mothers generally continued to take it for the first trimester after conception, thus exposing their offspring to abnormal amounts of testosterone. Drs. Baker and Erhard observed the female offspring of these women who had taken progestin. Although they had been socialized into the traditional female role, these girls were more assertive, dominant, and aggressive than other females. They preferred to play with boys, they preferred boys' toys to girls' toys, they eschewed the traditional female role and preferred careers to marriage. Although physically they were normal females, psychologically and behaviorally they were more like males.

This research has now been verified in three separate studies and, when combined with the anthropological and animal research, indicates that biological factors have a strong influence on the acquisition of sex roles. Other studies in different areas are also verifying biological contributions. The role that the hormone oxytocin plays in maternal behaviors and attitudes and the newer research showing innate sexual differences in the cerebral cortex have implications for sex role patterns.

Of course, it would be inaccurate to conclude that masculinity and femininity distribute themselves into rigid dichotomies. Some overlap between the sexes exists in all attributes. But the differences are strong enough to create reliable and predictable generalizations across cultures. And these generalizations form the basis of traditional sexual roles. They allow us to use our energy in the most efficient and satisfying manner. To fight against the traditional sex roles is to waste our energy for it is to fight against our own natures.

CURRENT TRENDS: THE ERA

The 1970s have been called the decade of the woman. It was a time when traditional sex roles were vehemently rejected and a new era of sexual equality was supposed to be on the horizon. The focal point of the new sexual equality was the Equal Rights Amendment (ERA). This proposed amendment was designed in part to legalize the new ideology of sexual equality and in part to eliminate unfair sex discrimination.

The ERA produced a cascade of vehement accusations and counter-accusations. Many of the supposed results of the ERA have been ridiculed, but one result is fairly well accepted among legal scholars: The Equal Rights Amendment, had it been passed, would have forced the government to draft women alongside men and to place women in combat positions on a par with men. More than any other factor, this contributed to the downfall of the ERA — and it's a good thing because other countries that have drafted women and used them in combat roles have quickly had to abandon the process. Israel tried it in 1948; but that country and others have found that using female soldiers is very inefficient. It actually causes the enemy soldiers to fight harder because they know that if there are women on the front lines who they can take as prisoners, they will have a source of sexual gratification. And obviously it would expose multitudes of women to sexual abuse. (Consider the abuse that American POW's in Vietnam were subjected to and the effects it had on their self-esteem. Think what it would have been like had they been women: On top of all the other mistreatment, sexual abuse would have been likely.)

But aside from the military issue, the ERA would not have solved the problems its proponents were aiming at. The issue of wage discrimination, for example, often emerged in debates over the ERA. The cry "59 cents for a dollar" indicated that on the average women earn 59 cents for every dollar that men earn. But that statement overlooked the fact that only when all male and female workers are lumped together with no consideration of training and experience differences do females earn that much less than men. Part of this sex difference in wages can be attributed to differences in educational background and type of work.

However, when education and training are equalized, sex differences in earning still remain. But how much of this difference can be attributed to unfair discrimination? Research designed to answer this question indicates that very little of the economic difference can be attributed to sex discrimination (Gilder, 1973). It is more likely that men earn more because they put more energy into their work. Innate sex differences in aggressiveness, initiative, and motivation account for at least some of the wage differences. The ERA and other such legislation will not alter these innate differences. The more likely result would be to give the government tremendous control over our lives. The government finds sex differences in wages so it steps in to eliminate those differences. But the wage differences won't disappear (based as they are on innate differences) so the government steps in again to assert even stronger control, and so on. This process could go on until the government becomes oppressively powerful.

But suppose the wage differences could be successfully eliminated. Would it be desirable? Not from the standpoint of our family and sexual relationships, if the research cited earlier in the chapter is accurate. The number of families in which females are the main providers would increase drastically, and along with it all the problems described earlier would also increase — male heart attacks, divorces, sexual incompatibility, spouse abuse, and marital dissatisfaction.

CONCLUSION

At the beginning of this chapter, I described three trends that have contributed to the idea that the traditional concepts of sex roles are outmoded. Those trends can now be reevaluated in the context of the evidence favoring the traditional sex roles.

Industrialization and an inflationary economy have precipitated changes in our sexual roles — at work and at home. It's difficult to assess to what extent these changes are the result of industrialization by itself or of changes in the family system (such as the skyrocketing divorce rate) that have accompanied industrialization. But the removal of productive work from the home has made it much more difficult for many women to find a satisfying balance between family and work.

But if the success and attractiveness of the home depend so much upon the woman's presence in it, then passively giving in to the new trends won't do anything to improve our family life or marital relationships. We must preserve as much of the traditional pattern as possible.

Of course, this is easier said than done. But some encouraging trends are already in operation. The new computer technology is opening up a variety of jobs that can be performed in the home. Some women are opting to do bookkeeping and secretarial work in their own homes, enabling them to devote more time to their families while they work. This is encouraging, but we could do more. Study after study has shown that married women with children prefer part-time to full-time work (Stinnett and Walters, 1977). We could push for industries to open up more part-time jobs. These innovations would make it easier for women to satisfy both family and work needs. But they are likely to occur only within the framework of a philosophy that recognizes the uniquely important contribution that women make to the home (i.e., the traditional sex roles philosophy).

These changes would be difficult to implement within the framework created by the new philosophy of androgyny. Proponents of androgyny generally value an equal sharing rather than a division of roles. But as I discussed earlier, an equal sharing of roles is impossible given the biological differences between the sexes and the rewards in terms of health, sexual enjoyment, and marital satisfaction that the traditional roles provide husbands and wives.

Further, the entire concept of androgyny is so fraught with inconsistencies that it seems a poor foundation upon which to build a philosophy of sex roles. For example, when Bem (1974) constructed the first inventory to measure androgyny, she decided to use only the positive qualities usually associated with masculinity or femininity. The androgynous individual, defined as someone who possesses a high degree of positive masculine and feminine traits, was supposed to be better adjusted than the "masculine" or "feminine" individual. If androgynous individuals do have higher self-esteem, then we can conclude that the more positive qualities you have, the better off you are. Hardly a new or profound conclusion.

Other problems have shown up in the research on androgyny, as Heilbrun's (1981) review makes clear. For example, males turn out to be much more androgynous than females. But if androgyny has something to do with sex role training, then the reverse should be true. The research has shown that males are given the more rigid sex role training (i.e., not allowed to engage in feminine behaviors) while females are generally not as often restricted to feminine sex role activities. Also, some of the research has led to confusing observations. Why it is, for example, that rapists turn out to be highly androgynous?

It would be a shame if advocates of traditional sex roles seemed to be saying that males and females are to develop only one side of their natures. Education, the world of work, children, and family life should be a part of both sexes' self-definition. We need the flexibility to adjust to changing circumstances.

But we also need some guidelines. The traditional roles provide us with the best standards to follow as we attempt to adjust to the changes in our society. It would be a tragedy to throw out the guidelines that have been shown to work in favor of a new ideology that is untested and riddled with inconsistencies. The traditional sex roles are the only patterns that are consistent with our biological heritage. No ideology can override the fact of our natures.

REFERENCES

BEM, S. (1974) "The measurement of psychological androgyny." Journal of Clinical and Consulting Psychology 42: 155–162.

EHRHARDT, A. and S. BAKER (1974) "Fetal androgens, human control nervous system differentiation, and behavior sex differences," in R.C. Freidman et al. (eds.) Sex Differences in Behavior. New York: John Wiley.

FORISHA, B.L. (1978) Sex Roles and Personal Awareness. New Jersey: Scott, Foresman.

GILDER, G. (1973) Sexual Suicide. New York: Quadrangle.

GOLDBERG, S. (1973) The Inevitability of Patriarchy. New York: William Morrow.

HEILBRUN, A.B. (1981) Human Sex-Role Behavior. New York: Pergamon.

HUTT, C. (1973) Males and Females. New York: Viking.

LAMB, M. (1976) The Role of the Father in Child Development. New York: John Wiley.

MEAD, M. (1975) Male and Female (1949). New York: William Morrow.

——— (1937) Letter. The American Anthropologist 39: 558–561.

RUBINSTEIN, C. (1982) "Real Men Don't Earn Less than their Wives." Psychology Today 16: 36–41

STINNETT, N. and J. WALTERS (1977) Relationships in Marriage and Family. New York: Macmillan.

Nontraditional Roles of Men and Women Strengthen the Family and Provide Healthier Sexual Relationships

JUDY LONG

Sex roles — a culture's images of attitudes, behaviors, and feelings felt to be appropriate to females and to males — operate in hundreds of interrelated ways to affect the way adult women and men live their lives in families. The effects of sex roles are neither elusive and "subtle" nor "merely symbolic." They permeate virtually all areas of life, from infancy throughout the life-span. Sex role scripts prescribe "sex-appropriate" dress and bodily posture as well as emotional reactions, occupational choices as well as marital choices, and a myriad of expectations regarding who gets the check in a restaurant and who gets the responsibility for the care of elderly parents. The expectations and the repertoire of sex-typed behaviors are taught and internalized by processes of sex role socialization. Its effects are the more powerful because most individuals remain unaware that our images of masculinity and femininity — including our own masculinity and femininity — are part of the culture and not, initially, part of the person. It is possible to analyze sex roles, processes of sex role socialization, and the process of social control that are linked with sex role conformity. Indeed, the past decade has seen the development of theory and research on this issue. New information thus gained permits the individual to reevaluate the elements of the sex role script and make conscious choices about her or his life-cycle. At present, however, the analysis and reevaluation of sex roles is not widespread.

In the absence of a reevaluation process, internalized sex role scripts guide decisions, reactions, and aspirations automatically, without a high degree of conscious awareness on the part of the individual. Although the later decades of the life-span are less completely scripted than the adolescent and early adult years, an individual can pass through many of the major life transitions on "automatic pilot," following what is typical and approved for his or her gender.

Traditional ideas about sex roles do not affect our lives only at the level of individual psychology. In addition to possessing internalized predispositions to behave and think in "sex-appropriate" ways, individuals are subject to social pressures to follow sex role scripts. Not only social expectations but also social sanctions — approval and success or ridicule and rejection — are organized along the lines of traditional sex role scripts. Finally, there are many institutional arrangements in society — structures a society has set up in order to conduct its business — that incorporate the society's images of what is appropriate to women and to men. Some societies provide public toilets on the street for men, but none for women. In other societies all public facilities are for men; women do not appear on the streets at all. In our own society, the lack of childcare facilities in organizations, factories, and business indicates that workers in these buildings are not expected to be parents.

The individual, social attitudes, and societal arrangements are all factors in the manner in which sex roles will affect the family life of women and men in the 1980s. Individuals may want to change in the direction of sex role liberation and find themselves swimming against the current as they encounter a traditional society and the social arrangements that embody traditional sex roles. The question of social change — the contrast between traditional and nontraditional sex role philosophies — involves all three levels: the individual, the social community, and social structure. In contrasting traditional and nontraditional sex role scripts in these pages, three aspects of intimate life will be examined: the person and sex role socialization; sexuality and the sexual relationship; and marriage and the sexual division of labor. An attempt will be made to look at each aspect across the life span.

SEX ROLES AND THE PERSON

The ideas of "femininity" and "masculinity" refer to roles, not to persons. However, in our society people are taught to think that "masculinity" and "femininity" are innate attributes of the person, as are maleness and femaleness. Given these cultural beliefs, the results of research on early childhood may be surprising to many. The extensive research which is now available tends to deflate cultural expectations. Thus, for example, in some measures boys show more dependence on the mother than do girls; in some studies the reverse is found; and most studies show no significant differences (Maccoby and Jacklin, 1974). Researchers have found differences not in the basic tendencies of boy and girl children, but in the expectations and reactions of adults toward them and the behaviors they exhibit. One of the major mechanisms involved in the creation of sex differences is the different reaction of others to the identical trait or behavior when it is manifested by a girl and by a boy. Differential reaction to and rewarding of the same behaviors when manifested by girls and by boys has been found in parents and teachers of young children. This sex-differentiating behavior appears to be unconscious, for parents and teachers report that they treat boys and girls the same.

As a result of what we have learned, research interest has shifted from cataloguing sex differences to the study of the mechanisms by which they are created. Processes of sex role socialization, backed up by differential rewards and punishments applied to girls and boys, are what produces the sex-typed behaviors and attitudes that most women and men can produce when the situation appears to call for it. The selectivity of sex typed behaviors in young children reveal the patterns of sanctions to which they have been exposed in this earliest phase of sex role socialization. Children learn that

adults want them to exhibit sex-typed behavior, so they do it to a
greater extent when adults are present than when they are alone.
Boys avoid "contra-sex" typed toys and activities to a greater
extent girls do. Girls are freer in their behavior, and hence exhibit
"tomboyish" traits, *before* puberty but are encouraged to drop them
to become "young ladies."

ADOLESCENCE

Traditional sex role socialization in childhood predisposes the
adolescent or young adult toward sex-typical choices at this stage
of development. In addition, pressures toward conformity increase
in adolescence. Both peers and adults exert pressure on adolescents for "sex-appropriate behavior" although these two sources
of influence may differ in many respects. There is evidence that for
girls especially, puberty stimulates parents to crack down and
reduce the freedoms enjoyed by girl children. New standards are
imposed, and social success rather than competence or autonomy
is rewarded. Girls often feel punished as parents change the rules
of the game: They are no longer interested in their daughters'
hard-won achievements — only in their social life (Komarovsky,
1946).

Sex role socialization of females in adolescence reduces their
scope. They are being shaped for a restricted sex role in adulthood, when the sex role script dictates that their major concern
should be husband, home, and family. In adolescence they are
shaped to participate effectively in the social assignments of dating
and courtship. A successful outcome is "catching" a good husband. Sex role scripts define what a good husband is.

Sex role socialization of males in adolescence also shapes them
for their adult roles. However, these turn outward — particularly
toward the occupational world — while those of the female, as we
have seen, turn inward toward the home. The experience of
females and males diverges increasingly as they adopt their adult
sex roles.

Both females and males have other concerns during adolescence
besides dating and mating. However, for females courtship and
marriage are the major concerns; Marriage represents the destination for women; for them (but not for men) marrying and living
happily ever after is traditionally the end of the story.

Courtship is a social activity that follows sex role scripts. To varying degrees, the personal feelings of adolescents follow the same scripts. This means that attraction, courtship, and falling in love follow certain scripts in our society.

A society like our own with highly polarized sex roles sets forth a very narrow ideal for male and for female. Our sex role ideals resemble the Ken and Barbie dolls which have become a multimillion dollar industry, with many profitable spinoffs. Fluffy females and well-built men do better in the mating sweepstakes; all females and males are rated according to how well they approximate these patterns.

Males who are big and presumably strong "make" females "feel feminine." Similarly, males who are older, more educated, and have better jobs are considered appropriate partners for females who are younger, less educated, and in less well-paid, prestigious, or demanding occupations. This combination has been the traditional mating pattern and remains so. The pairing of less competent females with more competent males is not a simple reflection of attraction between individuals alone. It has another dimension, telling us something about the way sex roles connect. The conventional type of pairing is perceived as complementary, perhaps "a perfect match." But the roles of female and male are neither symmetrical nor equal. Both the inequality and the dissimilarity have great importance in determining how a marriage based upon such a pairing will go. There are consequences for the marriage as a unit, and for the individuals who enter into it.

It is at this stage in the life-span — at the time of mating — that we hear old sayings such as "vive la difference" and "opposite attract." It may seem contradictory, given the negative values boy and girl children (but especially boys) have been taught to associate with the attributes of the "opposite" sex during early sex role socialization. If sex role scripts guide young adults into choosing partners who resemble the ideals of "femininity" and "masculinity," they are establishing marriage based on minimum overlap in their personal attributes. This has implications for the kind of intimacy they can attain. The issue of intimacy in the marital relationship is taken up in the next section, which focusses on marital sexuality.

Following traditional sex roles scripts in selecting marriage partners also has consequences for the form of the marriage itself. As we have seen, traditional scripts define separate worlds of women and men in their adult years. The implications of considering the home and family "woman's work" are spelled out in the third section of this chapter.

Although falling in love and committing oneself to a lifelong marriage may seem to the participants to be an intensely personal and subjective experience, they are in fact subject to much social observation, commentary, and sanction. When individuals violate the rule stated above in selecting a mate, they are subjected to social sanctions in the form of disapproval, ridicule, or being shunned. Because the rule is a sex role rule, the sanctions take the form of doubting or impugning the individuals' adequacy as female and male. If a man fails to choose an inferior as his partner but rather chooses an equal, he will be perceived as dominated, henpecked, homosexual, lacking in moral qualities, lacking in ability, or fixated at an infantile stage. If a women has unusually high achievements or abilities, she is warned that she will never find a husband. If she has a partner, she may find that he asserts "superiority" over her by putting her down, restricting her activities, or beating her.

ADULTHOOD

Problems resulting from following traditional sex role scripts are not limited to adolescence and early adulthood. For the processes of aging bring additional problems to persons who think of themselves in terms of traditional sex role scripts. The process of aging precipitates a crisis in women and men who are captives of traditional sex roles. Adolescence may be painful for most individuals as they suffer with their "inferiority" in comparing themselves to cultural standards. However, even those who approximate the cultural standards when young suffer from those same standards as they age. Indeed, those who are best adjusted to standards which are essentially adolescent may have the most difficulty in adjusting to expectations for adult role performance (Mussen, 1970) or have esteem drain away from them as beauty fades and pounds accumulate. A person-centered psychology leaves more room for accumulating competence and esteem over the life-span with the riches of experience than does a static sex role standard that gives highest esteem to Ken and Barbie dolls.

ANDROGYNY AND THE PERSON

Current information indicates that sex differences are created by man rather than by nature. The end product is a highly-polarized world of social arrangements and expectations in which there is little overlap between the functions and attributes expected of women and men. This is the world of traditional sex roles.

However, the raw material provides other possibilities. Human young of both genders share an enormous universe of similarity. Another way of saying this is that the distribution of measurable traits or characteristics that can be found among boy children overlaps greatly with that found among girls. This substantial overlap represents a fundamental androgyny in human young. Sex role socialization can build upon this overlay or seek to polarize the two distributions. Traditional sex role socialization involves the former strategy; nontraditional sex role socialization, the latter. Nontraditional sex role socialization takes advantage of the existing androgyny of young humans.

Androgyny refers to the coexistence in the person of attributes that have the social significance of being considered "masculine" and feminine." All individuals have this admixture of traits, the mix varying with individuals. The species characteristics boys and girls at birth, in infancy, and in childhood have much in common.

As both boys and girls develop from infancy, they exhibit the same active involvement with their environment, the same pleasure in mastering new competences, the same rhythm of risk taking and return to the security of contact with the parent. As they develop, children reveal differences, generally not tied to gender. They are tender-hearted and boisterous, daredevils and rebellious, careful and heedless. For in addition to the wealth of attributes that children have in common, there are individual differences. Some are shy and some are not; some are bullies and most are not. Some have exceptional talent. As a result of social learning, children develop skills, some individual and some required by the culture. They develop preferences, attitudes, idiosyncrasies, and prejudices. To some degree, individual characteristics affect the way adults will try to shape the child. The individual's development is in every case shaped by processes of socialization that fit him or her for participation in a particular culture. It is this shaping which is analyzed when we study sex role socialization. The traits that in latter life are associated with "masculinity" — assertiveness, persistence in goal attainment, competitiveness, lack of emotionality, and the like — occur and can be fostered in children of both sexes. Attributes that are thought to be "feminine" in adults — compassion, emotional expressiveness, responsibility, warmth, nurturance — occur and can be fostered in both girls and boys. The same is true of undesirable attributes like pettiness, vengefulness, or ruthlessness.

Traditional and nontraditional philosophies of sex role socialization differ both at their origin and at their destination. Traditional sex role socialization links any observed difference to gender, reinforcing a perception of polarity between the sexes by labeling and by sanctions. The child is taught to repudiate any attributes to the "opposite" sex. The child rearing practices of the traditional sex role philosophy are rationalized by reference to adult spheres of females and males which are perceived in polarized ways.

The nontraditional philosophy of sex role socialization views neither the raw material nor the destination as sex-polarized. Nontraditional sex role socialization accepts the fundamental androgyny of the child. It may try to foster attributes valuable for the society and the individual — integrity, assertiveness, nurturance, altruism, loyalty, bravery — as well as validating the attributes that an individual exhibits. However, it is not assumed that the individual's characteristics or behavior stem from gender. If it is approved, praise need not take the form of "good boy" or "good girl." Attributes and behaviors need not be linked to cultural labels such as "all boy" or "perfect little lady." Behavior that is disapproved of need not be labeled "sissy" or "weak," or "mannish" or "unfeminine." Nontraditional sex role socialization does not teach contempt for the other sex. It does not attempt to make girls and boys fit the stereotypes of their sex. Quite consciously, it avoids the double standard of punishing girls for traits that are admired in boys, and vice versa. Nontraditional socialization retains the valuable attributes which traditional sex role socialization would seek to eliminate; as a consequence, the young person is more androgynous and thus richer in resources than the traditionally moulded person. The nontraditional philosophy anticipates that the demands of adult life cannot be met effectively by someone who is "not playing with a full deck."

Two of the many ways in which traditional and nontraditional socialization differ have direct implications for the ways adults cope with family life. For one, adults are expected (and so children are trained) to be competent members of a household. Nontraditional sex role socialization emphasizes survival skills such as competence in sewing, cooking, finances, housekeeping skills, and home repair skills for both girls and boys. Neither is expected to be incompetent, relying on the other partner to manage whole areas of experience. The person-centered approach, with its emphasis on androgyny, envisions a person who is whole — not an incomplete fragment seeking completion by union with another.

The kind of union that women and men want to create — and maintain — is of central importance in this chapter. In our society it is the *quality* of the relationship on which people base their evaluation and their personal judgments of whether to go or stay. What most people mean by quality in a relationship is the quality of its intimacy: the extent to which partners are self-disclosing; to the extent to which they give and receive emotional support; the tenderness, compassion, tolerance, and respect they show one another. Perhaps one of the rarest components of intimacy is a full delight in the other person and her or his differentness from oneself. For one of the surest challenges to intimate relationships is that the partner change over a long life-span. When love is based on some version of self-centeredness — the need for someone to do certain things for us, the need for another to play a certain part so that we can play ours — it does not survive when the partner ceases to conform to our wishes.

Unfortunately, traditional sex roles facilitate the expectation that the female partner exists for purposes to be directed by the male. The wife and the household are satellites of the husband, and his wishes take priority. The consequences of this traditional sex role arrangement can be seen in the research on marriage, which will be discussed in the section on marriage.

Interestingly, today's young adults want and anticipate an intimate relationship in marriage that is androgynous in nature rather than traditional. During the sixties and seventies college students — the young spouses and parents of today — consistently expressed an ideal self image and ideal image of the other that was androgynous rather than following the polarized scripts of "masculine" and "feminine." Women and men admire the same qualities in others, and aspire to them in themselves. The kind of person they want to be and want to marry is both competent and tender, capable of interdependence and intimacy, and possesses strength and confidence. These are the "new generation"; will they live new marriages or old? The way they live their marriages will reveal the interplay of the individual and the social factors: their personal desires versus the societal patterns.

SEXUALITY AND THE SEXUAL RELATIONSHIP

The sexual relationship is a major part of marriage for contemporary young adults and enters into courtship as well. Current sexual standards are permissive in the sense that most college-age women and men believe sexual intercourse is acceptable behavior between people who, although not married, care about each other. Our dominant sexual standard does, however, link sex with love; there is less tolerance (particularly among females) for casual sex.

Sexuality is also part of individual development. Although our society makes it hard for young people to learn about many aspects of sexuality, there is an understanding that both women and men have sexual desires. Particularly after puberty, there is some tolerance for sexual experimentation among young people. Sexual standards hold that it is understandable for people who are in love to consummate their passion; and, if not explicit, there is at least the covert understanding that people are likely to fall in love more than once in a lifetime.

The quality of the sexual relationship is often regarded as an indicator of the quality of the relationship. And conversely, it is often assumed that people who love each other will automatically have a good sexual relationship.

Unfortunately, however, humans (like other primates) must learn their sexuality. It is not just "doing what comes naturally." Humans do not rut; they do not achieve fertilization through following a magical trail of pheromones. Even the mechanics of sexual contact must be learned. However, it is the quality of sex rather than the bare occurrence of sexual contact that most people mean by the idea of sexual relationship. Orgasm is taken as an indication of "success" in sexual contact, and volumes have been written on that topic.

As soon as we stop talking about rutting and start talking about qualitative aspects of the sexual relationship, we are talking about human attributes such as the meaning of the sex act, the sexual histories of two partners, and the sexual communication between them. Not surprisingly, sex roles provide the context within which most sexual learning of young people takes place. What they learn — not only how to perform sexually, but what and who is sexy, how to be sexy, the "facts of life," and evaluations of various recognized sexual statuses like "cheap girl" or "frigid wife" — is woven into sexual scripts that are orchestrated with their particular society's design for sex roles (Laws and Schwartz, 1977). Sexual attraction and sexual activity are approved for certain sexual statuses and disapproved for others. Thus older people of both sexes find it difficult to gain privacy and respect for their sexuality. Even though their sexual desire and capacity for intimate relationships are unaffected by the aging process, the expression of them is inhibited by the disapproval of younger people. A close examination of sexual scripts reveals that individuals who deviate from sex role ideals are denied their sexuality: obese, elderly, handicapped, or homosexual individuals are shunned or, in some instances, legally prohibited from seeking sexual partners.

For those who resemble Ken and Barbie — even a little — sexual scripts provide a guide through courtship, through the wedding day, and perhaps even through the honeymoon. However, there is little guidance to be had (from sexual scripts, from research on longlasting marriages, or even from 'old wives' tales") on maintaining and increasing quality of the sexual relationship in marriage. The excitement of courtship relies a good deal on novelty; familiarity breeds a lessening of frequency of sexual contact and perhaps of excitement and enjoyment as well. The need for skills in sexual communication (a vital subset of intimacy skills) is felt by many married lovers. Earlier experiences have not been of a sort to develop these skills. Research shows that unmarried males communicating with their peers about sex rarely talk about feelings, while females are likely to talk about feelings but omit specifics about sex. Much miscommunication between lovers results from the confounding of sex with love: Each is reluctant to tell the other exactly what is sexually arousing or satisfying if it differs from what the loved one has been doing. Of course, most young people are not prepared to explain their own sexuality fully; it will continue to develop through the life-span, and they will need to communicate about it.

The goal of sexual communication is not merely to achieve sexual satisfaction although sexual relationships do require tinkering and adjusting. Sexual communication is a major means of furthering intimacy between two partners. Intimacy is enhanced by sharing what is personal. In the case of sexual intimacy, partners need to know and understand each other as sexual individuals as well as enjoy their joining. Getting to know one another takes time and requires the ability to communicate feelings and to listen.

Partners need to talk about their sexual experience, preferences, fears, and dislikes, not only at the outset of their relationship but continually. The individual needs to learn her or his own sexual rhythms, as these change over time and circumstances. Sexual identity continues to develop throughout the life-span, and sharing self-knowledge is an ongoing part of intimacy. This requires sexual communication as a skill.

Sexual communication is a delicate matter. Many factors can add to the difficulties people feel in trying to express themselves regarding their own sexuality. Sex role scripts that make one feel ashamed or undercut the sense of one's basic femaleness or maleness can impede both self-discovery and sexual communication.

The quality of intimacy is central to the way people experience their partnership. Intimacy in its turn is based upon communication — not love, passion, or promises but an ongoing commitment which can feel like a lot of work. The way young people are socialized may greatly affect their competence in communicating and in maintaining intimacy. The social situation in which their relationship plays itself out also has the capability of enhancing or hindering intimacy. Traditional and nontraditional marriages offer two different patterns for long-lasting pair relationships.

TRADITIONAL MARRIAGE AND THE SEXUAL DIVISION OF LABOR

For most people the term "sex roles" refers to adult behavior and the spheres of men and women (what we have referred to as the destination of sex role socialization). "Traditional" marriage refers to a situation in which husband and wife are expected to perform different tasks in different spheres: a sexual division of labor. The husband works outside the home for wages, and the wife works within the home, unpaid. A corollary under this sex role script is that the husband has no responsibilities within the home and the wife has none outside of it. This pattern — this destination — has implications for all the major roles women and men generally take on in early adulthood (spouse, worker, parent) and for their lives in later phases of the life-span as well.

For men under the traditional division of labor, home is a place to spend leisure, to seek peace and quiet, and to receive personal services. For women, it is a workplace without the protection of an enforceable contract or the amenities of an eight-hour day, coffee breaks, sick leave, and days off. Research on the home as workplace shows that the housewife's work week is likely to be twice as many hours long as her husband's (Oakley, 1976). Job satisfaction among housewives is low (Oakley, 1976). The recent decades which saw a reduction in the paid work week of men brought an increase in the total workload of women as more women added a job to their domestic work week. One result is that leisure has all but disappeared for the working wife (Kreps and Clark, 1975). The present situation constitutes a dangerous health problem for women who are badly overworked. Research on household time budgets or domestic labor show that the wife and mother is getting by on too little sleep, and uses weekends and holidays (when the rest of the family is relaxing) to catch up on "her" housework. Sadly, when the wife and mother is outside the home in paid work, neither husband nor children step in to take any of the housework burden. Research shows that men and children contribute only minutes per week to household work, whether the mother is working part-time or full-time (Walker, 1970).

Although in theory spouses are partners under the traditional model, it has repeatedly been found that the one who earns the paycheck has the power. Competence displayed outside the home is more respected than that displayed within, and the inside worker is expected to show deference to the outside worker. As the marriage goes on, these power relations may become more pronounced. Research shows that the sex difference in marital power increases with the duration of the marriage, the number of children, and the wife's lack of economic activity outside the home.

The characteristics of traditional marriage fit well with traditional sex role socialization. "Man's world" and "woman's place" are polarized, overlapping very little in responsibilities, rewards, or even vocabularies. Communication is often a casualty when husbands and wives try to convey what is happening in their separate worlds — each has little experience with the other's world. Even when the wife works outside the home, she is not participating in her husband's occupational world. Occupational segregation by sex is so extensive in the United States that the vast majority of women and men work in jobs where most of all of their peers are of the same sex. Polarization between the sexes is more extreme in adulthood than in childhood for school children are, for the most part, in the same classrooms during the day.

Although husbands and wives are supportive of each other's roles (wives want their husbands to be successful, and husbands want their families to be happy), they have little real involvement in what the partner's role involves. They are prevented in part by early sex role learning. Boys have learned that "girl stuff" (and later, "women's work") is not "masculine" and that they should shun it. Girls have learned that participating or excelling in "masculine" activities can detract from their perceived femininity and will be frowned on by males. Many, perhaps most young people make the transition to marriage without reexamining the rules they followed as children.

Thus it is no surprise to find among adults that not only housework but the maintenance of the household and of the family itself is considered "women's work." Raising children is also considered women's work: Not only the care, feeding and supervision, but the demanding and delicate work of socialization, moral upbringing, and training toward self-sufficiency is left almost entirely to one parent alone. In the traditional "intact" home, the male breadwinner is an absentee parent and the "male head of household" is uninvolved in its operation.

Marriage under these conditions has negative effects on women's mental health (Bernard, 1972; Gove and Tudor, 1973; Chesler, 1972). In research comparing women and men, single and married, single women turn out to exhibit better mental health than married women. Married men (who enjoy the support of a helpmeet) benefit from marriage in mental health terms. Married women (who under the traditional script do not have a helpmeet) do less well than either of these groups. Interestingly, single men have the poorest mental health scores of any group. This is not surprising if we stop to consider that traditional sex role socialization does not equip men to be self sufficient, either in terms of domestic survival skills or intimacy skills. Interestingly, similar sex differences are found in later life, when bereaved women and men are compared. Men who are widowed appear to have more difficulty adjusting than women who are widowed, perhaps because of the functions their partner performed for them.

The movement for sex role liberation in the sixties and seventies arose in the contest of the failures and stresses of the traditional sexual division of labor in marriage. For a generation before the advent of the women's movement, marriages had been rupturing at an unprecedented rate. The "displaced homemakers" of today were the traditional wives of that generation. They accepted a sexual division of labor that disconnected them from the larger social world and gave them exclusive responsibilities for the house. But when the contract broke down they were unable to reenter the other world, get a new position like the old one, or collect any unemployment insurance.

Today we are aware of alternatives. The contrast between traditional and nontraditional sex role scripts provides options for intimate life-styles of today's and tomorrow's young people.

LIFE AFTER "HAPPILY EVER AFTER"

Space does not permit a full analysis of the ways in which traditional and nontraditional sex role scripts affect later phases of the life span: when children are schoolage; when they start to leave home; when all children are launched; the male mid-life crisis; female reentry; retirement; divorce; bereavement. However, a few issues may be raised as food for future thought.

The first issue inheres in the expanded life-span itself. Although at the turn of the century the life expectancy of a girl child was 57 years, it is now 75. The life expectancy of men remains lower but it, too, has expanded since our grandparents' time. Our lives will be longer than theirs, on the average, and we will be biologically younger at later ages than they were. Yet we still use their life designs. We know that the rate of social change has increased dramatically since our grandparents' day, demanding continual change and adaptation in response. Yet we act as though stability is to be desired and expected. In fact, what research has shown us is that many life transitions occur over the life-span, requiring changes in our ways of coping. Development continues into late life. In a marriage, individuals continue to develop, requiring adaptation on the part of the partner. In addition to individual change, spouses encounter the challenges of life transitions such as those mentioned above. These, too, bring change and may impact on the partners in different ways, making different demands on them. What all of this means is that past experience — or tradition — will be a poor guide for partners who are trying to maintain their relationship in changing conditions. They must rely heavily on today's communication to exchange information about themselves in the present time. Traditional sex role scripts provide often misleading information about what to expect and how to behave, thus short-circuiting communication. The latter part of life contains many challenges for which traditional sex role socialization does not prepare the individual.

A major contrast between traditional and nontraditional sex role socialization may appear when adults lose their partners through divorce or death. Here the way in which traditional sex roles have crippled women and men becomes apparent. Many men are ill-equipped to head a household and care for the needs of children and themselves. Many women have no information or experience about financial matters, about wiring and plumbing, about career planning, about the political and institutional systems of society. Many women who have been of the middle class all their lives find themselves living below the poverty line when divorce overtakes them. Individuals who were socialized in nontraditional ways and who have a more complete repertoire of skills have less to contend with when they lose a partner. They may be less likely to repeat their errors in a new partnership than are people who are desperate to replace a whole range of functions in their lives.

A question of major importance is the sex role socialization of the next generation. It appears that a good deal of the ability of today's adults to adopt more flexible or androgynous roles in their intimate relationships stems from the training they received in rejecting "contra-sex" attributes and experiencing them as alien. Even where the situation calls for role flexibility — as labor market and child rearing conditions in the future promise to do — individuals are finding it hard to respond adaptively. As we might predict from the relatively harsh sex role socialization boys receive in childhood, males show less flexibility in these matters than do females. A gap already exists between attitudes and expectations of

today's young adults about the kind of life-style and role partnership they want (Komarovsky, 1973). This gap will be hard on the
marriages of today's young adults.

Unless sex role socialization itself changes, today's infants will
be trained to tag most of their attributes with a gender label, to
believe that males are superior to females, that females and males
are different in all important respects and have different functions
in life, and to reject the attributes of the "opposite" sex. The
conservatism that can be seen in marriage forms is likely to occur
in child socialization unless parents become aware of the effects of
sex roles on their own lives and decide to change the direction of
those effects. Reevaluation of sex role scripts has the potential for
restoring to the individual the richness of his or her own
androgyny and, incidentally, enriches the model a parent can
provide for a child. However, reevaluation is an active, conscious
process that requires commitment.

THE FUTURE OF MARRIAGE
AND MARRIAGES OF THE FUTURE

It is difficult to predict whether marriages of the future will
follow traditional or nontraditional sex role scripts. In the forego-
ing discussion we have discussed factors that seem to facilitate
changes in sex role behavior and factors that seem to work in the
opposite direction.

Young people's own self images and their ideal other are
androgynous today, showing a good deal of overlap in admired
traits rather than polarized images of female and male. However,
these images are context free; they refer to individuals rather than
roles. It is still a question whether marital roles will accommodate
androgynous partners. The marital roles which young people
inherit are much more rigid than other roles they have enacted in
our fluid and affluent society.

Old patterns exert a powerful influence, even where partners'
ideals pull them toward more androgynous intimate relationships.
After all, most young people have had no chance to observe a
"liberated" marriage; the available models are likely to have been
traditional. As they make the transition from a pair to a family their

marriage will become more and more like that of their parents. The "new marriages" come to look very much like the "traditional" as husbands cut back on household work they shared before the baby came and wives cut back on paid work.

At their outset today's young marriages appear more nontraditional than those of their parents. Young people do their meeting and mating often in contexts in which females and males are at least nominally equal: in high school, in college, or in work situations where both are beginners and their career lines have not yet diverged. Moreover, research indicates that what attracts and stirs many young people is an androgynous other, not their "opposite." Attraction itself has the consequence of increasing perceived similarity between two individuals. All of these factors would lead to a prediction that marriages now being contracted will be more nontraditional in form and philosophy than those of a generation ago. After all, the majority of American women nowadays are in the paid work force at any given point in time; and increasingly their time out of the labor force, if any, is brief. The working wife as a permanent factor in American marriages should, in theory, exert an influence in the direction of nontraditional sex roles.

However, as we have seen, women's roles have changed in recent decades without a corresponding change in the form of marriage. More precisely, other family roles have not changed in such a way as to accommodate the new demands on women from paid work. This failure increases the pressure on women and on marriages.

If the structure of marriage does not change — particularly the division of labor — then the expectations of an equal partnership and the androgynous selves that young people bring to their marriages will suffer. In past generations marital and personal satisfaction were the casualties of unmet needs and expectations. Under present conditions it is more likely to be the marriage itself that falls victim to the lack of fit, as current and projected divorce rates testify. Another current trend is the percentage of college-age women who report that they do not intend to marry. If traditional marriage scripts do not fit many young people and marriage itself does not change, then both the popularity of marriage and its stability will continue to slip.

The sex role socialization today's young people have received may obstruct their ability to introduce change into their own intimate relationships. However, there are no grounds for undue pessimism. Many opportunities for continuing socialization for resocialization occur throughout youth and adulthood, even after the young parents have socialized their own children. If they have the opportunity to reevaluate sex roles early in life, however, their own and their children's chances for successful intimate relationships will be greatly increased.

REFERENCES

BERNARD, J. (1972) The Future of Marriage. New York: World-Times.

CHESLER, P. (1972) Women and Madness. Garden City, NY: Doubleday.

GOVE, W. and J. TUDOR (1973) "Adult sex roles and mental illness." American Journal of Sociology 52: 812-835.

KOMAROVSKY, M. (1973) "Cultural contradiction and sex roles: The masculine case." American Journal of Sociology 77: 873-884.

——— (1946) "Cultural contradictions of sex roles." American Journal of Sociology 52: 184-189.

KREPS, J. and R. CLARK (1975) Sex, Age and Work: The Changing Composition of the Labor Force. Baltimore: Johns Hopkins University.

LAW, J. L. and P. SCHWARTZ (1977) Sexual Scripts: The Social Construction of Female Sexuality. Hinsdale, IL: Dryden Press.

MACCOBY, E. M. and C. N. JACKLIN (1974) The Psychology of Sex Differences. Stanford: Stanford University Press.

MUSSEN, P. [ed.](1970) Carmichel's Manual of Child Psychology. New York: John Wiley.

OAKLEY, A. (1976) The Sociology of Housework. New York: Pantheon.

WALKER, K. (1970) Time-Use Patterns for Household Work Related to Homemakers' Employment. Washington, DC: U.S. Department of Agriculture Research Service.

SEX ROLES AND SEXUALITY

Questions

1. *Is it possible for males and females to be different yet carry equal rights and responsibilities?*

2. *Do women's moods and capabilities change each month due to their menstrual cycle? Are they more capable at certain times? Does the hypothalmus react differently in men and women? Do men have a monthly cycle?*

3. *What effect have the media and the women's movement had on traditional female roles? What connotations do we attach to the term "housewife"?*

4. *Should women be drafted?*

5. *Has the women's movement produced a "male crisis"?*

6. *How do sex roles control our behavior on the individual level? the social level? the institutional level?*

7. *Do our traditional sex roles limit our interpersonal and sexual relationships? Should men be dominant in a relationship? Is a strong woman aggressive or assertive?*

8. *What is the "Ken and Barbie syndrome"?*

9. *Must the nontraditional marriage become more traditional after the birth of a baby? Do both men and women have nurturing instincts?*

10. *Why do most single women exhibit better mental health than do most married women? Why do most married men enjoy better mental health than their single counterparts?*

Heterosexuality Is the Only Natural Form of Sexual Expression

JOSH McDOWELL

"A fulfilling love life — how can I have one?"

This is a question I find men and women asking across the continent. As I travel and lecture in major universities each year, I come into contact with thousands of students and faculty. We receive letters from television viewers and phone calls from concerned individuals. People everywhere want to know how to get the most fulfillment from love and sex.

There are a few simple principles which, if understood and applied correctly, can help produce a dynamic love life. These principles aren't as widely understood as you might think. This brief chapter will look at some of the purposes of sex, examine several principles of sexual fulfillment and make some remarks on the benefits of heterosexuality.

WHY SEX?

To begin with, it seems logical to ask a basic question: "why sex?" (Of course, some students I've met ask "why not?!") In his best-selling book, *Everything You Always Wanted to Know About Sex But Were Afraid to Ask* (1972), Dr. David Reuben discusses three distinct types of sexual intercourse. These parallel what I will call three purposes of sex (1972: 53–55). One of the main purposes of sex is pleasure. Sex is fun! Unfortunately, not everyone has always agreed. Before World War I, for instance, many authorities believed that "sexual feeling in young women in love was pathological and abnormal" (Brown, 1966: 129). Although some today still want to keep the pleasure of sex a secret, folks have known about it for ages! In fact, some of the best sex manuals ever written were produced several thousand years ago. Consider these remarks from one ancient sage:

> Drink water from your own cistern,
> And fresh water from your own well,
> Should your springs be dispersed abroad,
> Streams of water in the streets?
> Let them be yours alone,
> And not for strangers with you.
> Let your fountain be blessed,
> And rejoice in the wife of your youth.
> As a loving hind and a graceful doe,
> Let her breasts satisfy you at all times;
> Be exhilarated always with her love
> [Proverbs 5: 15–19].

One sociology professor in Illinois reads excerpts from another ancient Middle Eastern love song to the students in her "Marriage and the Family" courses each term. In one part of this love song, the writer lets us eavesdrop on a beautiful and passionate romance. First, the woman revels in her lover's attributes:

> My beloved is dazzling and ruddy,
> His hand is like gold, pure gold;
> His locks are like clusters of dates,
> His eyes are like doves,
> His cheeks are like a bed of balsam,

His abdomen is carved ivory
Inlaid with saphires.
His eyes are pillars of alabaster,
His mouth is full of sweetness.
And he is wholly desirable
[Song of Solomon 5: 10–16].

Later, the man praises her beauty:

How beautiful and how delightful you are,
My love, with all your charms!
Your stature is like a palm tree,
And your breasts are like its clusters
I said, "I will climb the palm tree,
I will take hold of its fruit stalks"
[Song of Solomon 7: 6–8].

No doubt about it, sex for those two was pleasurable. Dr. Reuben calls this aspect of sex "funsex." At a certain college on the West Coast there is a professor who is 84 years old. One day in sociology class a student asked him, "Tell me, sir, when does one stop enjoying sex?" He replied, "I don't know, but it's sometime after 84." Sex is meant to be pleasurable.

UNITY

Another purpose of sex is to promote a oneness or unity. Nearly 3,500 years ago, a learned Hebrew leader wrote, "For this cause a man shall leave his father and his mother, and shall cleave to his wife, and they shall become one flesh" (Genesis 2: 24).

A student at Duke University asked, "Why do some people make such a big deal out of sexual intercourse when all it is is mere physical contact?" This Hebrew writer was saying that when a couple unites sexually, much more is involved that "mere physical contact." According to his view, sexual partners (whether or not they are married) become "one flesh" with each other. Both give themselves to each other. They become united; they become one.

Another term often used to describe sexual union is the term "to know." When partners enter into sexual intercourse, they enter into one of the most private, personal relationships known to humans. Both people reveal intimate parts of themselves to each other. Each gains an interpersonal knowledge of the other. Sexual intercourse is designed to promote oneness and unity through this interpersonal knowledge.

Sex therapists Dr. William H. Masters and Mrs. Virginia E. Johnson touch on this concept in their book *Human Sexual Inadequacy* (1970). In their chapter on treatments for female orgasmic dysfunction, they explain that it frequently helps to assure the wife that once intercourse has occurred, she and her husband belong to each other sexually. They add, "When vaginal penetration occurs, both partners have literally given of themselves as physical beings, in order to derive pleasure, each from the other."

"They shall become one flesh."

PROCREATION

A third purpose of sex is procreation — propagation of the species. Reproduction, or "reprosex" as Reuben terms it, is of course how we all got here. In ages past and still in some cultures today parents have been concerned with multiplying the population. Most agree, however, that with world population climbing, our need is not to multiply the race but simply to continue it.

So then sex is for pleasure, unity, and procreation. But how can one get the most out of sex?

One way *not* to have most fulfilling love life is to focus on sexual technique alone. Please do not misunderstand. There is nothing wrong with learning sexual technique — especially the basics. An understanding of sexual physiology can definitely aid in a sexual relationship. Indeed, ignorance concerning sexual organs and their functions has produced a great deal of frustration in the past. This has been especially true when sexual myths have blinded men from helping women achieve sexual climax or women from feeling that pleasure in sex is good.

But technique alone is not the answer. A better technique does not guarantee a better sexual relationship. As Masters and Johnson state in their book *The Pleasure Bond*, "Nothing good is going to happen in bed between a husband and wife unless good things have been happening between them before they got into bed. There is no way for a good sexual technique to remedy a poor emotional relationship. For a man and woman to be delighted with each other in bed, both must want to be in that bed — with each other" (1976: 113–114).

If better technique alone is not the key to sexual fulfillment, what is? As my wife, Dottie, and I have found in our marriage and as many professional counselors agree (Masters and Johnson, quoted in Belliveau and Richter, 1975; Koch and Koch, 1976), the qualities that contribute to a successful sexual relationship are the same ones that contribute to a successful interpersonal relationship. Sex, you see, involves nearly every aspect of your being. It's not just a physical phenomenon; it is linked to your total personality. In fact, your most important sex organ is your mind!

Qualities such as love, commitment, and communication will help any relationship develop to the maximum. These are keys to sexual fulfillment. Let's consider them.

LOVE

A philosopher has defined love as "a feeling you feel you're going to feel when you a have feeling you feel you haven't felt before!" Maybe you can identify with that.

Consider several meanings of those romantic words "I love you." One meaning is "I love you *if*— if you do what I like, if you are lighthearted, if you sleep with me." This attitude attaches requirements to love. Love is given if the other person performs well. It says, "You must *do* something to earn my love."

Another meaning is, "I love you *because*— because you are attractive, because you are strong, because you are intelligent." This type of love is given on the basis of what a person *is*. It says, "You must *be* something to earn my love." Both types of love must be earned.

There is nothing wrong with wanting to be loved for what qualities you have, but problems can arise from having "if" or "because of" love at the basis of a relationship. Jealousy can set in when someone who is more attractive or more intelligent appears and the partner's affection shifts to the newcomer. People who know they are loved only for their strong points may be afraid to admit any weaknesses to their partners. The relationship becomes rigid and less than honest.

The best kind of love is unconditional. It doesn't say, "I love you if"; it doesn't say, "I love you because"; it says, "I love you, *period.* I love you even if someone better looking comes along, even with your faults and even if you change. I want to give myself to you. I place your needs above my own." This type of unconditional love is based on the character of the one who is loving rather than on the character of the one being loved; it is based on his or her ability to love rather than on the "loveability" of the partner.

UNCONDITIONAL LOVE

Real unconditional love seeks another's best, seeks to give even when nothing is given in return. Of course, I'm not advocating the denial of needs. We all have needs for love, acceptance, pleasure, and so on, and it is important that we be aware of those needs and have them met. But a paradox of life is that we receive love by giving love. If one partner in a relationship initiates unselfish love, most often the other will respond in kind. There must be a balance. Not a 50 percent-50 percent balance but a 100 percent-100 percent balance.

Is there anything in your life that you cannot share with your partner out of fear of even minor discomfort or rejection? If so, you'll have a difficult time experiencing maximum sex, because profound sexual intimacy requires 100 percent trust and giving. If there's any insecurity in your love, if there's any fear, the first place it will be manifested is between the sheets. In a maximum expression of true sexuality, we become completely vulnerable— we're wide open to the other individual. It is this very openness that makes possible maximum sexual gratification and sharing and this same openness allows for the deepest sort of hurt if we're not completely accepted. So, in a "love *because of*" relationship, you can never totally give yourself in sharing physical love because the risk is so great.

I was sharing this with a student audience on the East Coast when one of the women listening broke out crying. She was beautiful, and had been engaged to be married. In a car accident one side of her face had become terribly scarred; plastic surgery had been required to make repairs. Because her relationship was a "love *because of*" relationship, fear immediately entered her thinking and the entire relationship deteriorated. It was a classic case of "love *because of*." It was reflected in the phrase, "I love you and want you because. . ."; Much of the love we know in our lives is of this kind, leaving us very uncertain of its permanence.

When Dottie and I were engaged she wrote me a letter. In it she said, "Honey, I know that you accept me just the way I am. I don't have to perform for you. I don't have to do or be any certain thing. . . you just love me." And then she added, "Do you know what that does for me? It just causes in me a desire to be more of a women for you."

My wife loves me so much that I don't have to perform for her. Her unstoppable love triggers in me a natural desire to be the type of person she knows I ought to be. I don't have to be that way, I just want to. It's the natural response to her "love, *period*" kind of love for me.

Probably you can see how unconditional love will help a sexual relationship. In order for sex to be most fulfilling, it should be experienced in an atmosphere of caring and acceptance. Partners are bound to make mistakes — no one is perfect. It is important that both be willing to accept, forgive, and give in an understanding way, regardless of the other's shortcomings. When sex is viewed in this context, it becomes not a self-centered performance but a significant expression of mutual love.

COMMITMENT

In addition to love, a second quality that is essential for a strong relationship and a fulfilling sex life is commitment. I'm not merely talking about commitment to a piece of paper (the marriage license) or an institution (holy matrimony) although I believe those are important. I refer to a deep, lasting commitment to another person as a human being. If two people are totally committed to each other, their relationship will be strengthened. If you know that your partner will support you and show concern and not desert you under pressure, the two of you will be able to function as a team. Trust brings you closer together.

In football, when a quarterback steps up to the line of scrimmage and sees a wall of giant defensive linemen ready to gobble him up, one of the reasons he's willing to take the ball from the center is that he knows there are five offensive linemen who are committed to protecting him. The same is true in a relationship. Mutual commitment gives both a feeling that the other partner is on his or her side. Without it, neither will be able to live with maximum confidence that the relationship is secure. The fear may exist that should one encounter a trial, the other may not be there for support. This uncertainty can erode their bond.

Total, permanent commitment is important in sex too. It brings security to each partner. It frees both from feeling they have to strive to perform sexually to keep each other. Sensing a conscious or subconscious pressure to perform well in bed so as not to lose a partner's affection can cause great fear. One or both can worry that a sexual "blunder" might end in a severed relationship. Performance fear is one of the greatest causes of sexual failure (Belliveau and Richter, 1975), so a lack of commitment can backfire and produce a lack of sexual satisfaction. Psychiatrist Alexander Lowen in his book *Love and Orgasm* (1975) writes, "In the absence of a total commitment to the sexual act and to the person who is one's partner, a satisfactory experience cannot be expected" (p. 191). Commitment helps to breed satisfaction.

COMMUNICATION

Besides love and commitment, a third quality that is essential for a strong relationship and a fulfilling sex life is communication. Even if partners share love and commitment, they must consistently communicate it by what they say and do. Simply saying, "I love you" can do wonders. And it helps to say it often. One exasperated husband complained, "I can't understand why my wife wants me to tell her I love her all the time. I told her I loved her the day we got married and until I take it back, it stands the same!" Obviously this is one man who has a lot to learn about communication.

Showing love by your actions also helps to strengthen a bond. Kind deeds and occasional gifts work like glue. Dividing up the household chores, even if it means sacrifice, gives partners an opportunity to say (through their actions) "I care about you."

Verbal support and encouragement to pursue an outlet that one finds meaningful can increase excellence and fulfillment. "I'm behind you all the way. I think you are a fine writer, speaker, counselor, athlete, student, businessperson" and so on. Words like these from an understanding mate can provide the impetus needed for success and draw the couple together.

Sexual partners who want maximum fulfillment should seek to develop open, honest, clear communication, especially in the bedroom. For example, the woman should tell her man what pleases her and not expect him to read her mind. The man should do the same. Open, honest verbal interchange about sexual needs and preferences can help turn a warm relationship into a sizzling romance. In response to the question, "What can a woman do to initiate sexual intercourse?" David Reuben writes of "almost unlimited" possibilities. Then he recommends, "Even in bed a wife should let her husband know what she wants and how she wants it. It helps a man to perform better if he is sure he is gratifying his partner" (1972: 76). It works both ways.

If a problem arises in our relationship, we've found the need to talk it out and forgive rather than give each other the silent treatment and stew in our juices. Feminist writer Gloria Steinem says that "sex is a form of communication" (1976: 47). I agree. You can bet that if partners are harboring resentment or not communicating with each other verbally it will show in their sex life. Sex will become a source of anxiety, a bore, or perhaps even nonexistent during that time.

How can you have a fulfilling sex life? By developing a strong, close relationship with your partner. As one professor expresses it, "Sexual foreplay involves the round-the-clock relationship."[1] In other words, you must concentrate on the total relationship.

THE VITAL DIMENSION

There is an additional factor necessary for sexual fulfillment. I believe it is the vital dimension in a dynamic relationship. It has to do with relating to your partner as a total person. Human lives have three dimensions: (1) the physical (your body); (2) the mental (your mind — intellect, emotion, will); and (3) the spiritual (your spirit). In order to have a complete relationship, it is important for the couple to relate on all three levels: body to body, mind to mind, spirit to spirit. If any level is missing, the relationship is incomplete.

One older student at a large southern university illustrated this graphically. (In his mid-forties, he had returned to school to get his degree.) After hearing a lecture on love and sex, he said,

> My wife and I have been married for 25 years. We've had a
> physical relationship, somewhat of a mental relationship, but no
> spiritual relationship at all. I can see now that many of the
> problems of the last 25 years could have been avoided if we'd
> related on all three levels.

The spiritual area is very often the vital dimension in a successful relationship. I would like to propose that the God who designed sex, even the plumbing for it, can be a significant factor in our sexual fulfillment. As one friend quipped, "A God who made sex can't be all bad!"

Some people picture God as a mean, long-bearded ogre who looks down over the rim of heaven and shouts to us humans, "Hey! Are you having any fun down there?" Then when we sheepishly reply, "Well. . . (glup). . .yyyesss," God says, "Well, cut it out!" The God of the biblical documents is not like that at all. He is a God of love and is infinitely concerned with our well-being. He's not down on sex — it was His idea in the first place.

Granted, some Christians have made some pretty horrendous statements about sex in the last 2,000 years. One church leader said that sexual intercourse in marriage for any purpose other than procreation was a "degrading act of mere self-gratification" (Brown, 1966: 129). Another, in the 1500s, believed it was "inexcuseable for a wife to touch or even look at her husbands genitals" (Feucht, 1961: 86). Still another in the fourth century cautioned "that the Holy Spirit left the room when a married couple engaged in sexual intercourse" (Small, 1974: 62–63).

However, these warped ideas are not found in either the Old or New Testament. The biblical documents present a very positive view of sex and sexuality. For instance, the spicy love songs quoted earlier in this article were taken from the Bible. One of the best sex manuals ever written is the Song of Solomon in the Bible.

SEX AND SPIRITUALITY

Fortunately, more and more people are realizing that sex and spirituality can mix well together. For example, in September of 1975, *Redbook* magazine published the results of a study of female sexuality. The study, conducted by a professional sociologist, involved 100,000 women and was called the most extensive since the Kinsey report (of the late 1940s and early 1950s). One of the things the researchers attempted to learn was whether a correlation exists between the intensity of a woman's religious convictions and pleasure in sex. Based on the reports of the women themselves, they concluded:

> *Sexual satisfaction is related significantly to religious belief.* With notable consistency, the greater the intensity of a woman's religious convictions, the likelier she is to be highly satisfied with the sexual pleasures of marriage [Levin and Levin, 1975: 52].

Of course, I'm not using this study in an attempt to prove nothing about the truth of religion or sexual values. I merely cite it to draw attention to the fact that a large number of people today do associate strong spiritual beliefs with pleasure in sex. If they've found something good, perhaps it's worth investigating.

In our marriage, Dottie and I have found our bond strengthened through our individual relationships with Jesus Christ. We've found the inner strength to love each other unconditionally (or "less-conditionally"). We've found an increased trust and commitment to each other. Our faith has given us a security that frees us to be increasingly open and honest in our communication. Knowing that God forgives us of every sin frees us from being burdened with guilt. And the inner power He offers helps us daily to develop as increasingly fulfilled individuals and partners.

Some might scoff at the idea that Christianity can offer realistic alternatives to modern individuals. They dismiss it as a myth or fairy tale. I can understand their skepticism because while I was a university student, I set out to destroy Christianity. I thought it was a big farce and I wanted others to be as aware of this travesty as I was. But as I tried, I could not intellectually refute Christian truth. As a result of intensive investigation, I came to the conclusion that Jesus of Nazareth was who He claimed to be — the Son of God, the Messiah.

In 1959, during my second year in the university, I trusted Christ as my Savior — the One who died and rose again for me. I invited Him to come into my life and give me a fulfilling life. He began to change my mind and my thought forms. Within a year and a half, He fulfilled me from the inside out. In fact, He so renewed and changed me that my sexual perspective changed. He made it possible for me to truly "give" in a relationship without demanding something in return. That's when I learned the basic differences between "love *if*" and "love *because of*" on the one hand, and "I love you, *period*" on the other.

After graduate school, I continued to compile evidences for the validity of Christianity. Eventually these were published in the two volume series, *Evidence That Demands a Verdict* (McDowell, 1972, 1975). I would refer you to those volumes for more detailed information on that subject.

WHY HETEROSEXUALITY

Some today ask, "Why should heterosexuality be considered the only natural form of sexual expression?" The best way I know to answer is to point out that sex was God's idea in the first place. Moses, a Hebrew leader, wrote, "God created man in His own image . . . male and female He created them" (Genesis 1: 27) and "For this cause a man shall leave his father and his mother, and shall cleave to his wife; and they shall become one flesh" (Genesis 2: 24). When I buy an automobile, I assume that the engineers who designed it know best how to operate it. This is why I read the owner's manual that the manufacturer supplies. It tells me what type of fuel to use, how to break the car in, how to operate the controls, when to perform routine maintenance, and so on. Similarly, if one views God as the "engineer" who designed humanity, it makes sense to follow His blueprint for living. His unconditional love for us makes Him worthy of our trust. He knows what will fulfill us most; these things He labels "right." And He knows what will hurt us; these things he labels "wrong." This is the main reason why I choose monogamous heterosexuality: God recommends it because He knows it will be most fulfilling. In other words, He designed us to operate best in that way.

Another reason I hold this position is that in our marriage (and in those of countless other couples), these same principles have proven to provide fulfillment. Of course, we're not claiming perfection. We both make mistakes every day and have a lot to learn. But we find that as we grow together we develop and mature in ways that would seem to be difficult or impossible outside of our mutual commitment and common faith. And we view each other as teammates. Our arrangement does not force us into rigid roles in which one partner is dominant and the other is subordinate. Rather, we prefer in each attempt to demonstrate concern for the other. As Paul, a first century Christian, wrote in advising husbands and wives, "Submit to one another" (Ephesians 5: 21). In other words, spouses should attempt to outdo one another in showing concern. Such advice seems appropriate for any relationship.

There are numerous variations on monogamous heterosexuality that could be discussed — including premarital sex, extramarital sex, cohabitation, as well as others. Space necessitates brevity here but I would refer you to two books that discuss those issues from a biblical perspective: *Givers, Takers and Other Kinds of Lovers* (1980) by Josh McDowell and Paul Lewis, and *How to Unlock the Secrets of Love, Sex and Marriage* (1981) by Rusty Wright and Linda Raney Wright.

One practical aspect of monogamous heterosexuality is that the plumbing fits. Another is the potential plus factor it presents to the family, a basic and foundational unit of society. Furthermore, as Dr. John White, counselor and Professor of Psychiatry at the University of Manitoba, points out, longevity is more characteristic of monogamous heterosexual relationships (1977: 112).

Heterosexual relationships on the whole seem to be much more gratifying, according to psychiatrist Alexander Lowen (1975: 75) and others.

Some have suggested that nonheterosexual orientation and behavior result from physical differences in hormones, genes, and chromosomes. On this, Dr. White remarks, "Science has so far searched vainly to find [such] a physical basis" (1977: 116). He goes on to say,

> Scientific evidence seems to suggest that while our sex hormones may account (at least in part) for the fact that we exhibit sexual behavior and that we experience sexual urges, our sex hormones *do not necessarily determine either the kind of sexual behavior we indulge in or the sex of person we choose as a partner* [1977: 116].

"But," asked one young person, "suppose you've tried many heterosexual relationships, found none of them fulfilling and then finally find happiness with a member of the same sex?"

The biblical God is pictured as having infinite knowledge of humans and their potential partners. He knows more about what contributes to a fulfilling and successful match than any number of trial runs could ever show. With all that infinite wisdom, He still recommends heterosexuality. Regardless of the level of happiness a person may *think* he or she has reached, God says He can make life better. It certainly seems safer to trust the counsel of a wise and loving Creator than one's own limited sample of personal relationships.

That positive note seems an appropriate one on which to conclude a discussion of a biblical view of heterosexuality. Jesus of Nazareth made a significant statement about human liberation that relates to this whole issue. Part of it is inscribed in stone on buildings at several major universities across the United States. His statement sums up this perspective on successful living and relationships. He said,

> you shall know the truth, and the truth shall make you free. . . . If therefore the Son shall make you free, you shall be free indeed [John 8: 32, 36].

NOTE

1. This statement is taken from Dr. Emily Dale, a Professor of Sociology at Illinois Wesleyan University, Bloomington.

REFERENCES

BELLIVEAU, F. and L. RICHTER (1975) Understanding Human Sexual Inadequacy. New York: Bantam.
BROWN, D. G. (1966) "Female orgasm and sexual inadequacy," in R. Brecher and E. Brecher (eds.) Analysis of Human Sexual Response. New York: Signet.
FEUCHT, O. E. (ed.) (1961) Sex and the Church. St. Louis: Concordia.
KOCH, J. and L. KOCH (1976) "The urgent drive to make good marriages better." Psychology Today, September: 34.
LEVIN, R. J. and A. LEVIN (1975) "Sexual pleasure: The surprising preferences of 100,000 women." Redbook, September: 52.
LOWEN, A. (1975) Love and Orgasm. New York: Macmillan.
MASTERS, W. H. and V. E. JOHNSON (1976) The Pleasure Bond. New York: Bantam.
——— (1970) Human Sexual Inadequacy. Boston: Little, Brown.
McDOWELL, J. (1975, 1972) Evidence that Demands a Verdict, vols. 1 and 2. San Bernardino, CA: Campus Crusade for Christ.
——— and P. LEWIS (1980) Givers, Takers and Other Kinds of Lovers. Wheaton, IL: Tyndale.
REUBEN, D. (1972) Everything You Always Wanted to Know about Sex but were Afraid to Ask. New York: Bantam.
SMALL, D. H. (1974) Christian: Celebrate Your Sexuality. Old Tappan, NJ: Fleming H. Revell.
STEINEM, G. (1976) "Is there sex after sex roles?" Ms., November: 47.
WHITE, J. (1977) Eros Defiled. Downers Grove, IL: Inter-Varsity Press.
WRIGHT, R. and L. R. WRIGHT (1981) How to Unlock the Secrets of Love, Sex and Marriage. Eugene, OR: Harvest House.

There Are Many Natural Forms of Sexual Expression

JOHN A.W. KIRSCH

The basic element in both secular and religious arguments against nonheterosexual sexual behaviors is that because sex is designed for reproduction, behavior detracting from that end is biologically unnatural and therefore perverse. In an age when science commands special attention, that line of reasoning may seem decisive; yet whether one should accept certain behaviors just because they seem natural (or reject others because they do not) is really a question of ethics, not science. I shall explore that question later, but will first show that both the premise and conclusion of this argument are partly wrong: Sex has uses other than procreation, and behaviors that are apparently nonprocreative may nonetheless contribute to reproductive success.

Author's Note: I am grateful to many colleagues, students, and friends for their patience and numerous discussions of the issues and evidence considered here, but especially to James Rodman, Peter Bottjer, Peter Alpert, Catherine Badgley, and James Weinrich.

Arguments about sexuality, like all arguments, often hinge on a failure to agree on the meaning of terms. The simplest sense of the term "natural" (critical to this discussion) is "what is found in the world"; but the doctrine of natural law that underlies much religious discussion of sexuality involves also the inferred purposes of natural phenomena, a composite description of human characteristics, and a prescription of what, on all these grounds, correct human behavior should be. These aspects of "natural (which are not the only ones; see Boswell, 1980) are often confused. I shall consider chiefly the descriptively natural, but will not hesitate to speculate on the function of observed behavior from the perspective of an evolutionary biologist. Most of my discussion will deal with homosexuality, since that is at once the best-studied and most dramatic example of nonprocreative sexuality. Even so, as one professionally concerned with the problems of classification, I am uncomfortable with the implication that we are dealing with a single phenomenon or single developmental pathway: The range of behavior labeled homosexual even in human beings (to say nothing of other species) probably includes some fundamentally different responses to the challenges of forming relationships; accordingly, any discussion of what homosexuality "means" can hardly be simple.

ARGUMENT AND EVIDENCE

THE NATURE OF BIOLOGICAL EXPLANATIONS

Nonprocreative sexual behavior does occur, and quite widely, among animals other than ourselves. Some especially pertinent examples will be discussed later, but extensive listings can be found in Ford and Beach (1951), Karlen (1971), or West (1977). However, facts in isolation are meaningless and are rarely even collected without a theoretical reason for doing so. Here our interest is in showing that homosexual, bisexual, autoerotic, and other such "nonreproductive" behaviors play some role in the lives of animals engaging in them.

The most general explanatory theory in biology is that of evolution through natural selection: Given that organisms are capable of reproducing far beyond the capacity of the environment to support them and that the members of any species vary among themselves in ways that are heritable, it follows that the individuals best adapted to their environment are those which live longest and leave the most offspring. The eventual result will be that the species as a whole comes to resemble genetically its best-adapted members; as the environment changes, so may the direction of evolution. Over time this simple mechanism — so like what animal and plant breeders employ artificially — has resulted in an enormous number and variety of species.

The critical point is that adaptedness is assessed in terms of greater or lesser procreation. Using reproduction as a criterion of adaptedness sometimes seems a strange explanatory device to nonbiologists because it concerns the "ultimate" cause of any organism's activities — producing more offspring than its competitors — rather than the "proximate" or immediate reason for doing what it does. It may well be that two birds, for example, pair for life because they love each other; but an evolutionary biologist would rather say that the mating assures greater reproductive success over the long term, and that birds have therefore been selected to behave *as if* they were in love. (Indeed, the methods of studying animal behavior usually exclude inferences that animals have and are aware of emotions or motives.)

If the measure of evolutionary fitness is reproduction, behaviors that don't seem to serve this end are difficult to account for in evolutionary terms: How could exclusive homosexuality, for one, remain part of the sexual repertoire of any species? Even the time and energy taken from procreation by a bisexual organism would seem to put it at a disadvantage with respect to completely heterosexual ones.

ENVIRONMENT OR INHERITANCE?

One answer might be that such nonprocreative activities are a minor and pathological component of behavior, appearing only under unusual circumstances and indeed rendering the practitioners unfit. Of course, that is exactly the traditional sort of explanation for human homosexuality, but such explanations do not adequately account for the wide occurrence of homosexuality in different human cultures, to say nothing of the fact that siblings reared in the same home may grow up to be either homosexual or heterosexual. And of course, complicated psychiatric scenarios can scarcely apply to most animals. Reproductive abnormalities in rats (including cannibalism as well as homosexuality) are regarded as responses to over crowding; Aristotle suggested that the Cretans of his time similarly practices homosexuality as a population control method.

The essential condition for any evolutionary explanation of nonprocreative behaviors, however, is that there is an inherited influence accounting for the occurrence of those behaviors. The pioneering sex researchers of the late nineteenth and early twentieth centuries favored notions that homosexuals were a "third sex," physically or emotionally intermediate between male and female; that they were individuals whose biological sex was misconstrued at birth; or that hormonal imbalances were responsible for unusual sexual interests.

No one has ever demonstrated convincingly that there are any consistent physical differences among persons of differing sexualities, nor can the rare cases of true hermaphroditism or wrong gender-assignment[1] apply to the majority of gay and bisexual persons. Recently, the idea that gay people may have low (or high) levels of the sex hormones appropriate to their biological sex has again become popular (see Naftolin and Butz, 1981). The evidence is equivocal: Low testosterone in males, for example, may be a *result* of sexual activity rather than the cause of the direction that activity takes. What *is* true is that exposure to an excess of male hormones during fetal life can produce many of the external signs of maleness in a female. (Sex itself is genetically determined by a particular pair of chromosomes which are of the same shape and size in females but differ in males; whether an individual is "chromosomally" male or female is determined at conception.) Such masculinized females are sometimes raises as boys, sometimes (after surgical alteration of the genitals) as girls. Providing that their parents are consistent in how they treat the youngsters, these children accept the assigned gender and develop attraction to the "opposite" sex — although the girls usually behave in ways that our society regards as "tomboyish" (Money and Dalery, 1976). These natural experiments show that any notion of a genetic basis for nonprocreative sexuality must be reconciled with an enormous contribution from learning.

All behavior is genetic in the sense that the design of the nervous system sets limits on what an animal can do, but there is a real difference between suggesting that nonprocreative behavior might be part of the possible repertoire of a species and that nonprocreative individuals are distinct genetically from those which are strictly heterosexual. A good bit of the homosexual behavior observed in various animal species has been regarded as simply being within the range of capabilities of all individuals, and, moreover, as having little to do with reproduction at all.

Animal behavior is nothing if not efficient: The meaning of specific acts may differ according to context, and abbreviated or ritualized sexual behavior is particularly likely to find its way into nonsexual situations. Mounting of one animal by another of the same sex is usually a statement of physical or social dominance, while an invitation to mount is taken as an expression of submission or appeasement. The mount may be followed by a few thrusting movements on the part of the mounter, whether male or female, but penetration and orgasm are rare in the wild (if not in the laboratory, which hardly counts: Consider the peculiarities of human behavior under conditions of incarceration). Impressed with such "uses" of sex, one school of psychotherapy regards human homosexuality as an acting out of metaphorical dominance (described by Karlen, 1971).

Evolutionary explanations for the existence of a behavior are stronger if genetic variation between individuals can be demonstrated because then the proposition that one type of behavior might be differently adapted than another can be directly tested. By far the best evidence for genetic variation among people of distinct sexualities comes from studies showing that if one member of a pair of identical twins is homosexual, the other usually is as well; fraternal twins, on the other hand, both show homosexual preference at about the level expected from the frequency of homosexuality in the general population (reviewed by West, 1977).

NATURE AND NURTURE: TOWARD AN INTEGRATION

Studies of gender reassignment and concordance for sexuality in twins are, respectively, the best lines of evidence for divergent views on the importance of the environment or genetics in determining sexual preference. Certainly none of the facts can easily be dismissed, but the usual response of proponents of either position is to look for methodological flaws in the investigations supporting the other point of view — or to pay lip-service to the idea that genes and the environment actually work together. The categorical distinction between "nature" and "nurture" has never been a real one, but few viable mechanisms for how they might interact to determine sexual preference have been presented. To the best of my knowledge, the following one is original.

Suppose that the putative hereditary factor affecting preference determines *not* that one will be attracted to the opposite (or the same) chromosomal sex, but to the gender other than (or the same as) that one *imagines* oneself to be, most people having the genetic predisposition toward the opposite gender. Indeed, it sexual preference is to be largely a matter of training, it would be efficient for the results of learning to be genetically directed in just this way: Fewer mistakes should occur, and it is certainly simpler than if there were genes acting separately to direct the preferences of each biological sex. Under this hypothesis the high success rate of gender reassignment is readily understandable. Since homosexuals constitute only about 5 percent of the population, very few of the gender-reassigned people would be expected to posses and actualize the rarer genetic disposition to prefer their assigned gender. Moreover, this notion of how nature and nurture interact explains why the sex of childhood playmates is a strong predictor of later homosexuality, those who play mostly with the opposite sex tending to become gay; or why (more generally) people are not usually attracted sexually to siblings or others with whom they grew up (correlations examined by Werner, 1979). The reason is simply that familiarity breeds identification, and the "gayness" in these individuals is really a preference for those *thought* to be sexually different. In fact, the latest Kinsey Institute study (Bell et al.; 1981) shows that the strongest factor in explaining homosexuality is some history of "gender nonconformity" in childhood (that is, manifestation of behavior regarded as appropriate to the opposite sex). Significantly, this history does not statistically explain *all* homosexuality. Finally, the hypothesis suggests why most societies are enormously preoccupied with defining and inculcating gender roles.

Of course, even diseases are natural and some diseases are genetic. Just the fact that proclivities toward nonreproductive sexual behavior can be inherited doesn't prove them to be of evolutionary value. But if they are not, then once more we must ask how they can persist — apparently, for humans, at much the same frequency — through successive generation? Why hasn't natural selection eliminated them? To understand the answers proposed to these questions requires first a reconsideration of what sex may be all about.

TWO EVOLUTIONARY HYPOTHESES

THE MEANING OF SEX

It has become common among biologists to say that sex is not "for" reproduction at all. Most plants and animals reproduce without it, relying instead on budding, cloning, or other methods that do not involve a second individual. Since a clone does not differ genetically from its parent, such methods make a great deal of sense if the organism is already quite well adapted.

But one cannot count on the environment remaining always the same; what is well adapted today may not be tomorrow. What sex is really "for" is creating new ways of meeting changing environmental demands.

To see that point requires a little genetics. All sexual organisms have two complete sets of "genes" (or bits of DNA) organized into a much smaller number of paired chromosomes, one member of each pair being inherited from each parent. (A special kind of cell division takes place in the formation of eggs or sperm such that only one of a pair enters an egg or sperm cell; for that reason the number of chromosomes does not go on doubling with each generation.) Genes frequently occur in two forms, or *alleles*— as in the case of genes determining eye color (blue or brown), hair quality (straight or wavy), or being right or left handed. For any particular characteristic one form may "dominate" the other, so that an individual inheriting a "dose" of the eye color gene for blue and one for brown will have brown eyes; but in some cases, like blood group AB, both alleles are expressed. Those who inherit identical alleles are said to be *homozygous*, while those with different alleles are *heterozygous*. Because of the allelic differences, mated heterozygotes[2] can produce three different kinds of offspring: two sorts of homozygotes, and heterozygotes like themselves.

Mutations — often a result of imperfect copying of the DNA during the cell divisions producing eggs or sperm — are the original source of different alleles; but considering that the grandparents on each side might have contributed different alleles to the mother and father, that the two parents might be genetically distinct from each other, and that the resulting combination of genes for different *characteristics* is to some extent a matter of change, the greatest source of variation between individuals clearly comes simply from mixing alleles at reproduction. Impressed with that, evolutionary biologists have concluded that the *chief* function of sex is precisely the generation of variation. One reason for believing this conclusion true is that species which can reproduce either alone or through sexual union usually reserve sex for special occasions — "hard times" that would seem to require some new solution to environmental problems, achieved in part by combining the alleles of differing individuals.

Of course, birds and mammals are "stuck" with sex, and it would be sophistry to argue that sex is not *also* vital to reproduction in these species. But it remains true that sex has to do with more than just making near copies of parents; indeed, exact duplication is technically impossible. Accordingly, there is a conflict between preserving a genetic combination that "works" and altering it as insurance against the future; that tension may lead organisms to adopt surprising and devious means to reproducing their combinations of alleles as nearly as they can. This observation leads to some of the explanations that have been advanced to account for the existence of nonprocreative behaviors. Two will be discussed, one of which has great generality; the other is more peculiarly human.

In both instances, however, I do not mean to imply that behavior shared by humans and other animals is necessarily a common inheritance, but rather that it represents a similar response to the same biological problem. In other words, I shall be arguing from analogy, which is permissible here since we are considering questions of function or purpose. Thus, examples from worms or birds do sometimes possess relevance to explaining human behavior. Of course, the argument is stronger when the animals are closely related to humans, as many primates (such as apes or monkeys) are. But it would be easy to overstate the importance of close relationship: Gorillas have a distinctive social organization, and hence differ from humans in many of the reasons for their behaviors.

HETEROZYGOUS ADVANTAGE

Specialization is common in animal evolution; but it is often useful to be versatile, and that versatility may have a genetic basis. The essence of the more general hypothesis is precisely that having a dose of each of two alleles makes the possessor somehow more fit than homozygous individuals. The textbook example in humans is sickle-cell anemia: Those homozygous for this condition produce only a kind of hemoglobin (the oxygen-carrying pigment in blood) which causes distortion of the red blood cells and clogging of small blood vessels — the condition being usually fatal. A heterozygote bearing alleles for normal as well as the sickle-causing hemoglobin (both of which are expressed) still produces enough regular hemoglobin to survive; and it happens that the presence of some sickle cells confers resistance to malaria. Thus, in parts of Africa where malaria is a problem heterozygotes are likely to live longer and produce more offspring than either kind of homozygote: Those homozygous for sickle-cell hemoglobin die from it; those homozygous for normal hemoglobin may succumb to malaria. However, when heterozygotes mate with other heterozygotes, the chance is 50% that new homozygotes of one or the other sort will be produced, so that numbers of reproductively less fit individuals are continually added to the population. In short, a genetic trait that by itself clearly ought to be eliminated by natural selection (sicklers rarely live long enough to reproduce) nonetheless persists because in combination with the alternative allele it confers a special benefit.

Now, it is a long jump from the elegant simplicity of this example in molecular genetics to sexual orientation, but an analogous situation exists with regard to sexual behavior in a group of worms parasitic in the guts of vertebrates, the Acanthocephala (Abele and Gilchrist, 1977). When males mate with females, each male deposits not only sperm but a vaginal cap which prevents other males from inseminating that female. However, some males copulate with other males, leaving no sperm but only a cement seal on the genitals. The absence of sperm makes it unlikely that mistakes in recognizing females are involved, but the effect of the seal on the other male is to prevent him from copulating with females. The male that indulges in some homosexual behavior thus promotes his reproductive success by eliminating competition from other males. That not all males "rape" others suggests genetic differences among acanthocephalans, although controlled breeding experiments would be needed to substantiate that conclusion. If there is such variation, then bisexual worms can be considered the carriers of an evolutionarily disadvantageous trait — homosexuality (disadvantageous because homozygotes for that trait would leave no offspring whatever) — from which those carriers nevertheless benefit.

Nothing quite so genetically simple is likely to obtain for humans, but an explanation for homosexuality along these lines has been proposed (Hutchinson, 1959). The studies of twins noted above along with much anecdotal evidence about the occurrence of homosexuality and bisexuality within families do indicate a genetic influence. Moreover, the "uses" of sexual behavior and hence the special advantages of a bisexual capability may be less obviously related to reproduction. Considering that homosexual mounting can be a statement of social position, it may be that the dominant members of an animal society are dominant partly because of their genetic ability to make such a statement more effectively. In the wild, the leading members of baboon, monkey, or ape societies are not necessarily ones who coerce their rivals, but individuals who are able to form effective coalitions. Adolescent social primates often form "gangs" of males or females, and recent field studies of langur monkeys (cited by Weinrich, 1982) reveal that young males of this species engage in frequent homosexual behavior which is rather difficult to interpret in the usual terms of dominance and submission. One possible explanation is that such homosexual involvements solidify relationships that, in the future, will be important to cooperative endeavors.

However reasonable this supposition, exclusive homosexuals seem to be rare in the wild. Yet such individuals should occur at least as a consequence of mating among heterozygotes. The place to look for them is probably not among social primates — for whom sex is a small part of life and child rearing is often a community concern — but rather among species that form monogamous, long-term relationships. Such relationships ought occasionally to occur between two individuals of the same sex.

Long-term monogamy is characteristic of many birds, and in fact males of some species of manakins do establish lasting pairbonds because it is only by cooperating that they can produce a courtship display attractive enough to interest a female. Again, one can regard this kind of pairing as not homosexual at all, but an example of "lesbian mothers" is known in Western Gulls (Hunt and Hunt, 1977). Some females of this species form a relationship in which both contribute to a clutch of eggs. Normally these eggs are sterile, but occasionally a male gull will copulate with one of the pair, and some eggs do hatch. The females then raise the young as a heterosexual pair would. Were the mother not paired with another female, however, these chicks would not survive.

Even in the case of the gulls one can argue that homosexual behavior really has something to do with increasing their reproduction. Is it possible that some individuals may *never* reproduce, yet have their supposed alleles for homosexuality selected and maintained by evolution? If so, this would be fundamentally different from situations where exclusive homosexuals were tolerated by natural selection merely because of the advantage their genes conferred on bisexual carriers (as in the worms) or where the homosexuals just happened (as in the birds) themselves to reproduce.

KIN SELECTION

The theory of kin selection was devised to explain exactly the sort of paradox presented by nonreproductive sex — instances where the behaver performs acts that are detrimental to his or her survival but which may be beneficial to other members of the species. Familiar examples include the member of a group that utters an alarm call which calls attention to her or himself but allows others to flee the predator (and breed another day) or the selfless individual who risks death to save a threatened brother or sister.

The essence of his selection is that such altruistic behavior most frequently occurs among related individuals. What is really at stake in evolution is less the duplication of the individual than of his or her alleles. Because close relatives are statistically more likely to share alleles than distant ones, behavior that facilitates the reproduction of a close relative even to the detriment of the altruist has much the same effect as if the altruist had personally reproduced. Thus, the occurrence of sacrificial acts is explained by the value they have in promoting reproduction by individuals who, as a concomitant of relationship, possess copies of the altruist's alleles. The evolution of such behavior can be considered an extension of the solicitude parents have for their offspring (again, because those offspring bear copies of the parents' genes), and therefore altruism is more likely to occur in species that are quite social.

Wilson (1978) has suggested that homosexuality may be associated with altruistic behavior in humans, arguing that homosexuals in early human societies might have performed helpful functions for their kin group. One useful service would have been nurturing the members' children, thus freeing parents for other activities (including more reproduction than they would otherwise have been able to manage). In primitive human societies — which, as best we can reconstruct them, probably consisted of bands which survived by hunting and gathering — such "helpers at the nest" would have been very welcome; aid in rearing young by females (and sometimes males) without offspring is common among social primates. But the kind of help provided by nonreproducing individuals need not have been limited to child care, and one of Wilson's main lines of evidence comes from work of Weinrich showing a strong association between homosexuality and the performance of medical or ritual functions (as by the often-homosexual shaman or berdache of many native American tribes); these functions probably do affect the reproductive fitness of other individuals.

FROM BIOLOGY TO ETHICS

As this brief survey shows, there are examples of homosexual and bisexual behavior among a wide range of animals, including your own species and related primates. It seems unreasonable to suppose that these all represent mistakes in development, environmentally induced pathologies, or even genetic diseases, if only because of their wide occurrence and continuity through time. Rather, it is theoretically possible that alternative forms of sexual expression are of positive significance in animal evolution. Although reproductive fitness is the definition of evolutionary success, there are many ways of perpetuating one's genes; some, like kin selection, need not even involve reproduction of the individual possessing the alleles in question. While kin selection may have special relevance to humans, the hypothesis of heterozygous advantage has a generality that is also appealing. There is no reason to suppose the explanations are mutually exclusive, of course, and both mechanisms may help to explain the appearance and persistence of apparently nonreproductive behavior in human beings.

Nevertheless, these hypotheses remain only intriguing ideas with tenuous empirical support, and some biologists have expressed grave reservations about the arguments themselves (Futuyma, 1980; Kirsch and Rodman, 1977). To most scientists, a theory is only so good as the tests that can be devised to disprove it, and few tests of the ideas presented here have yet been carried out. For example, it if could be shown that bisexuals do *not* generally produce more offspring than heterosexuals, it would be strong evidence against the heterozygous-advantage hypothesis. (Of course, that test would have to be carried out in a situation where population growth was greater than zero!)

The severest tests than any theory of genetic determination face are the successful results of gender reassignment, which provide seemingly conclusive evidence that sexual orientation is simply a learned preference. But I have suggested above how such results may be reconciled with the evidence for a genetic component. These cases provide a reminder that maleability is the essence of human behavior. Moreover, sexuality cannot be entirely teased apart from the rest of human activity. Even less can one kind of sexuality be explained in isolation from the others: Homosexuality and heterosexuality are complementary aspects that undoubtedly function together in promoting human reproductive success.

Nevertheless, while an organism may be an integrated whole, its parts can still be under separate (if limited,) genetic control. Demonstrating unequivocally that there *is* some genetic influence on sexual preference is the first priority for anyone pursuing an evolutionary explanation of sexuality. That the evidence is still insufficient to convince everyone is partly because if has only recently become acceptable to consider nonpathological explanations for statistically deviant sexual behavior. Biologists, no less than nonscientists, are constrained by prejudice in how they see the world and in the choice of problems they examine.

Whatever the precise explanations for the occurrence of non-procreative sexualities, such behavior is certainly biologically natural. This question remains: What difference does (or should) that make to our attitudes about those who practice alternatives to heterosexuality? At the very least, the naturalness of homosexual, bisexual, and autoerotic behaviors means that the basis for negative attitudes cannot be that such variants are "against nature." Some other type of argument — religious, philosophical, or political — must be invoked. But, to the extent that biological facts are the basis for natural law, religious arguments at least lose some of their force; and lacking the support of revelation, abstract philosophical arguments against nonprocreative sexuality build on an even less secure base. In addition, Boswell (1980) has shown that supposed scriptural sanctions against homosexuality depend upon ambiguous interpretations or mistranslations, and there is no history of consistent or determined clerical opposition to gay people before the fourteenth century. The objections of some early church fathers were less moral than political — a way to attack enemies or the adherents of rival cults. That religious objections are an historically fundamental part of Christian dogma is, accordingly, doubtful. Moreover, even fundamentalists now agree that the purposes of sex go beyond procreation (Schroeder, 1981); to argue, as they do, that heterosexual bonds facilitate the stability of the family and the growth of children is really not in conflict with the kin selectionist view that — in the extended family — homosexual bonds may contribute to the same goals.

While we cannot condemn nonheterosexual behaviors as unnat-ural, neither can we say that people ought necessarily to act on their homosexual or bisexual urges *because* those urges are biologi-cally natural. Yet one should at least consider the consequences of failing to act naturally. Physical laws place constraints on possible behavior: One may not, for example, ignore gravity with impunity; and for gay and bisexual people the effect of denying their true sexuality and affections are scarcely less dramatic.

But if the biological natural constrains and sometimes directs behavior, it should not dictate ethical codes. One misuse of the kin-selectionist hypothesis would lie in requiring altruistic acts as the price of homosexual indulgence. Clearly, the aim of human beings ought no longer to be reproduction at the fastest possible rate (if indeed it ever was). The human condition has changed in two million years, and it is as much our ethical responsibility to recognize when it is appropriate to act against our biology as when it is needful to live within biological limits that, like the law of gravity, cannot be disregarded.

NOTES

1. "Gender," or more exactly, "gender identity," is the sex you (or others) think you are. This may not always be the gender implied by chromosomes or anatomy.
2. "Heterozygous" is the adjective; "heterozygote" is the noun.

REFERENCES

ABELE, L. G. and S. GILCHRIST (1977) "Homosexual rape and sexual selection in acanthocephalan worms." Science 197: 81–83.
BELL, A. P., M. S. WEINBERG, and S. K. HAMMERSMITH (1981) Sexual Preference: Its Development in Men and Women. Bloomington: Indiana University Press.
BOSWELL, J. (1980) Christianity, Social Tolerance, and Homosexuality. Chicago: University of Chicago Press.
FORD, C. S. and F. A. BEACH(1951) Patterns of Sexual Behavior. New York: Harper & Row.
FUTUYMA, D. (1980) "Is there a gay gene? Does it matter?" Science for the People 12, 1:10–15.
HUNT, G. L. and M. W. HUNT (1977) "Female-female pairing in western gulls (Larus occidentalis) in Southern California." Science 196: 1466–1467.
HUTCHINSON, G. E. (1959) "A speculative consideration of certain possible forms of selection in man." American Naturalist 93: 81–91.
KARLEN, A. (1971) Sexuality and Homosexuality; New York: Norton.
KIRSCH, J.A.W. and J. E. RODMAN (1977) "The natural history of homosexuality." Yale Scientific 51, 3: 7–13.
MONEY, J. and J. DALERY (1976) "Iatrogenic homosexuality: Gender identity in seven 46, XX chromosomal females with hyperadrenocortical hermaphroditism born with a penis, three reared as boys, four reared as girls." Journal of Homosexuality 1: 357–371.
NAFTOLIN, F. and E. BUTZ [eds.] (1981) "Sexual dimorphism." Science 211: 1245–1360 (N. 4488).

SCHROEDER, D. D. (1981) "Is it true some are 'born that way'?" The Plain Truth 46, 8: 31–36.

WERNER, D. (1979) "A cross-cultural perspective on theory and research on male homosexuality." Journal of Homosexuality 4: 345–362.

WEINRICH, J. D. (1982) "Is homosexuality biologically natural?" pp. 197–208 in W. Paul et al. (eds.) Homosexuality: Social, Psychological and Biological Issues. Beverly Hills, CA: Sage.

WEST, D. J. (1977) Homosexuality Re-examined. Minneapolis: University of Minnesota Press

WILSON, E. O. (1978) On Human Nature. Cambridge: Harvard University Press.

MODES OF SEXUAL EXPRESSION

Questions

1. *What has technology done to change our feelings about sexuality and the purposes of sexual intercourse?*
2. *Why are homosexuality and masturbation considered unnatural?*
3. *What are the ingredients that make up a truly fulfilling sexual relationship?*
4. *What influence have religious teachings had on our sexuality?*
5. *Are interpretations of the Bible changing to meet the needs of our sexually open society or vice versa?*
6. *What arguments are made against the ideal that sex should be purely for procreation?*
7. *Why is monogamous heterosexual intercourse seen as the ideal?*

Individual Choices

The two issues covered in this section
include the functions of sexual intercourse
and the relationship between sex and
marriage. Again, the basic question revolves
around whether the conventional relationship
or alternatives should be the model. Should
sex occur primarily in order to foster
procreation and should sex occur only in
marriage? Traditionally, both bride and
groom were expected to enter married life
with no previous sexual experience and
refrain from extramarital experiences
thereafter. Would we have a better society if
we could return to this ideal? Has the more
recent emphasis on individual choice been
beneficial or harmful to the people involved

and to society? As the issues are somewhat different we have divided the question of sex within marriage into two parts — one dealing with sex before marriage and the other with sex after marriage.

FUNCTIONS OF INTERCOURSE

III–A

The Primary Purpose of Intercourse Is Procreation

VIRGINIA A. HEFFERNAN

The marriage teaching of the Roman Catholic Church asserts that the primary purpose of intercourse is procreation. Because the Church is the principal proponent of this concept, the statement has to be set in the context of Catholic theological teaching for it to make sense in the modern day. Consequently, I will endeavor here to give a historical overview of Catholic teaching on sexuality, to give the full flavor of contemporary Catholic documents with the precise English translations, and to discuss how today's Catholic married couples apply this teaching.

I must clarify, first of all, that from the perspective of the Catholic Church this doctrine is a teaching for *marital* sex. Intercourse outside of marriage is considered immoral, with or without procreative intent. If a pregnancy results from nonmarital sex it cannot be interpreted as justifying the sex. Furthermore, at no point in recorded history have the Church fathers insisted that only the fertile may have intercourse. Intercourse is not forbidden to the sterile, to the already pregnant, or those past child-bearing age.

In its most basic interpretation, the statement is a recognition of the procreative potential in sexual intercourse. The first "fact of life" we are taught is that sexual intercourse causes pregnancy. From this biological fact the Church has moved through a torturous route — from rejection of sex for pleasure, even in marriage, to a contemporary appreciation of the pleasure bond of marital sex and a licitness to limiting sex activity to the sterile portions of the menstrual cycle.

HISTORICAL OVERVIEW

The non-Catholic readers can perhaps understand how far we have come, when we remember that Catholic women were not permitted to comment on their experience in regard to conception and have these comments considered by the magisterium until the 1960s. For twenty centuries there appears to have been no interest in the views of any Catholic women on this subject. No one had ever consulted the people who actually bore the babies. As we shall see, Pope Paul VI gave that testimony only minimal attention when he made his statement on contraception in 1968.

The early Church was not interested in procreation. It was assumed that Christ would soon return and there was no point in continuing to replenish the earth. In the New Testament marriage is presented as good and sexual intercourse as holy. This image is used as the model of Christ's love for his Church. This valuation of marriage and marital intercourse was not specifically linked to procreation — that is, it was not specified as an obligation. However, procreation is used symbolically as the image of joy that will be experienced when Christ returns. The present day couple, sharing the joy of deliverying their own child, can understand this biblical image.

The belief that procreation is the primary purpose of sexual intercourse is not evident in the New Testament writing. It was the evolving Church that introduced this idea. Some of the subjects that would be touched on eventually included the intention with which married sex may be sought; the lawfulness of marriage by the sterile; the role of pleasure in marriage.

According to I Corinthians 7:3–6, marital intercourse is the right of both husband and wife. This has posed a constant corrective on the Church fathers who asserted that intercourse was permissible only with procreative intent. The marriage "debt" as it has been called, was to become a modern issue for women who did not care to always be obligated to their husbands. Although this scriptural passage makes it clear that wives are also entitled to sex, the implicit attitude was that virtuous women weren't really interested in sex.

Ironically, it is from a pagan source — Greek philosophy — that the early Church's attitude on sex is derived. It is the Stoics that we have to thank for the essentially negative attitudes about sexuality that come up through the Christian heritage. From *The Nature of the Universe* (Sec. 44) — a Pythagorean treatise — we have the following: "The sexual organs are given man not for pleasure, but for the maintenance of the species." The Stoics did not connect intercourse with love, and this became a profound influence on the Christian doctrine on marriage as well as contraception. Greek philosophy was attractive because of its appeal to reason over nature. This ascetic approach would coincide with the higher value placed on consecrated virginity than on marriage.

One of the many historical ironies is St. Augustine's attack on the use of the rhythm method to avoid pregnancy. What was once viciously condemned has become the only method approved by the Catholic Church for family limitation. He believed it established marriage as only a means to satiate lust rather than to procreate. The question could still be raised: If procreation is the primary purpose of sexual intercourse, why is it all right to confine sexual activity to sterile periods?

St. Augustine had a horrendous struggle with what the Church calls "concupiscence" (sexual desire). All Christians, Protestants and Catholics alike, are heirs to his distortions. He believed that only procreative intent could justify lust, and he was even a little suspicious of that. He made strong condemnations of pleasure and passion in marriage. Augustine did believe marriage had three goods: offspring, fidelity, and symbolic stability. The rendering of the aforementioned marriage debt was a part of stability. You could, if you must, allay concupiscence.

Peter Abelard was the first married man in the Western Church to contribute to the theology of this issue — and this did not occur until the eleventh century. (I have already noted that it took twenty centuries before married women got in a word.) But because Abelard was considered an unrepentent sinner, his words were not influential. By the thirteenth century avoidance of children in marriage was referred to as fornication, adultery, and homicide.

The above historical information was drawn from Noonan's comprehensive *Contraception* (1965).

CONTEMPORARY THEOLOGICAL PHILOSOPHICAL VIEWS

I shall move ahead seven centuries to the contemporary Catholic teaching on sexual activity. I shall present the official statements and some of the philosophy upon which they rest, and explain how these statements are interpreted in Church marriage regulations and in the lives of believing couples.

The Second Vatican Council was the Church's revolutionary move into the modern world. *Gaudium et Spes* (1965), known in English as the *Pastoral Constitution of the Church in the Modern World*, is this Council's treatment on marriage and the family. The following passage from this document is illustrative of the Church's position:

> Marriage and conjugal love are by their nature ordained toward the begetting and educating of children. Children are really the supreme gift of marriage and contribute very substantially to the welfare of their parents. The God Himself Who said, 'it is not good for man to be alone' (Genesis 2:18) and 'Who made man from the beginning male and female' (Matthew 19:4); wishing to share with man a certain special participation in His own creative work, blessed male and female, saying 'Increase and multiply' (Genesis 1:28). Hence, while not making the other purposes of matrimony of less account, the true practice of conjugal love, and the whole meaning of the family which results from it, have this aim: that the couple be ready with stout hearts to cooperate with the love of the Creator and the Savior. . . . Marriage, to be sure, is not instituted solely for procreation . . . marriage persists as a whole manner and communion of life — even when, despite the desire of the couple, offspring are lacking [Sec. 50].

I will come back to these themes presently.

It was *Humanae Vitae* (1968), an encyclical of Pope Paul VI, that caused the explosive rupture in Catholic circles. In spite of the findings of the Birth Control Commission appointed by Pope John 23rd, Pope Paul VI chose to ignore the majority and emphasize the centuries-old ban on contraception.

The commission's majority view held that a couple could select from several means of birth control and still foster marriage as a community of fruitful love. The majority believed the issue to be one of procreation versus a depreciation of the child bearing principle rather than a quarrel over the terms of limitation (*Tablet*, 1967). The criticism has frequently been made that the only reason the natural means of limitation were approved by the Pope was because he did not think such methods would work anyway, and thus procreation was guaranteed. Cynicism aside, the reason is an adherence to the position originally derived from the Greek philosophy.

Please note, however, that the papal encyclical does reveal a distinct shift from the anti-sex beliefs of some theologians discussed earlier. In Section 2 of *Humane Vitae* we read, "Also noteworthy is a new understanding of the dignity of woman and her place in society, of the value of conjugal love in marriage and the relationship of conjugal acts of this love."

Pope Paul VI supports the dual significance of the marriage act:

> This particular doctrine . . . is based on the inseparable connection, established by God, which man on his own initiative may not break, between the unitive significance and procreative significance which are both inherent to the marriage act.

> The reason is that the fundamental nature of the marriage act, while uniting husband and wife in the closest intimacy, also renders them capable of generating new life . . . and this as a result of laws written into the actual nature of man and woman. And if each of these essential qualities, the unitive and the procreative, is preserved, the use of marriage fully retains its sense of true mutual love and its ordination to the supreme responsibility of parenthood to which man is called [Sec. 12].

> If therefore there are well-grounded reasons for spacing births, . . . the Church teaches that married people may then

take advantage of the natural cycles immanent in the
reproductive system and engage in marital intercourse only
during those times that are infertile, thus controlling birth in a
way which dos not in the least offend the moral principles
which we have just explained. What is explicitly condemned are
contraceptive actions which interfere with the natural generative
process — either before, after or during. The couple may
cooperate with nature but not artificially bypass natural
consequences [Sec. 16].

Even married philosophers in today's Church sometimes echo
the Augustinian heritage. Germain Grisez insists that orgasm must
be subordinate to the procreative purpose. (Grisez, 1964) Sexual
desire for one's wife is not considered a higher good. If a couple
wish to control fecundity, then the sexual desire must be sup-
pressed to be awakened only at the proper time in the cycle. Even
then, it is unity — not one's own desire — that has priority. Such a
philosophy is not completely consistent with the teaching of I
Corinthians — that a couple have a duty to meet each other's
needs — but it is consistent with the ancient Catholic teaching that
desire must be controlled by reason. From this position, sexual
intercourse may be an expression of unity but it is a lesser good if
it is sought only for the release of sexual tension. At the time
Grisez was writing in this vein, he had been married for 13 years
and had fathered four children. He professed to be living what he
was teaching.

In even more recent theological writing (Dennehy, 1981) we still
find these principles. Dennehy explains it in this fashion:

The dignity that this tradition sees in human sexuality has its
explanation in the fact that it is regarded as the creaturely
analogue of the creative power of God. Having made man and
woman in his own image and likeness, he invites them to
participate in his own providence. In the sex act, they
cooperate with him in the creation of a new human life [1981:
10].

[T]he sex act is an expression of love and generosity. It is at
this point that the Church's insistence on the impossibility of
separating the unitive and procreative aspects of the sex act
derives its intelligibility. For this is the act in which a man and
a woman express their mutual love and in so doing donate

themselves to each other in such way as to procreate another human being. Because love is by its nature creative, the expression of their love for each other, which the act makes possible in a unique way, is inextricably tied to that act's openness to procreation. . . . to say that in marriage a man and a woman become two in one flesh is not simply to speak metaphorically; it is to state a literal truth as well [pp. 10–11].

Joseph de Lestapis, S.J., has summarized Karol Wojtyla's *Love and Responsibility* (Karol Wojtyla is now Pope John Paul II):

Since man is a rational being, his tendency to extend the participation of his consciousness to all areas of his activity is consistent with his nature. It is the same with the tendency toward conscious maternity and paternity. The man and the woman having conjugal relations should know at what moment and how they can have a child. In fact, they are responsible for each conception–responsible to themselves and before the family they are thus creating or increasing.

According to the order of the nature what is the sexual relationship between man and woman? To this question reason responds: "With the man, conjugal relations are always tied to procreation, with the woman, they are connected to it periodically." In sexual relations, the man always serves procreation by furnishing seeds of life in an overabundance. The nature of woman, on the contrary, fixes the number of possible conceptions in a precise and, one could say, 'economical' way [1981: 128].

Gerald Coleman (1983) has written the following: "*Humanae Vitae* affords the distinction between primary and secondary ends of marriage in favor of marital love which intrinsically possesses a connection between union and fertility. [The Pope] is calling the couple to be open to God."

The modern theologian-philosopher in conformity with Catholic teaching continues to emphasize the procreative value of sexual intercourse. There is an unbroken line for this from the time of the early Church fathers. The modern emphasis has placed the unitive value as an equal value but continues to stress the procreative because it reflects the natural bodily and reproductive functions and also because it fulfills a religious function.

THE LIVED REALITY OF CATHOLIC MARRIAGE

The sacrament of matrimony is a social sacrament. It is not just to unite a man and a woman and put a blessing on sexual activity. It is a sacrament of community with a purpose that goes beyond the couple. When a couple approaches a priest seeking marriage, they will be asked about their intentions of participating as part of the Catholic community. If they answer in the negative, they may be advised to seek marriage rites elsewhere.

If the couple indicates that they do not intend to ever have children, they are supposed to be refused marriage in the Catholic Church. There are exceptions to this rule (such as health problems) but a general attitude of being closed to new life would be considered an impediment to valid marriage.

Like the Deuteronomist, the Catholic is expected to "Choose life!" If life is worth living, is it not a precious gift to be passed on? Within the Church marriage and the family is the basic unit of faith. It is to the family that the basic work of perpetuating the faith belongs. The Catholic couple is exhorted not only to procreate but to educate their children so that the faith can continue. The teaching of mothers and fathers carries the message far more than the exhortations of priests and nuns. So entrenched is the idea of the family as the basic unit that parishes usually count their "families" rather than individual members.

Periodic continence — the only sanctioned method of the family limitation for Catholics — is not a popular life-style. Cynics ask if anyone lives this way. Indeed, they do.

Natural family planning proponents are close to being a religious sect of their own. Couples who choose this method because of preference for natural methods have a high degree of satisfaction with it, as my own research indicates (Heffernan, 1977). Of all the methods of fertility control, this requires the most sharing; this sharing will be a continuing thread throughout a couple's life. Pinpointing the time of ovulation has become accurate enough so that the method has a high degree of success for couples willing to live with periodic continence.

This is also an indication that "responsible parenthood" has become the norm — you must be a parent if you can, but you can space and limit your family according to your own situation.

This norm prevails also for the vast number of contraceptive users among Catholic couples — children are part of the plan, but they can be spaced and limited according to the couple's situation.

We are a very long way from St. Augustine, but the argument is still unresolved in Catholic circles as to whether conception can be impeded by artificial means. There is still an uneasiness about passion and an insistence that sexual desire be controlled by reason — even in the marriage bed. A modern theology of sexuality is still far from being worked out. Surely this time the process will include women, as women can be theologians even if they cannot become priests.

Andrew Greeley has examined the relationship between religiosity and sexual fulfillment in young Catholic married couples (Greeley, 1980). Contrary to the impression this discussion of Church sexual attitudes might give, he found that the more religious a couple is the more sexually fulfilled they are likely to be. There were strong correlations between such measures as frequency of prayer and warm religious images. (Warm religious images would include seeing God as gentle, patient, and comforting.)

Few theologians have understood or even sought to understand the full dimensions of sexuality in marriage. With the retrieval of the Church's scriptural heritage, the issue has become even more focal. The Old Testament provides a basic structure for an understanding of sexual ethics. Man and woman together reflect the image of God — not man alone. Marriage and fecundity are good.

Sexuality comes to its full meaning within the dynamics of marriage. The sexual component bears a special task in the irrevocable community of a man and a woman. The force that draws a man and a woman together to form this community possesses a special creative charge. This creativity is expressed not only in children but in the love which continues to nurture the relationship.

It would appear that the nurturant quality of marital sexuality is least understood in terms of traditional Catholic teaching. It is not possible to regulate moments of reconciliation or reassurance by female biological rhythms. Sexual intercourse is the supreme act of physical unity far surpassing other gestures of affection. This unity helps produce the atmosphere of a loving community in which the children can thrive.

This teaching, that the primary purpose of intercourse is for procreation, will continue to be an overarching principle for Catholic marriage. It is the literal symbol of the two-in-one flesh image given us in Genesis and it is a sign of hope for the future, and is equally well expressed by having one child as by having ten. It is already lived this way here in the United States.

REFERENCES

The Birth Control Report (1967) Majority View. London: The Tablet, April 22.

COLEMAN, G.D., S.S. (1983) "Marriage: The vision of HUMANAE VITAE." Thought 58 (March).

DE LESTAPIS, J., S. J. (1981) "A summary of Karol Wojtyla's LOVE AND RESPONSIBILITY," in R. Dennehy (ed.) Christian Married Love. Ignatius Press.

DENNEHY, R. [ed.] (1981) Christian Married Love. Ignatius Press.

GREELEY, A. M. (1980) The Young Catholic Family. Chicago: Thomas Moore Press.

GRISEZ, G. G. (1964) Contraception and the Natural Law. Milwaukee: Bruce.

HEFFERNAN, V. (1977) "Attitudes of some couples using natural family planning." Communio 4 (spring).

NOONAN, J. T. (1965) Contraception. Cambridge: Harvard University Press.

Pope Paul VI (1968) HUMANAE VITAE. (English trans.: The Pope Speaks, 13, Fall.)

Second Vatican Council (1965) Pastoral Constitution on the Church in the Modern World. Washington, DC: National Catholic Welfare Conference.

Sexual Intercourse Serves Many Purposes Which Are Equally Acceptable

JEANNINE GRAMICK

Being engaged in the sensitive area of church ministry with the lesbian and gay community for the last 10 years including advocacy for the civil rights of this disenfranchised group in the political arena, I am immersed in three explosive topics which one tactfully avoids at chic parties to obviate disruptive argumentation. The more I work to secure rights, to eliminate sexual stereotypes and myths, and to calm irrational fears with reasonable information, the more I become aware that the three "hot" topics of religion, sex, and politics are intimate bedfellows. How many serious discussions of sex, for example, conclude with some reference to religious teachings which have attempted to direct human sexual behavior through moral guidance? And as anyone privy to the internal machinations of organized religion will admit, dogmatic pronouncements completely devoid of clerical politics is a fiction.

No matter how manifestly objective the social scientist, philosopher, or psychologist wishes to appear, family background, social experiences, and personal biases impact on any "objective" reasoning. As much as I would delight in claiming that the rational arguments I shall set forth below are impersonal, value-free, and dispassionate, I must truthfully admit that such is not the case. That is not to say that my subsequent dialetic regarding human sexuality is without reason or logic but merely that it has been inevitably affected by a personal value system evolved from a complex religious and political history.

In this article on sexuality and values, I shall specifically explore the purposes of human sexual intercourse. Human beings engage in sexual intercourse for a variety of reasons; for example, for love, children, pleasure, material gain, aggression, or fulfillment of an obligation, to name a few. These subjective intentions, however, may not constitute a purpose intrinsic to the sexual act itself. Does genital intercourse retain a meaning independent of the participants' motivations? Assuming that is does, what then, one will ask, is this intrinsic purpose? Is there more than one? Are there, in fact, many purposes for human intercourse?

First, I shall present a brief historical overview of the traditional Christian teaching on the procreative purpose of sexual intercourse.[1] Second, I shall review various definitions of nature on which the traditional argument is built and critique the inadequacies of these notions. Third, I shall defend two additional purposes of human intercourse. I shall conclude with a concise personal postscript.

PROCREATIVE PURPOSE: THE HISTORICAL UNDERPINNINGS

Traditionally, the Christian churches (which dominated the intellectual, social, and economic life of Western civilization until modern times,) have staunchly taught that procreation is the proper end of human sexual intercourse and must occur only within the marriage context. How did such a conviction evolve? In the first two centuries, Christian leaders found in the rigorous Jewish beliefs on sexuality and especially in the secular Stoic ideals a basis for their doctrine on purposeful intercourse.

Fiercely independent and distrustful of human feelings, the Stoic philosophers exalted reason and posited that there exists some universal natural law against which to measure the intrinsic worth of human acts. Because a person should not be dependent on bodily wants or needs, sensual desires were to be controlled by reason. Temperance and moderation in all bodily desires satisfied the requirements of rationality and the natural law to which humans must conform. The Stoic shibboleths of "nature, virtue, decorum, freedom from excess"(Noonan, 1965: p 46) were enthusiastically embraced by early Christian thinkers as maps for their ethical sexual journey. Erotic passions, regarded with suspicion even within marriage, represented an uncontrolled dependence on another person. Marriage itself was justified because it was the necessary context for raising children and thus conformed to the natural law for the propagation of the human species. A reasonable aim and purpose for marriage made evident by nature was procreation. Within the Stoic system of values of reason and moderation, coition for reproduction within marriage made perfect sense.

Of course, the Stoic doctrine on the relationship between genital intercourse and marriage was heard by willing ears and may have developed within the Christian community even if Stoicis had never arisen. In some of his epistles St. Paul refers to nature when specifying sexual sin. But it is unlikely that "nature" for Paul referred to some universal law to which human beings must conform; Paul rather uses the word in the sense of what is common, usual, or characteristic of an individual or group (Boswell, 1980). Stringent Jewish values on sexuality were affirmed by Stoic philosophy. Although the great value placed on sexual fertility among the Jewish people is not identical with a philosophy of sexuality based on procreation, the principles — far from being incongruous — are rather complementary.

Harmonized with rigid Jewish sexual customs, the Stoic doctrine dominated the thought and teachings of the early Christian leaders. A basic mistrust of emotion and affection coupled with an unwillingness to appear dependent on another person preempted any consideration of love as a purpose of marriage or intercourse. The paramount standard became nature, not love.

While not the originator of the principle of procreation as the sole justification for sexual intercourse, St. Augustine was certainly its most influential proponent. From the early and high Middle

Ages until modern times, attitudes on sexual morality in Western civilization have been dominated by Augustinian thought. Although minor developments occurred at various historical points, it is impossible to exaggerate the power and persuasiveness of this fifth-century theologian. Augustine taught that as celibacy is preferred as a "higher state" of life than Christian marriage, virginity within marriage is more noble than intercourse. In a world in which women were not permitted to be the social or intellectual equal of men, Augustine could write, "I do not see what other help woman would be to man if the purpose of generating was eliminated" (Noonan, 1965: 129). From the time of Augustine until the beginning of the nineteenth century, only minor variations on the basic procreational theme were voiced.

Within the Augustinian analysis of human sexuality the questions of recognizing or approving the marriage of an aged or sterile couple was discussed at great length but remained fundamentally unresolved. Although the practice of blessing such heterosexual unions devoid of any possibility of generating new life was permitted since earliest church times, such couples either were enjoined to refrain totally from sexual intercourse under penalty of sin or were permitted intercourse in order to avoid fornication. As unions of homosexual couples were not similarly blessed, a double standard existed whereby childless sexual unions were sanctioned, — in practice if not in theory — in one case but not in the other (Kosnik et al., 1977).

With changing sociological conditions and improved technology, it became evident that an increasing number of European Christians were not adhering strictly to their religious tenets in sexual matters. Declining birth rates were recorded in many European countries by the end of the nineteenth century, and there was good reason to contend that the principal reason was contraception. Advocacy for birth control developed in England and in the United States in the last one hundred years; by the twentieth century the movement supporting contraception had become international.

In the twentieth century a visible transformation occurred in the professional worlds of law, medicine, and religion. United States judicial and legislative actions prohibiting the use, sale, or importation of contraceptive devices eventually ceased by mid-century. Except for Catholic institutions, the majority of medical schools were providing courses on contraception by the 1930s. Following the lead of the Anglican Church, which recognized at its Lambeth Conference that means of contraception other than complete abstinence may be used, the authoritative bodies of most major Christian denominations began to rethink and to change their official prohibitions against contraceptive devices. Except for the Roman Catholic Church which still officially opposes any means other than abstinence, substantial agreement exists among the Christian community regarding the permissibility of some form of birth control. Within the last decade, however, surveys revealed that more than 80 percent of the American Catholic population do not accept this official Catholic doctrine, thus causing a grave credibility crisis in Catholic leadership. That official church, state, and medical judgments shifted only after a change in popular opinion and subsequent public action is an interesting sociological observation.

DEFINITIONS OF NATURE

Given that the legal and medical institutions initially supported the leadership of the religious establishment in opposing information, use, and acceptance of contraceptives and that the official Catholic Church still remains a major moral force in its prohibition, it is incumbent upon us to examine the religious arguments that maintain a necessary link between sexual intercourse and biological generation. The classic explanation hinges on the Stoic exaltation of natural law. Between the fifteenth and nineteenth centuries most theologians writing on sexuality divided sexual sins into two categories: those in accordance with nature (i.e., open to procreation) and those contrary to nature (i.e., inhibiting procreation). Thus anal and oral intercourse, masturbation, bestiality, coitus interruptus, and intercourse during pregnancy were considered unnatural; adultery, fornication, and rape were considered sinful but natural.

Four distinct concepts of nature were used historically in Christian disputations on sexuality. Appealing to the human's biological heritage, the first sense of the term natural was equated with animal behavior. St. Thomas Aquinas, for example, considered contraception "against nature, for even the beasts look for offspring" (Noonan, 1965: 242). Like the early Church Fathers, the scholastic theologians selectively chose their analogies of what was natural in order to reinforce views already held. So at times, natural was described as what was different from the animals. For example, the position in intercourse of the woman beneath the man was thought to be natural because any other position was comparable to "brute animals" (Noonan, 1965: 241). Can an insistence on a "natural" position in intercourse reflect an antediluvian belief in the supposed "natural" superiority of man over woman? A consistent application of patterns of animal sexual behavior would have revealed that animals do indeed engage in modes of sexual expression that do not admit of generation.

A second sense of nature rests on a structural argument. As the vagina is an obvious receptacle for the penis, any use of the male sexual organ other than for the deposit of semen in the appropriate vessel was deemed unnatural. An examination of the male and female bodies in which the parts manifestly "fit" showed the truth to be self-evident; axioms require no demonstration. Such reasoning illustrates an argument by limitation or restriction. The fact that one form of linkage is obvious and rather common does not render alternative modes "unnatural." Because human genitalia fit together in one way does not preclude other ways of sexual matching.

A third, but similar, description of what is natural was one proposed in functional, rather than structural, terms. An obvious — and therefore natural — physiological function of the genital organs is reproduction. But to maintain that a particular bodily organ serves only one purpose seems provincial at best. In the human evolutionary development, hands serve as a means of grasping, not of walking. Yet who would object that hands be used in conveying greetings or other emotional messages because such actions are contrary to the nature of hands? Would anyone deny that the mouth, whose primal function is food ingestion, has a second and socially higher function of verbal communication? Would proponents of a single purpose theory refuse to admit that another purpose of the penis is demonstrated in the biological process of elimination of urine?

Sexual moralists today almost unanimously acknowledge more than one purpose of human sexuality and human intercourse by differentiating between the reproductive and unitive functions of human sexuality. Many theologians (Keane, 1977; Kosnik et al.,

1977; Nelson, 1978; Pittinger, 1970) maintain that the two functions need not be present simultaneously in every act of sexual activity in order to render the action ethically responsible.

In addition to these three concepts of nature based on animal behavior, structure, and function, a fourth understanding of nature involved what a human being *should* be, not what animals might do nor how certain organs functioned or were structured. An object's nature consisted in that which made it essentially or actually what it was or what God intended it to be. The key question, of course, is what is the divine purpose? Do such arguments merely interpret human preference and prejudice as God's will? Along with divine intent, one must also examine human motives to determine whether insistence on the unnaturalness of contraception, homosexuality, or masturbation is merely a reflection of an unconscious desire to legitimate the existing social order. Unexamined cultural assumptions influence human perceptions and judgments; what is conveniently regarded as natural is often an expression of a deep-seated cultural bias. Such appeals to God's intent are at least questionable and can lead to such absurd deductions as "If God wanted beings to fly, God would have given them wings. Therefore, the airplane is unnatural." While the faith of those who hold these positions cannot be questioned, their interpretation of human sexuality certainly can and should be.

A current understanding of nature is one which is dynamic and constantly in flux. Aristotle taught that fire by its nature moved away from the center of the universe. When science demonstrated the Copernican theory in which the earth was no longer viewed as the central planetary body, the Aristotelian concept of the nature of fire was revised. Similarly, the ancient Greeks believed that every earthly object was composed of earth, air, water, or fire. But a deeper understanding of physics and chemistry demanded a more sophisticated explanation of the nature of any object in the universe. As species of living objects themselves are gradually being transformed by evolution, the human perception of such objects' natures is continually adapting and in need of revision. Even slight variations in successive generations of a species influence the constantly developing human understanding of nature.

Unless rigid or static, a construct of human nature popular in 500 B.C. or in A.D. 1300 is not identical to a contemporary perception of human nature which incorporates scientific advancement and current data from the behavioral sciences. Accurate knowledge regarding human reproduction was not discovered until after 1875. Basing their philosophical and theological arguments in the context of the biological data of their day, our religious forebears can be exonerated for their understandably limited analysis of human sexuality. But with the quantum leaps that have been achieved in biology, psychology and sociology, the twentieth-century believer must subject traditional religious arguments about nature to more thorough and critical analyses. Today's personalist interpretation of human nature is not bound by a static view reminiscent of Freud's "biology is destiny" but rather is struggling to free itself from biological imperatives.

LOVE AND SEXUALITY

In addition to the obvious biological purpose of human intercourse stressed by the Western Christian tradition, there is certainly an equally obvious affectional purpose — namely, human love. The human collective consciousness of the relationship between personal love and sexuality is a relatively recent historical development requiring centuries to unfold and expand in broad proportions. This is not to say that for centuries no individuals engaged in genital intercourse because of human affection for each other but rather that a notion linking love and sexuality did not come into societal awareness until the appearance of twelfth-century courtly love rhapsodized by the French troubadours. Celebrating the sexual pleasures of woman and man in extramarital romance up to but not including genital intercourse, the troubadours divorced the procreative purpose from genital acts. Courtly love brought to social consciousness an awareness that a sexual experience can be a meaningful human encounter (Richardson, 1974).

The integration of marriage and romantic love arose in the seventeenth century as part of a more comprehensive social revolution that posited that societal structures should be adapted to meet human needs instead of vice versa. The Quakers and the Puritans began to teach that the primary purpose of sexual intercourse (within marriage, of course) was communion. Children, believed to be an added but nonessential good, did not legitimate marriage and sexual expression but completed them. But Western Christian thought did not easily follow the Puritan and Quaker lead in relating love and genital expression.

Perhaps this religious languor can be attributed to the supposed spiritual superiority of celibacy and to the fact that Christian teachings on marriage and sexuality were formulated almost exclusively by males committed both institutionally and personally to a celibate life-style. A society in which mating customs revolved around property, children, and social class rather than around love and affection as important marital values may also help to explain but certainly does not exonerate the theological delay in integrating marital intercourse with love.

A substantial theological development in this regard occurred only after World War I. Dietrich von Hildebrand, the first married layman to contribute substantively to the Catholic tradition on marriage and sexuality, repudiated a mere biological approach and declared that love must be a necessary element of marital intercourse. After twenty centuries Christian theologians were beginning to acknowledge that genuine expressions of human love constituted a moral justification for sexual relations.

If in the centuries following the Middle Ages the connection between love and sexuality began to grow, it is only in the modern period that love is viewed in terms of psychological intimacy (Calderone, 1971). In an often lonely and fragmented modern life-style, the hunger for intimacy and meaning becomes not an occasional desire but almost a constant need. Physical and emotional attractions can spark a further drive for a more significantly intensive union. Many persons seem to be searching for a private communion with another human being who can be companion, friend, and lover and with whom a mutuality and sharing of lives will help to dispel some of the desolate feelings of isolation inevitable to human living. When such a person is found, there is a desire to express the psychological union and closeness in sexual way. Equally important is the desire for pleasure and ecstacy which sexual union brings. Genital actions then become signs or expressions of genuine love which includes the enormous satisfaction of receiving pleasure and of giving oneself to another person in complete love.

But what is love? Certainly it is not a reduction to a sentimental caricature nor an over-emphasis on a spiritual or angelic bond.

Pittinger (1970) characterizes love by at least five elements: commitment or dedication, a desire to give, a readiness to receive, an anticipation of a newness or a refreshing surprise in the relationship, and a mutual sharing or union.

Commitment or dedication involves a willingness to entrust oneself to another, to let another stand by us, and to take responsibility for the other. Commitment engenders a feeling of safety or security, a confidence in knowing that each partner will not let the other down. Masters and Johnson (1976), the most popular sexual researchers in America today, view some form of commitment as an essential part of truly satisfying sex.

In genuine love there is a self-giving of the human personality, of body as well as mind. But such openness and pure gift in which nothing is hidden or cautiously held back is balanced by the other's gift of honesty and openness and by one's humble willingness to receive. Receiving, however, is not a requirement for loving. Love is not a business venture, not an investment involving prudent risk and expectations of high dividends from which one pulls out if adequate returns do not accrue. The receiving which is part of loving is a confession of one's own insufficiency and guards against the domination of constant unilateral giving.

Those who are "in love" experience an eagerness and expectancy that seeks the creative and inexhaustibly novel wonders of the other. As the love relationship continues and deepens through years of "ups and downs," there may be long periods when the newness and fascination seems to have worn thin. But a living love does not permit a lethal monotony to suffocate a significant relationship. The lover expects and unconsciously creates by enticing allurement an atmosphere of delight which releases new energy. This expectation tempts, stimulates, and excites the other in a self-fulfilling prophecy.

Finally, love is a union or communion of two whole, integrated persons — not one needing the complementarity of the other. Communion signifies an interdependence and mutuality of two mature adults in which sharing does not blur each one's individuality or distinctness.

But is not such a description of love idealistic? Yes, certainly. As human beings in the process of becoming who we are meant to be, "the important question is whether we are *on the way there*, not whether we have in fact arrived" (Pittenger, 1970: 46).

SEXUAL PLEASURE

Not to be denied or underrated, the sexual ecstasy of human intercourse experienced individually through the ages was brought to Western social consciousness also only in the twentieth century. The importance of sexual pleasure or satisfaction as a human value can be traced, among other factors, to a post-Victorian sexual revolution, the women's equality movement, and an improved technology which lessened (if not virtually eliminated) pregnancy fears. No less than the ancients' Adonis and Aphrodite, the contemporary paradigms of the American sexual revolution — the Playboy/Playmate couple — parade across the globe as sexual-identity models. Acknowledging that the Playboy philosophy reflects a traditional patriarchalism and exploitation of sex, the Presbyterian theologian Herbert Richardson nonetheless singles out Playboy's positive contribution to the evolutionary conceptual-ization of sexual life. In a unique and surprising fashion, Richard-son maintains that the Playboy/Playmate symbol portrays the attractive and alluring woman as a friend and equal to man:

> The Playmate is not of interest simply for her sexual functions alone. The photo montage that surrounds the playmate portrays her in a variety of everyday activities: going to work, visiting her family, climbing mountains and sailing, dancing and dining out, figuring out her income tax. She is, first and foremost, the Playboy's all-day, all-night pal. . . .
>
> The Playmate likes mountain climbing, working for a living, and being independent. The Playboy likes to cook (he's a gourmet chef!), enjoys shopping for cosmetics and fashionable clothes (for himself!), and even is interested in playing "mother" to the kids. The Playboy LIKES children. Imagine that! [Richardson, 1971: 90–91].

While Harvey Cox rejects the Playboy "girlie" philosophy as "departmentalized sex" and therefore "basically antisexual," it is nonetheless true that the worldwide success and popularity of the Hefner enterprise underscores a human desire to recognize socially — even to legitimate institutionally — the pleasures of sex. The mass media sexual image, which is both an indicator and an influencer of public opinion, signals a version of sexuality as entertainment/recreation and brings a note of freedom and frankness to otherwise stuffy and clinical discussions of sex. Whatever its shortcomings, the signification illustrated by Playboy's monthly magazine has enabled even rigid moralists to admit the permissibility of enjoying sex. Cox's protestations notwithstanding, the "gospel [of Playboy] frees us from captivity to the puritanical 'hatpin brigade'" (Cox, 1965: 176). An authentic gender maturity wraps the box of sexual responsibility with appealing and seductive ribbons. One need not be a hedonist to acknowledge that sex is fun. Sexual partners can be, indeed hopefully are, erotic stimulants for each other.

As a civilization Western society is discovering or rediscovering the playfulness of sex — a sex that can be filled not only with passion and intensity but also with merriment, surprise, and delight. When children play, their imagination and resourcefulness come alive. By repressing the fun-loving pleasure principle, too many adults risk becoming less human. The sexual interlude of the bedroom game can transform serious and mundane lives into a fantasy and festival of play. For the professional basketball, tennis, or hockey player, and for the dancer, comedian, or nightclub entertainer, even the play which seems casual, spontaneous, and effortless requires a patient and disciplined practice. So also frolicsome sexual loveplay takes practice — the practice of prolonged foreplay for each encounter as well as the practice of years of experimentation for skillful interaction. But the pleasurable rewards are well worth the persistent efforts. The novelty and excitement of rich and playful lovemaking become an endless exploration of the spiritual and sensual mysteries of one's partner (Greeley, 1975).

A PERSONAL POSTSCRIPT

Three distinct purposes of sexual intercourse have been delineated: biological, affectional, and recreational. Is the presence of a specific one of these purposes necessary to an ethical use of one's sexual powers? That depends, of course, on one's symbolic value system. As I remarked at the beginning of this article, virtually no presentation — no matter how much one consciously attempts to be objective — is totally value free. Even an exposition of indisputable factual information suffers from selectivity. Why are some facts chosen for enumeration while others are ignored? In keeping with the limits of objectivity, I wish to end with a personal postscript on the meaning of human sexuality gained from my decades of dealing with religion, sex, and politics.

The sociologist Ira Reiss (1960) has suggested two basic models of sexual attitude and behavior: body-centered and person-centered. The body-centered perspective compartmentalizes sensual pleasure; sex is merely orgasm and physical satisfaction. In the body-centered standard sex as a tension release is an end in itself; it is the gratification of an uncontrollable appetite. On the other hand, a person-centered sexual expression does not deny or denigrate the body but demands an integration of erotic instinct, affection, and commitment; sex is used as an expression of a relationship. Person-centered intercourse manifests esteem, tenderness, reverence, and respect for the human dignity of the other person.

I stand in favor of a person-centered ordering of sexual attitudes and behaviors. Within such an organization, fulfillment is not achieved through *mere* physical gratification because genital pleasure alone cannot impact the total personality. But let there be no misunderstanding of my position: I stand wholeheartedly in favor of playful sexuality, of laughter, lightheartedness, and pleasure. I stand in favor of a person-centered sexuality in which the central values of love and affection are expressed with tenderness, kindness, and care. Complete enjoyment depends upon *mutual* enjoyment.

Sexual intercourse with whom? Adults can learn much by watching the interpersonal dynamics of children. With whom do children play? With friends they like and care about. So also I believe that sexual play becomes human when the lovers are also friends who truly care about each other. Some who search for the ultimate in human sexual satisfaction would argue in favor of multiple significant relationships. To them I reply with Elliston's (1975) conclusion in his clever defence of promiscuity: "What the dialogue . . . achieves in breath, it may lose in depth: having talked with many, we may discover that our most meaningful dialogue can be carried on with one (pp. 239–40). When all is said and done, "the intentionally lifelong relationship is intrinsically more valuable . . . [than] intentionally temporary relations" (p. 240).

Within a person-centered approach to structuring human sexuality, such questions as "Is this specific sexual act right or wrong at this time?" or "What is the purpose of human sexual intercourse?" are really moot. The central issues need to be recast. The goal of the entire sexual behavior process becomes mutuality.

What are the possible ties between human intercourse, love, pleasure, marriage, children, and other human values? Society is yet searching for the archetypes which flesh out our sexual ideals. Using the knowledge of the collective consciousness, each one must forge a satisfactory sexual ethic for oneself. "Freedom for mature sexuality comes to man [sic] only when he is freed from the despotic powers which crowd and cower him into fixed patterns of behavior" (Cox, 1965: 178).

I believe that there are no sure universal norms or laws by which to regulate or control sexual behavior between consenting adults. To legislate sexual rules runs the risk of oversimplifying some complex human issues. For me, the kind of sexual expression — even within marriage — is correlated to the depth of mutual affection and felt intimacy. For me, there is a vision that can make sexuality human — a vision that regards coition between human beings as more than biological copulation. What makes sexuality human is precisely the meaning or the significance which humans can invest in sexual acts.

NOTE

1. See John T. Noonan, Jr.'s comprehensive historical development of Western Christian thought on contraception upon which I substantially depend.

REFERENCES

BOSWELL, J. (1980) Christianity, Social Tolerance, and Homosexuality. Chicago: University of Chicago Press.
CALDERONE, M.S. (1971) Sex, Love and Intimacy. New York: Siecus.

COX, H. (1965) The Secular City. New York: Macmillan.

ELLISTON, F. (1975) "In defense of promiscuity," in R. Baker and F. Elliston (eds.) Philosophy and Sex. Buffalo, NY: Prometheus Books.

GREELEY, A. (1975) Love and Play. Chicago: Thomas More Press.

KEANE, P. S. (1977) Sexual Morality: A Catholic Perspective. New York: Paulist Press.

KOSNIK, A., W. CARROLL, A. CUNNINGHAM, R. MODRAS, and J. SCHULTE (1977) Human Sexuality: New Directions in American Catholic Thought. New York: Paulist Press.

MASTERS, W. H., and JOHNSON, V. E. (1976) The Pleasure Bond. New York: Bantam.

NELSON, J. B. (1978) Embodiment: An Approach to Sexuality and Christian Theology. Minneapolis: Augsburg Publishing House.

NOONAN, J. T., Jr. (1965) Contraception. Cambridge, MA: Harvard University Press.

PITTENGER, W. N. (1970) Making Sexuality Human. Philadelphia: Pilgrim Press.

REISS, I. L. (1960) Premarital Sexual Standards in America. New York: The Free Press.

RICHARDSON, H. W. (1971) Nun, Witch, Playmate. New York: Harper & Row.

FUNCTIONS OF INTERCOURSE

Questions

1. *If the Catholic Church says that sexual intercourse is only for procreation, then what about sterile couples and menopausal women?*

2. *The Catholic Church sees the rhythm method or natural family planning as the only acceptable means of birth control. What are the advantages and disadvantages of this method?*

3. *If the purpose of sexual intercourse is procreation, then aren't unmarried couples who conceive children fulfilling that purpose?*

4. *If marriage and intercourse between sterile or aged couples is sanctioned, why are homosexual couples denied these rights?*

5. *What has changed our thinking about human sexuality away from religious doctrines to what it is today?*

6. *What are all the possible purposes of sexual intercourse?*

SEX AND MARRIAGE

IV–A

Sex Should Occur Only within Marriage

WALTER R. SCHUMM
GEORGE A. REKERS

Inasmuch as other scholars have presented a great many effective traditional arguments for keeping sexual relationships (herein abbreviated as simply, "sex") within marriage, our intention here is not to repeat their theological (Grounds, 1968; C.S. Lewis, 1960), ethical (Geisler, 1971; Murray, 1957), social and health-related (Miles, 1971; Scanzoni, 1975) reasons in detail but to focus instead on selected issues of self-interest with which the reader may be less familiar. We assume that our readers will pursue other sources concerning historical and cultural variation in premarital and extramarital sexual attitudes and behaviors (Reiss, 1980; Singh, 1980), including the changing vocabulary reflecting presuppositions associated with various sexual activities (Rekers and Braun, 1981). Excellent reviews of the literature on sexual behavior are available concerning premarital sexual behavior (Clayton and Bokemeier, 1980) and nontraditional sexual behaviors (Murstein, 1978; Macklin, 1980; Macklin and Rubin, 1983). Critiques of the quality of sex research, among other types of family studies research, are available elsewhere as well (Schumm et al., 1980; Schumm, 1982). We shall present some points in favor of our assigned position statement, disagreeing with what is probably the majority opinion among secular social scientists.[1] Throughout this process, however, we wish to avoid even the appearance of condemning anyone who may choose to disagree with our position or arguments in either attitude or practice. Our position is derived from our particular values. Therefore, it seems quite reasonable to us that other very scholarly persons could use equally valid or even better logic starting from a different set of values and presuppositional premises, and thereby arrive at quite different conclusions from ours.

Jurich and Jurich (1974) presented an interesting research report in which they contrasted moral maturity with preferred premarital sexual standards among 160 upper division undergraduate students from eight coeducational colleges in the northeastern region of the United States. They found that proponents of the traditional standard (no sex before marriage), the double standard (sex is okay for males but not for "good" females), and the permissiveness-without-affection standard (sex is okay anytime, with anyone) scored equally low on moral maturity, while those students who favored the other two standards — permissiveness with affection (sex is okay when two people feel affection for each other) and nonexploitiveness without affection (sex is okay if neither person is trying to exploit the other, if there is a mutual understanding of the level of commitment entailed) — scored at moderate and high levels of moral maturity, respectively . It seemed surprising to us that those students who were the most religious and tended to opt for the traditional standard seemed to be among the *least* morally mature. In the process of evaluating Jurich and Jurich's (1974) study, the senior author devised a schema associating certain logical prerequisites with each sexual standard (Table IV–A.1).[2]

At the most basic level, the permissiveness-without-affection standard requires the physical consent of the other party, without which the activity could be classified as sexual assault or rape. The double standard achieves a somewhat higher level, with consideration given to the gender of the parties and the reputation of at least one of the parties. Of course, the double standard is biased sexually in favor of the male party. Permissiveness with affection adds a requirement for mutual affection or perhaps even love, at

TABLE IV–A.1 Prerequisites for Sexual Intercourse/Activity Versus Different Sexual Standards

	Permissive Standards			Conditional Standards		Commitment-Oriented Standards	
	Permissiveness without Affection	Double Standard	Permissiveness with Affection	Nonexploitive Permissiveness without Affection	Semi-traditional	Traditional (Modified)	Traditional (Ideal)
Religious commitment/covenant							?
Legal commitment/contract							X
Public commitment/engagement						X	X
Personal commitment/cohabitation					X	X	X
Nonexploitiveness/communication				X	X	X	X
Perceived love/affection			X	?	X	X	X
Consideration of reputation		X	X	X	X	X	X
Physical consent	X	X	X	X	X	X	X
Physical presence	X	X	X	X	X	X	X

least as perceived by the two persons. The nonexploitive-permissiveness-without-affection standard takes into account the mutually desired level of limiting prerequisites for intercourse of the parties, with an implicit assumption of some serious, honest communication having to occur between the two persons in order to establish the absence of at least overt exploitation.[3] We have identified the next standard as semitraditional, corresponding to the phenomenon of cohabitation which parallels traditional marriage in many respects only without the legal or public type of commitment that accompanies marriage. However, cohabitation does involve a personal commitment that is self-evident in the fairly weighty decision required to assume a relationship of living together. Of course, there are different types of cohabitation (Ridley et al., 1978) that may involve greater or lesser degrees of personal commitment, ranging from liaisons of convenience to essentially trial marriage. The next standard is the traditional standard; we have subdivided it into two categories to reflect a modified application of the standard which is to engage in intercourse after an official engagement, and the traditional ideal of abstinence until after the wedding ceremony. Although traditional marriage generally corresponds to the ideal traditional standard, we make a distinction between the civil, legal contract and the possible religious vows which may involve an unconditional covenant that features both persons promising to love each other regardless of what happens, even if the marriage should prove very disappointing. We assume that under normal conditions the prerequisites are ordered hierarchically, that there is a systematic progression in complexity of prerequisites as the standards change from permissiveness without affection to the traditional standard and with the prerequisites of more liberal standards generally included among the prerequisites of more conservative standards.[4]

PERSONAL VALUES AND SEXUAL CHOICE

It is clear that one's evaluation of the costs and rewards associated with different sexual behaviors does influence one's actual or projected choices (Bukstel et al., 1978). But what determines how one perceives and evaluates the various possible costs and rewards? We believe that one's personal values are primary determinants and that, therefore, it is essential that any such values be made explicit in the discussion of sexual choice. As we noted previously, given different value presuppositions two individuals using equally valid logical deduction and inference could arrive at entirely different conclusions and decisions regarding their personal sexual choices and regarding the relative advantages and disadvantages of various forms of sexual activity under certain conditions. Furthermore, values themselves may be derived from a variety of sources.

A popular lyric asks, "How can anything that feels so right be wrong?" Several such popular sources of values have important limitations. Majority rule or sociological norms are inadequate, we think, because such have justified slavery or pogroms in certain nations at certain points in history. Statistical norms (such as the Kinsey studies) can reveal what does occur most frequently but not necessarily what should be occuring. Even psychological guilt feelings are inadequate guides for ethical decision making as well, given the occurrence of "false" guilt feelings over apparently innocent situations (e.g., a person might feel guilty for being a single parent after their spouse died of cancer) and of minimal guilt feelings over obviously criminal actions (e.g., as when a psychopath kills others with no apparent remorse). In summary, while these sources of values are sometimes useful considerations, we cannot accept them as sufficient by themselves.

Scholarly ethical thinkers down through western intellectual history have generally taken one of two basic starting points for deriving human values. One viewpoint gaining adherents in twentieth-century Western and Eastern thinking is the materialistic presupposition that human existence and personality (including sexuality) are ultimately a product of preexisting energy or mass plus time plus chance. With this starting point, a humanistic ethic is built upon evolutionary concepts of the survival of the fittest, social responsibility, mutual consent, preservation of the human race, reason, and the greatest happiness in a situation. We wish to acknowledge that many intellectual and well-intentioned individuals work diligently to build a moral framework based on situationalism and an intended benevolent humanism.

The other basic ethical starting point used by scholars down through the Western civilization has been based in the theistic presupposition that human existence and personality (including sexuality) originate from the eternal preexistence of an infinite-personal Creator. The Judeo-Christian answer to the origins of human life explain human personality as a creation of God who is the source of love, meaning, significance, trust, and communication. From this perspective, the source for ethical value judgments regarding the acceptability for various sexual relationships resides in discovering the Creator's purpose and design in creating human beings as sexual creatures.

Having wrestled with the pros and cons of these two starting points, we have concluded that the theistic presupposition provides answers to the human questions of "Who am I? What is love? Where did human personality come from? What is sex? What is right?" where the materialistic presupposition is inadequate.

However, regardless of which starting point you choose — the materialistic view or the theistic view — you must start with a basic mystery: "Where did the first bit of mass or energy come from?" or "Where did God come from?" Our only point here is that it is no more or less scholarly or intellectual to start from either the materialistic or the theistic presupposition — both of our intellectual options leave us with some unanswered questions.

Within the limitations imposed by context, errors in translation, and errors of individual interpretation, we prefer to accept the authority of the Bible as the best guide for sexual decision making, as well as for many other areas of life. We consider Scripture to be important not because of tradition or institutional affiliation but because, after reasoned study, we make the assumption that they contain the wisdom of the Creator regarding the human condition and effective ways of relating to others interpersonally. In particular, we turn to the life of Jesus as a guide for our own value system. Several values were important in his life, values that we seek to incorporate more and more faithfully in our own lives. First, Jesus trusted in the word of his Father, that God's law as revealed in the "law and the prophets" was worth serious consideration (Luke 16:16–17, 18:20). In contrast, many people today pay minimal attention to the claims of revelation from God in either the Old or New Testaments, often overlooking them without first subjecting them to careful examination. Second, Jesus did not consider his mind or body something to be used at his own sole discretion but that it should be an instrument for service as God the Father directed (Luke 22:42). Third, Jesus considered both long- and short-term consequences in his decision making (see Matthew

5:10–12, 7:24–27; 16:24–26; Proverbs 16:2, 25 and Galatians 6:7–9 for related ideas). Jesus also seemed to remain skeptical about people's stated motives and intentions, apparently recognizing that self-deception/and deception of others are not uncommon (Matthew 15:7–9; Luke 14:32, 16:15, and 20:23). However, contrary to these values, we find many people asserting their total rights to their bodies and decisions, doubting the importance of long-term consequences of sexual decisions and assuming that fraud and exploitation in sex are not too difficult to detect outside of committed relationships. Nevertheless, despite such differences, we must side with Jesus in refusing to condemn people who adopt alternative sexual life-styles with which we disagree, even though many fundamentalist religious leaders in Jesus' time and now are willing to denounce them with something approaching fanatical eagerness (John 4:16–27, 8:1–11; Luke 15:2). In summary, it seems reasonable for us to conclude that sexual choice should involve an evaluation of short- and long-term consequences as they pertain to oneself, others, and God.

From these values, we deduce several implications for sexual choice. First, the Bible does cogently address the appropriateness of a variety of sexual behaviors under various conditions although we recognize that it does not use the same specific terminology regarding contemporary sexual standards that we have summarized. Second, we all have a heavy responsibility to use our bodies in the best interest of others, not to mention responsibility to honor God; just because something is gratifying to oneself alone in no way suffices to make it the right thing to do. Third, we feel obligated to weight the obvious immediate gratifications of sexual activity against any potential long-term consequences that might accrue to ourselves or others. In particular, we must take special heed to the danger of consciously or otherwise overlooking long-term consequences through various rationalizations that only serve our immediate self-interest sexually. Finally, we maintain that it is possible to disagree with others' values while not condemning them or adopting a superior attitude towards them even though others may doubt this (Knapp, 1975) and even though research instruments assume that disagreement and condemnation go hand in hand (e.g., Larsen et al., 1980). For example, even though we disagree with homosexual practice, we firmly believe it is possible to enjoy the company of homosexuals, to be nondefensive towards them, and to fully accept them without condemnation (Rekers,

1982a, 1982b). We do not claim to always succeed in such an attitude, but we hope to be able to imitate the way Jesus dealt with such situations.

EVALUATING SEXUAL STANDARDS

For convenience of discussing the ethical standards, we have divided them into three basic groups (Table IV–A.1). The first group, which we label permissive, consists of the permissiveness-without-affection standard and the double standard. Among these standards, there are relatively few restrictions placed on sexual activity. The second group of standards, which we shall call conditional, includes the permissiveness-with-affection standard, the nonexploitive-permissiveness-without-affection standard, and what we have called the semitraditional standard. Standards within this second group place prerequisites on sexual intercourse in varying degrees. The third group of standards, which we shall label as commitment-oriented, includes the two versions of the traditional standard. We recognize that the placement of the semitraditional standard is somewhat arbitrary as at least some forms of cohabitation do involve considerable commitment; however, we felt that the qualitative difference between private and public/legal commitment justified the distinction.

Because our assigned task is to argue the traditional sexual standard (see Chapter IV–C by Catherine S. Chilman for an argument for the advantages of sex outside of marriage), we will discuss some of the disadvantages of commitment-oriented standards. We do recognize many apparent advantages of sex outside of marriage — which had been amply illustrated elsewhere (Murstein, 1978; Newcomb, 1979) — including sexual gratification, companionship, economic gain, relief from boredom, and so on. We do not intend, as Reiss (1981: 274) suggests many do, to imagine that only negative consequences accompany what we consider to be sexually wrong.

PERMISSIVE STANDARDS

Historically, permissive standards for sexual activity have simply been dismissed as immoral. Today, however, greater social acceptance exists for simple body-centered sexuality (Reiss, 1981) although many people who approve of it reject it for themselves in practice (Maykovich, 1976). More approval tends to be given to permissive premarital sexual activity than to permissive extra marital sexual activity, which may be an indirect result of differential Old Testament sanctions which have historically shaped values in Western culture (Deuteronomy 22:22–29).

Warnings against permissive sexuality in terms of the health risks of pregnancy and sexually transmitted disease are probably in today's society like cheap locks on bicycles parked in public — good for keeping honest people honest but ineffective in stopping determined thieves. In other words, such warnings are probably most effective for discouraging those who don't really want to get involved sexually from becoming involved. However, many people do not fully appreciate one limitation in current contraceptive technology, even in those cases in which it is used with permissive sexuality. At present, there is no such thing as a "sure bet" contraceptively. Those devices such as the pill that are the most highly effective for preventing conception (realizing that none is 100% effective) actually may increase the risk of contracting certain types of venereal disease to which one may be exposed. On the other hand, those methods such as the condom with foam that are more effective at preventing venereal disease are relatively less effective (in practice if not in theory) at preventing conception. In other words, there is to some extent an inverse relationship between contraceptive effectiveness and prophylactic effectiveness. With these trade-offs, there remain certain levels of health risks associated with sexual permissiveness, including the risk of contracting the incurable and often painful genital herpes. The second author, as a clinical psychologist, has counseled many young people who have incurable venereal diseases from premarital intercourse—some of whom have even given up hope of marrying, not wanting to expose someone they love to the pain of the disease.

A second concern we have pertains to the reasons for which some people choose to engage in permissive sexual activity. Research during the past decade (Macklin, 1980) has consistently supported the idea that a substantial number of people engage in permissive sexual behavior such as extramarital sex as a way of dealing with other problems, such as a disappointing marriage characterized by reduced sexual interaction. Although not all persons do so for such reasons, enough do to lead to a consistent, moderate statistical relationship between marital dissatisfaction and extramarital involvement. We also agree with Schmidt (1982) who has expressed concern that people too often try to compensate for personal feelings of emptiness, boredom, of self-doubt by casual participation in the ecstasies of sexuality. We are concerned that such short-term solutions may exacerbate existing personal problems, leading to a rather destructive and spiraling escalation of those difficulties. Furthermore, at best the satisfactions from permissive sexual liaisons may compensate enough for the initial dissatisfaction as to discourage concerted attempts to remedy the factors causing the initial dissatisfaction. Instead of trying to improve their marital communication in order to improve their sex life, spouses may settle for an occasional sexual fling to maintain a desired overall satisfaction level. Much extramarital sex therefore ironically undermines the achievement of the highest forms of sexual fulfillment.

Third, we are concerned that permissive sex may adversely affect a person's reputation and their ultimate range of choice in potential marital partners. At least one recent study (Istvan and Griffitt, 1980) suggests that the desirability of highly sexually experienced women for marriage is quite a bit less than for mere dating, *even among men who are highly experienced themselves*— a manifestation perhaps of the double standard at work. As Josh McDowell says in his university lectures on "Maximum Sex," a lot of guys who won't buy used furniture are themselves in the antiquing business (McDowell and Lewis, 1980). Among inexperienced subjects, highly experienced partners were seen as much, much less acceptable than other inexperienced partners (for dating and for marriage). We hope that our readers will not fall for the "Of course I'll respect you in the morning" line, because it is not true in most cases. In fact, Weis and Slosnerick (1981) have observed a significant association between sexual permissiveness and a tendency to disassociate sex and love.

We do recognize with Reiss (1981) that this sort of double standard is sometimes subtly encouraged, even in religious circles — a situation that we deeply regret. One only has to remember that it was the *woman* who was caught in adultery who was brought to Jesus for execution by the Pharisees (John 8:1–11); one wonders what became of the male party.

Although we view permissive standards as more acceptable than sex without physical consent (rape) and more honest than getting married *only* to legitimize sexual relations, we have grave reservations about the practical wisdom of permissive sexual activity, even apart from our purely ethical concerns.

CONDITIONAL STANDARDS

In America, conditional standards receive much wider acceptance than do the permissive standards. We suggest that most Americans, excepting perhaps the very religious, accept some form of conditional standard. The senior author recalls a comment by Eleanor Macklin during a visit to Kansas State University while he was a graduate student that essentially stated that half of all college students would cohabit at some time, one-fourth would if they had the opportunity (but they didn't), and the remaining one-fourth were just too religious. Indeed, even we find the conditional standards *more* acceptable than the permissive standards because they recognize more of what we view as important elements of strong interpersonal relationships. In one aspect we agree with Reiss (1981) who, although an advocate of body-centered sexuality, admits that person-centered sexuality is better and that fraud and force have no place in sexual interaction.

However, we differ from Reiss (1981) in our estimation of the danger and actual extent of sexual exploitation, especially of women. Faced with concrete, indisputable, short-term benefits in a very active sexual relationship, we question how many people will have sufficient presence of mind to adequately weigh potential long-term costs for themselves or the other person. No doubt some will feel quite content with their decisions years later, but we suspect that the majority do not and would have made different decisions if they had been able to accurately anticipate all of the consequences of their decisions. Many times two persons may think they are both following the same conditional standard when in fact one party has no intentions of the same long-term relationship as does the other (Newcomb, 1979). The conditional standards *beg* for exploitation to occur, with the immediacy of substantial short-term gains making it all too easy to rationalize one's behavior, to overlook or minimize things that are important to building a relationship in the long run, or to disregard the long-term welfare of oneself or the other person. Unfortunately, it is easy to deceive even oneself about one's intentions or the true meaning of one's words. If one realizes that the easiest way to quick gratification of one's sexual tensions in a relationship is to say certain combinations of words (e.g., "I really love you" or "I really do think we ought to consider marriage someday"), then it becomes very easy to think "Well, I really do love her sort of, in my own way (even though she may not think of it quite the same way)." It is amazing how cheap such terribly significant but empty words can become in such situations.

We also need to ask, "What effect do conditional standards held before marriage have on later marriage?" Premarital sexual attitudes and behavior are highly correlated with projected extramarital sexual behavior (Bukstel et al., 1978). The story of "sure, I've messed around, but once I get married I will never do it again" should be accepted with great caution. We are concerned that even if a person avoids some form of exploitation in the premarital relationship that exploitation might occur later after marriage when expectations concerning extramarital sexual activity could be violated.

We think that it is ironic that Reiss (1981) and others associate traditionalism with a sexual inequality bias when (in our observation) it is the conditional standards rather than the traditional standards that leave the women most vulnerable to sexual exploitation. Requirements on the male to make a commitment ("put up or shut up") would seem to be a deterrent to easy "lines" about how much affection or personal commitment might be involved in exchange for sexual favors. We would argue that the traditional standards are the ones that best promote sexual equality.

We are also concerned about the potential for premature sex to inhibit communication in a developing relationship. While it is tough to communicate, it's easy to make love; thus, it is all too easy to soon have an imbalanced relationship (Lucado, 1983). How easy is it to continually avoid dealing with touchy but important issues through various levels of sexual activity, even at levels below sexual intercourse. Once an imbalance develops between emotional intimacy and physical intimacy, the effect can spiral in an escalating fashion as more and more sex is needed to offset growing anxiety about the underlying strength of the relationship.

However, many feel that the conditional standards permit one to test a relationship prior to making the commitment to marry someone. Of course, as long as someone knows that they are being scrutinized for signs of "incompatibility," there is probably a tendency to avoid letting down one's guard to reveal the "real me," which occurs quite often after marriage. Therefore, we doubt for theoretical reasons that premarital testing can ever be completely effective. Yet it would seem to be an attractive way of ensuring that one at least does not marry a totally unsuitable partner. However, current research, even by those who have expected otherwise (Watson, 1983), tends to find little support for the proposition that even cohabitation, — the closest parallel to marriage — can help one select good or bad partners in a way that will ultimately increase one's eventual marital satisfaction. Likewise, we know of no research that supports the ability of cohabitation or premarital intercourse to strengthen a weak relationship although it is possible for relationships that were strong to begin with to survive premarital intercourse (Kirkendall, 1961). In this regard, the wife of a Professor at Purdue University stated a profound truth in her comment, "You aren't married until you're married." Conditional standards often suggest that the marital state can be established outside of marriage, at least in terms of the relative rewards and costs; however, we feel that such aspirations are simply unrealistic if not misleading, and too often are a way of trying to "kill the goose for its golden eggs" rather than being content with the more gradual development of an intimate sexual relationship.

However, the conditional standards are not without positive aspects, especially as compared only to purely permissive standards. Yet the commitment-oriented standards offer greater rewards in the long run, as well as tending to minimize some of the profound risks that are inherent in the conditional standards.

COMMITMENT-ORIENTED STANDARDS

Unfortunately, much religious family-life education is faulty in that it relies upon unbiblical precepts about sexuality that were adopted by the early, medieval church (Bullough, 1977; Scanzoni,

1975). Too often commitment-oriented standards have been presented in exclusively negative terms (i.e., no sex before marriage) rather than in positive terms. This is the reason we are no longer surprised at Jurich and Jurich's (1974) finding that adherents of the traditional standard scored lowest on moral maturity — the average such student probably seldom encountered a very sophisticated approach to sexual morality within their religious socialization, probably hearing mostly negative injunctions and sanctions regarding specific forbidden behaviors.

In contrast, we are interested in more than what is merely permissible; we are concerned about what makes for the *best* sex, not just "good" sex. We are convinced by observation, logic, years of marriage counseling experience and available evidence that commitment-oriented standards yield the highest probability of long-term benefits within the context of real life with its daily frustrations and responsibilities. Sex detached from mundane constraints as in a brief affair may feel more sweet at the time (Proverbs 9:6–23; 20:17), but Stafford (1983) has eloquently described a better alternative:

> Let me now get to the heart of my subject. I have been married for five years, and I am not going to try to kid you that sex in marriage is always like life in a *Playboy* fantasy. You've probably guessed that already, having rarely seen your father come to the breakfast table grinning like Hugh Hefner.

> But the problem is not marriage. The problem is life. Life is not like a *Playboy* fantasy. Not for anybody, not even Hugh.

> What messes up sex is people. It turns out, in practice, that while the technique of great sex is tricky, the demands on your personality are much, much more critical. You have to love another person. It isn't easy, day after day. The initial thrills, the newness, disappear. Your differences can make getting along difficult. You lose self-consciousness with each other, and that's good. But if you are the least bit lazy, the lack of self-consciousness easily becomes complacency, not even trying to please each other. You have to cope with what you don't like about the other person and with what you don't like about yourself. This all affects sex. It does for anybody, married or not. It's just that some people split up before they even get

started at the hard parts of achieving great sex — and great love.

But marriage, Christian marriage, makes you stick with it. When splitting up is not a serious consideration you have the best chance to find satisfaction, love, and yes, even great sex. Because you keep on working at it, year after year.

But in the process, you find out that sex was something different from what you thought. It is greater, and lesser, than you ever imagined. Great as sex is, it shrinks in comparison to the greatness of the love of your partner that hides nothing, knows everything, shares everything, and loves all the more. Sex becomes almost incidental, as just one part of the wonderful experience of true oneness with another human being.

But in this oneness — this love — sex is also greater than you thought. It is more than thrill and pleasure. It has tied you into the deepest springs of love, love that has no limits and no end. This best sex is like a wonderful food. The sensations it offers — the smells, the tastes, the feelings — are fantastic. But the way it nourishes and heals you is even better.

I am not trying to kid you. Sex in marriage isn't always, or even usually, like that. But it is sometimes. And from what I know, you can find the best sex nowhere else. It is very much worth waiting for with all your patience, and very much working toward, with all your energy.

Sex reserved for marriage facilitates an exclusive association of sexual pleasure with the marital relationship and *only* the marital relationship; a couple can then genuinely say, "This is something unique in space and time to our relationship alone. No one else has or will ever share it. It is something of ourselves and for ourselves that is very, very special, for us alone to cherish and enjoy." We question whether something quite precious is not lost when a couple cannot honestly say such things about their relationship.

Such a viewpoint will strike many, we assume, as quite unrealistic. Yes, that and the idea of a lifelong commitment are unrealistic by ordinary standards, we agree. As C. S. Lewis (1960: 101–102) once said,

> My own view is that the Churches should frankly recognize that
> the majority of the . . . people are not Christians, and
> therefore cannot be expected to live Christian lives. There
> ought to be two distinct kinds of marriage: one governed by
> the State with rules enforced on all citizens, the other
> governed by the Church with rules enforced by her on her
> own members. The distinction ought to be quite sharp, so that
> a man knows which couples are married in a Christian sense
> and which are not.

For Christians, the marital relationship is an act of faith, of faith in
the God who will provide the necessary wisdom and strength to
make even the seemingly incompatible marriage endure and
promote the personal and mutual growth of both spouses. Furthermore, it serves as a model of the covenant between God and his
people, something much different qualitatively from a mere legal
contract (with various implicit or explicit escape clauses). In the
type of covenant of which we are speaking, each party commits
themselves not only to an enduring relationship but to the other
party's long-term welfare, specifically, personally, and unconditionally. We do not say, "I will hang around as long as you make
me feel reasonably happy, after that I might leave." Rather, we say,
"I will be here for you, with you regardless of what you may say or
do, even if it means you take the opportunity of my vulnerability to
exploit me" — to loosely paraphrase the wedding vow which
expresses enduring commitment "for better or for worse." It is an
agreement not to be entered into lightly. But we feel it offers the
greatest potential for personal growth and fulfillment of the many
alternatives for sexual relationships that are available. We believe
that sex is a wonderfully appropriate vehicle for celebrating such
an intimate and lasting love relationship, and that this kind of
marriage is the most desirable environment in which to conceive
and nurture children.

A final concern that must be addressed especially for the
religious reader is the question of sexual involvement short of
intercourse that is best given the different prerequisites. In other
words, for those who reject the notion of premarital or extramarital intercourse the question "How far should one go sexually,
outside of the marital relationship?" may arise. We have known
very strict colleagues to suggest that even kissing should be
reserved for marriage; however, we recognize that some intermedi-

ate level of activity is much more likely in today's society. The question becomes how to decide what is right for any given relationship. Many religious people end up doing just about anything except actual intercourse (sometimes called "technical virginity"), finding various ways of obtaining orgasms with each other in other ways (Mahoney, 1980). We have some concerns about such decisions even though our concern probably seems ridiculous to those who are debating only whether to engage in intercourse per se.

First, there is the problem of diminishing returns. Once a certain level of sexual arousal is reached, only the next level seems to offer promise of deeper excitement. It can be amazingly difficult to return to a previous, lower level of physical involvement short of breaking off a relationship completely. In this process, delicate points of emotional growth (as well as communication) can be overshadowed by the more alluring promises of sexual gratification or exploration. However, as Lucado (1983) has expressed it, "It is more vital to explore your partner's soul than their body."

Second, heavy premarital petting will build up associations between sexual arousal and ordinary dating so that when marriage occurs, foreplay is not something truly unique to the marital relationship but only a repeat of earlier experiences whose mental associations may interfere with full sexual enjoyment even if intercourse itself has been reserved for marriage. Thus, in some cases, sex can remain a painful reminder of a foolish summer or the cheap way one used to trade self-respect for social attention. The second author has counseled many married persons who have complained bitterly that no one had forewarned them that premarital permissiveness would have this unintended and distressing side effect. Sex can remain at the level of mechanical approaches that one used to provide one's partners with temporary thrills. In retrospect, the senior author would have adopted a much more conservative approach to premarital sexual exploration as a way of maximizing the full emotional development of relationships that tended to, as it was, proceed further in physical intimacy than was merited by their emotional depth and to minimize the unnecessary pain that often resulted as a consequence of that imbalance.

So we conclude with this: Sex is not equally acceptable within and outside of marriage because there is a genuine difference in personal consequences when all of the prerequisites for an ideal sexual relationships (listed in the left side of Table IV–A.1) are present as compared to situations where any of these prerequisites are missing. A sexual relationship has its greatest benefits for the person, the couple, and any potential children resulting from their physical union when *all* of these features are present: mutual physical consent, consideration of reputation, genuine love and affection, nonexploitiveness with communication, personal commitment to living together, public commitment, legal commitment with the protection of a state marriage license and a religious commitment by a covenant vow. Unacceptable risks to the welfare of both parties are present when any of these ingredients for a maximum sexual experience are missing.

This chapter by no means represents the final word on sexual ethics, even for the religious. We encourage our readers to study carefully the books we've listed in our reference section and others as well. We do hope that our presentation will provoke intelligent discussion comparing our position to the other one and serve as a vehicle for facilitating responsible independent sexual decision making by our readers to whom we extend our appreciation and our earnest concern that you too will experience the best that the gift of sexuality has to offer.

NOTES

1. Upon hearing that we were undertaking such a controversial chapter, more than one of our colleagues attempted to dissuade us from it, arguing that it would be scholarly "suicide," especially for the non-tenured senior author.

2. The standards are applicable to both premarital and extramarital relationships with either heterosexual or homosexual patterns (in terms of behavior and attitude, Matthew 5:28).

3. Reiss (1981) has challenged the casual use of the term exploitation, arguing that it is difficult to operationalize; that is, who is to say that someone is being exploited, if the relationship is a voluntary one? Are professional athletes being exploited? We define exploitation as situations in which one person thinks the relationship means one thing in terms of commitment and grants privileges accordingly while the other person accepts the privileges knowing that no similar commitment to the other exists on their part. Instances of incest involving a parent with a minor child provide another type of example where exploitation is inevitable.

4. Exceptions are obvious, of course, as some may get married with minimal levels of personal commitment, communication, nonexploitiveness, or affection.

REFERENCES

BRAUN, M. and G. A. REKERS (1981) The Christian in an Age of Sexual Eclipse. Wheaton, IL: Tyndale.

BUKSTEL, L. H., G. D. RODER, P. R. KILMANN, J. LAUGHLIN, and W. M. SOTILE (1978) "Projected extramarital sexual involvement in unmarried college students." Journal of Marriage and the Family 40: 337–340.

BULLOUGH, V. L. (1977) "Sex education in medieval Christianity." The Journal of Sex Research 13: 185–196.

CLAYTON, R. R. and J. L. BOKEMEIER (1980) "Premarital sex in the seventies." Journal of Marriage and the Family 42: 759–775.

GEISLER, N. L. (1971) Ethics: Alternatives and Issues. Grand Rapids, MI: Zondervan.

GROUNDS, V. (1968) "The new morality: Why wait for marriage?" pp. 41–50 in Essays on Love. Downers Grove, IL: Intervarsity Press.

ISTVAN, J. and W. GRIFFITT (1980) "Effects of sexual experience on dating desirability and marriage desirability: an experimental study." Journal of Marriage and the Family 42: 377–385.

JURICH, A. P. and J. A. JURICH (1974) "The effect of cognitive moral development upon the selection of premarital sexual standards." Journal of Marriage and the Family 36: 736–741.

KIRKENDALL, L. A. (1961) Premarital Intercourse and Interpersonal Relationships. New York: Gramercy.

KNAPP, J. J. (1975) "Some non-monogamous marriage styles and related attitudes and practices of marriage counselors." The Family Coordinator 24: 505–514.

LARSEN, K. S., M. REED, and S. HOFFMAN (1980) "Attitudes of heterosexuals toward homosexuality: A Likert-type scale and construct validity." Journal of Sex Research 16: 245–257.

LEWIS, C. S. (1960) Mere Christianity. New York: Macmillan.

LUCADO, M. (1983) "A case for presexual marriage." His 43, 4: 8–11.

MACKLIN, E. D. (1980) "Nontraditional family forms: A decade of research." Journal of Marriage and the Family 42: 905–922.

——— and RUBIN, R. H. (1983) Contemporary Families and Alternative Lifestyles: Handbook on Research and Theory. Beverly Hills: Sage.

MAHONEY, E. R. (1980) "Religiosity and sexual behavior among heterosexual college students." Journal of Sex Research 16: 97–113.

MAYKOVICH, M. K. (1976) "Attitudes versus behavior in extramarital sexual relations." Journal of Marriage and the Family 38: 693–699.

McDOWELL, J. and P. LEWIS (1980) Givers, Takers and Other Kinds of Lovers. Wheaton, IL: Tyndale.

MILES, H. J. (1971) Sexual Understanding before Marriage. Grand Rapids, MI: Zondervan.

MURRAY, J. (1957) Principles of Conduct. Grand Rapids, MI: Eerdmans Publishing.

MURSTEIN, B. I. (1978) Exploring Intimate Lifestyles. New York: Springer.

NEWCOMB, P. R. (1979) "Cohabitation in America: An assessment of consequences." Journal of Marriage and the Family 41: 597–603.

REISS, I. L. (1981) "Some observations on ideology and sexuality in America." Journal of Marriage and the Family 43: 271–283.

REKERS, G. A. (1982a) Growing Up Straight. Chicago, IL: Moody Press.

—— (1982b) Shaping your Child's Sexual Identity. Grand Rapids, MI: Baker Book House.

RIDLEY, C. A., D. J. PETERMAN, and A. W. AVERY (1978) "Cohabitation: Does it make for a better marriage?" The Family Coordinator 27: 129–136.

SCANZONI, L. (1975) Why Wait? A Christian View of Premarital Sex. Grand Rapids, MI: Baker Book House.

SCHMIDT, G. (1982) "Sex and society in the eighties." Archives of Sexual Behavior 11: 92–97.

SCHUMM, W. R. (1982) "Integrating theory, measurement, and statistical analysis in family studies survey research." Journal of Marriage and the Family 44: 983–998.

—— W. T. SOUTHERLY, and C. R. FIGLEY (1980) "Stumbling block or stepping stone: Path analysis in family studies." Journal of Marriage and the Family 42: 251–262.

SINGH, B. K. (1980) "Trends in attitudes toward premarital sexual relations." Journal of Marriage and the Family 42: 387–393.

STAFFORD, T. (1983) "The best of sex." Campus Life.

WATSON, R.E.L. (1983) "Premarital cohabitation vs. traditional courtship: Their effects on subsequent marital adjustment." Family Relations 32: 139–147.

WEIS, D. L. and M. SLOSNERICK (1981) "Attitudes toward sexual and nonsexual extramarital involvements among a sample of college students." Journal of Marriage and the Family 43: 349–358.

SEX AND MARRIAGE

IV–B

Sex Should Not Occur outside of Marriage

ED WHEAT

Whenever human beings discuss the conditions under which sex *should* occur, they admit by implication, at least, that they are more than animal organisms. Could one imagine a dog or a fruit fly having sexual scruples? Generic man may share his nervous and sensory system with the animal world, but only humans have the capacity to make rational choices based on ethical and moral considerations, and only humans have the need to discover the meaning of sexuality.

Issues in human sexuality exist because of this search for meaning. Responsible men and women obviously will decide when, where, and if they will engage in sexual intercourse, and who their sexual partner will be. But every decision is based on some sort of criteria, faulty or otherwise, and discussions arise over which criteria to follow in making sexual choices. The real questions are; Which view of sex most accurately reflects the meaning of our sexuality as men and women who know ourselves to be more than animals? and, which guidelines will enable us to satisfy our deepest emotional and spiritual needs?

The long march of history indicates that human beings have, for the most part, failed to apprehend a meaningful view of their sexuality. Consider, for example, the contrast of Victorian repressions (manifested by the Queen, herself, who wrote to her daughter, "The animal side of our nature is to me — too dreadful") set against today's book-writing, magazine-publishing, film-making hedonists who urge us to claim our orgasmic rights at any cost, the only criterion being "Whatever turns you on!"

While those Victorians seem painfully inhibited and uninstructed — sex to them being something shocking that men did and good women endured for the sake of motherhood — today's hedonists seem simplistic and even mindless in their pursuit of physical gratification. Ironically, they share a common misunderstanding. Both present-day Victorians who are embarrassed by sex (even in marriage) and the swingers who reduce all sex to casual genital encounters believe that sex is an expression of the animal nature. If Victorians are disturbed by the thought, the swingers are titillated. Both are tragically mistaken.

If we look farther back into a past which still casts its shadow on views of sexuality held today, we can find in the first centuries A.D. a strangely distorted philosophic approach to sex, both in theory and practice. Secular thought produced the Platonists who repudiated the body in favor of "spiritual" love, and the Gnostics who embraced the dualistic premise that matter is inherently evil and thus the human body is evil. Although those holding this view condemned both marriage and coitus, they often practiced sexual licentiousness as a show of contempt for the body.

To add to this confusion of philosophy and practice, it was common practice to frequent the pagan temples which were, in effect, houses of prostitution and debauchery in the name of "worship." Although this was their practice, true goodness was attributed to those who had renounced sex forever. In secular thought virginity became the symbol of spirituality after the pattern of the ancient vestal virgins of Rome, while sex in marriage was regarded as unholy and impure.

These views are worth noting today because they found their way into the early Christian church and have had their effect upon Western culture. Religious leaders of that time, influenced by secular thought, plunged into asceticism, exalted celibacy, and derogated the sexual side of marriage. In the process, the biblical perspective of human sexuality was almost lost, and until very recent times the "religious" view of sex has been largely negative, both in and out of marriage.

The mind-set that prevailed is illustrated by Jerome's warning: "He who loves his own wife too ardently is an adulterer"; by Augustine's teaching that the processes of conception and birth were shameful; and by Gregory's injunction against pleasure in intercourse, for, he claimed, it was a husband and wife's enjoyment of sex that tainted the act! Not surprisingly (given these teachings) the church of the Middle Ages attempted to regulate and restrict sexual activity in marriage by requiring abstinence five days out of seven. (Sex was reluctantly allowed on Tuesdays and Wednesdays.)

Of course, regardless of the philosophic climate, men and women have continued to have sex through the ages. However, a sharp dichotomy has existed between their practice and their perspective. This is perhaps reflected in today's society in which parents are still embarrassed to discuss sex with their children but will allow them to watch the world of sex on television — a world of sexual innuendo and suggestively clad characters; a world devoid of tenderness and commitment. A *TV Guide* report observes the following:

> Some children may even develop the impression that sex is
> more closely related to violence and vulgarity (note the number
> of prostitutes on prime time, or of scenes suggesting rape)
> than to love and intimacy [Singer and Singer, 1982: 33].

Television is but mirroring today's culture in which sexual liberation has brought no more happiness than did sexual repression in the last century. In demanding sexual freedom without meaning, we have (as the Old Testament prophet said) hewed out broken cisterns for ourselves in which there is no water. This is well expressed by Dwight Hervey Small:

> With greater availability has come greater meaninglessness; this
> meaninglessness touches all of life, for we are sexual beings,
> and sexuality is basically the power to relate as persons [1974:
> 11].

Even a brief survey of past and present reveals a strange array of views on sex — most of them injurious to the welfare and happiness of mankind. People are prone to believe that sex is animalistic and embarrassing; that it is merely a genital exercise done for the fun of it; that the human body is evil and should be hidden, even from one's mate; or, conversely, that it should be flaunted in public to inspire lustful admiration; that the process of conception is somehow shameful; that sex in marriage is dirty — impure, unholy, and unmentionable; or that adulterous affairs are particularly exciting; that enjoyment of sex displeases God; or that sexual pleasures should be pursued as the supreme good. The twentieth century has been marred and our own society impoverished by a self-centered preoccupation with sex in which physical gratification is the chief goal and orgasmic rights are demanded apart from any moral standard. Although not all hold these views, the quality of life has been altered for everyone.

These are but symptoms. The real problem lies in a fundamental misunderstanding of the origin of human sexuality, its nature, purpose, and function. As a result, sex, for the greater portion of the human race, has become like a bent key that will no longer fit into the lock. When twisted out of shape by misunderstanding and misuse, human sexuality cannot achieve the purpose for which it was intended. It cannot function according to its design.

As a medical doctor, certified sex therapist, and marriage counselor, I work daily with people who are trying to repair and restore their relationships. They are attempting to function again according to a design which they hunger for even before they consciously know that it exists. I have found this design in one ancient, yet contemporary, book that addresses the basic problem of mankind with an insight and relevance that leads the reader to think, "This book understands me!" Although this book occupies a place of universal respect for its wisdom, too few people really understand its contents. I speak of the Bible, a collection of 66 writings from Genesis (the book of beginnings) through the New Testament. Many authors contributed to it over a time span of thousands of years, but the Bible speaks with a single voice concerning human sexuality and offers a perspective that comprehends the full meaning of our sexuality; gives room for us to satisfy our deepest emotional and spiritual needs; preserves us from false inhibitions on the one hand and empty excesses on the other; and enables us to experience the richest pleasures and genuine thrills of sexual love as they were meant to be experienced. The biblical perspective provides a balanced criteria for the sexual choices every responsible individual must make and can answer the question, Should sex occur only within marriage?

Through a consideration of several key passages, we will attempt in these few pages to assemble sufficient data to summarize what the Bible says concerning the origin, nature, purpose, and function of human sexuality — the areas in which misunderstanding has so frequently occurred. The Bible begins with one fact assumed: There is a self-existent God who is the Source of all life. It does not seem to have occurred to any of the writers of the Bible to try to prove or to argue for the existence of God. Everywhere and at all times it is a fact taken for granted. We will begin at the same point: "In the beginning God" (Genesis 1:1).

The Bible deals with the origin of sexuality in the first chapter, teaching that it was designed by God the Creator and is therefore "Very good":

> So God created man in his own image, in the image of God created he him; male and female created he them. And God blessed them, and God said unto them, Be fruitful, and multiply and fill the earth. . . . And God saw every thing that he had made, and, behold, it was very good [Genesis 1:27,28,31].

The word "man" here denotes *two* sexual beings made for intimate union with each other. In the original Hebrew "man" is *adam*, but not the proper name, Adam. Nor is it a collective which emphasizes men as a group. It is, instead, a generic term separating mankind as distinct from the animals. *Adam* definitely does not refer to man as a male biological creature distinct from woman, for another word, ish, is used to make this distinction, as in Genesis 2:23. Two other words differentiate "male" and "female" in this passage. When the writer says, "God created man in his own image," it is clear that both male and female were included — the two sexual beings together forming the whole human being who reflects God's nature and possesses qualities similar to God's. Scholars sometimes call the man and woman "The Adam."

A reading of Genesis 1 will indicate that all other parts of creation have been pronounced "good." It was not until man and woman were created as sexual beings endowed with the mysterious qualities and attributes of masculinity and feminity that God called his creation *very* good. We have only to imagine how colorless and uninteresting a world would be in which there was just one sex. Then we can appreciate the goodness of a plan that devised sexuality — two kinds of beings, similar, yet complementary, who express their total being in a profoundly satisfying union of persons, even as their bodies merge in an act that is both physically enjoyable and spiritually fulfilling. As Elisabeth Elliot has said, "The idea of male and female was God's idea. None of us would have thought of it."

It should be noted that the natural outcome of sexual intercourse — procreation — is also good. God's first word to his new creatures makes it clear that their *relationship* was sexual for he commanded them to exercise that sexuality — to be fruitful and multiply. His blessing upon the couple which evidently formed a part of their wedding ceremony eliminates any suggestion of sexual activity as evil in itself because such activity is the very means commanded by the Creator to carry out his will for humanity.

The origin of sex and its nature, then, cannot be separated, according to biblical perspective. Procreation is presented as a normal part of God's good creation, and our sexuality is presented as a good gift from God, intended for our blessing. To celebrate the gift with thanksgiving seems a reasonable response. This, in fact, is taking place as the church turns to the Bible for sexual guidelines. One observer reports the following:

> In my role as a sociology professor, I find that Christian young people resonate with the idea of sexuality as God's gift to be received with thanksgiving, offered in faith back to Him in its fulfillment, and celebrated in His holy presence [Small, 1974: 16].

The New Testament underlines another aspect of the nature of human sexuality: Sex was not only good at its origin, but when enjoyed in the context of marriage according to the Creator's design sex is both pure and valuable. The author of the letter to the Hebrews writes, "Marriage is honorable in all, and the bed undefiled, but fornicators and adulterers God will judge" (Hebrews 13:4).

Three words here require special attention. The word translated as "honorable" means most precious, costly, of great price. The word translated "bed" is, literally, *coitus*— a plain reference to sexual intercourse. And the word "undefiled" signifies freedom from contamination — purity. In one cogent sentence, the Bible says that marriage — God's chosen environment for the expression of sexuality — is most precious, of indescribable value, and that sexual intercourse in that setting is so pure that it could take place (and does!) as an act of worship.

This scripture depicts the marriage bed as a sort of "holy of holies" where husband and wife meet privately to celebrate their love for each other. But if sex is holy in that setting, it is no less enjoyable physically. We were created as sensual beings with piercing desires, and our bodies were intricately designed to experience exquisite sexual pleasures. The Bible places high value on the human body for its own sake as "wonderfully made" by the Creator (Psalm 139:14) and inhabited by the incarnate Saviour. The same body that enters into the passionate, physical delights of intercourse with one's marriage partner is described as "the temple of the Holy Spirit" (1 Corinthians 6:19). How far this takes us from the pagan philosophy that sees the human body as an evil thing worthy of contempt!

But no complacent glow of general well-being is allowed to delude the individual into misusing his sexuality. The same verse (Hebrews 13:4) that presents the worth and purity of sexual intercourse in marriage adds an uncompromising warning for those who would contaminate God's good gift by engaging in sexual intercourse outside of marriage: "fornicators and adulterers God will judge." Apart from its theological implications, this statement certainly indicates that sex outside of marriage brings something undesirable upon one's self and one's partner. The couple obviously incur the loss of all blessings and benefits designed by God for those who partake of the sexual gift according to his plan.

Psychiatrist John White points out that sex outside of marriage means a loss of freedom — an exchange of freedom for enslavement:

Fornication is wrong because it defeats God's purpose for your sexuality. It replaces freedom with bondage and closes the door to the deepest intimacies of all. . . . Far from being mean and restrictive about sex God wants you to experience the fullest possible enjoyment of it consistent with your happiness. He wants to make you sexually free. You can only enjoy sex in freedom. "The body is not meant for immorality, but for the Lord" (1 Corinthians 6:13). In other words, the purpose of your sexuality was that you might know intimate love (which is wider and deeper than physical sex) within the secure and growing framework of marriage. Any other use of it will not free you but enslave you. You have only two option: to be free within God's purposes for you or to be a slave to sex, to yourself and to others outside of his purposes [1977: 61–62].

From the secular viewpoint, *Newsweek* sees the "swinger's" loss as a loss of personal growth and emotional development:

The longer that many "swinging" singles play their roles, the harder it seems to unlearn the script, to break off the quest for new conquests and the conditioned adjustment to a paucity of communication and commitment. . . . Inordinately indulged, prolonged singlehood tends to deaden the emotional and sexual palates, freezing its disciples in a state of suspended adolescence [1973: 57–58].

Perhaps a part of the judgment spoken of in Hebrews 13:4 is the loss of ability to love genuinely. One is reminded of Dostoevski's remark: "I ponder, What is hell? I maintain it is the suffering of being unable to love." One may also lose the ability to enjoy sex; that, too, is suffering. As Rollo May has commented,

If sensuality has to carry the whole weight of the relationship, it becomes cloying. If sex is only sensuality, you sooner or later turn against sex itself (1969: 313).

But individuals who claim to make their sexual choices on the basis of situational ethics and those who protest that they can live together in love without the commitment of marriage may feel that these warnings do not apply to them. It is necessary to return to Genesis and more closely examine the purpose of human sexuality. Procreation and pleasure are worthy purposes, but the primary objective, according to Scripture, is a healing of man and woman's essential loneliness through the mysterious unity of the one-flesh relationship in marriage. This truth appears in the second chapter of Genesis. Genesis 1 has declared the fact of the creation of "the adam — male and female. Genesis 2 goes back to describe the process by which this occurred. Stephen Sapp notes this:

The story seems to build to an intended climax in the creation of the woman whose elaborate creation is in marked contrast to the relatively perfunctory creation of the animals (and even of the man himself) [1977: 13]!

In other words, the woman arrives with the sort of narrative fanfare that indicates her crucial importance to man and to the plan of God: "And the Lord God said, It is not good that man should be alone; I will make him an help fit for him" (Genesis 2:18).

With so many good things in creation, only one was said to be not good: man's incompleteness, his loneliness, his need for a companion worthy of him. The "helper" spoken of here did not mean a subordinate but a partner for the Hebrew word refers to a beneficial relationship where one person aids or supports another person as a friend and ally. In fact, the same word is used of God himself in Psalm 46:1 where he is called our *helper*, "a very present help in trouble." The Hebrew word also contains the idea of "alongside him" or "corresponding to him" with the idea of similarity as well as complement. The translator Delitzsch renders this as "the mirror of himself, in which he recognizes himself" (Sapp, 1977: 13).

Obviously, this kind of a partnership could not be a thing of the moment. A passing encounter or even a live-in relationship of several years duration could never fulfill the intentions of the Creator who had devised human sexuality to solve the great problem of the human race — loneliness. Only the one-flesh relationship in the permanent context of marriage could accomplish the Creator's stated purpose.

The woman's appearance on the scene resulted in the man's delighted response with what is surely the world's first love song: "This is now bone of my bones, and flesh of my flesh" (Genesis 2:23).

Hebrew scholars say that Adam was expressing a tremendous excitement, a joyous astonishment: "At last I have someone corresponding to me, who is perfectly suited to me! I have finally found the one who can complete me, who takes away my loneliness, who will be as dear to me as my own flesh"

The creation account concludes with the most concise and comprehensive counseling session ever presented on marriage:

"Therefore shall a man leave his father and his mother, and shall cleave unto his wife; and they shall be one flesh" (Genesis 2:24).

These words sum up the entire teaching of Scripture on marriage and place the sexual relationship at the very heart of marriage. Marriage is to begin with a leaving of all other relationships and to result in a lifetime spent in cleaving (literally, sticking like glue so that the two cannot be separated without damage to both). In the setting of a permanent relationship with both man and woman leaving all else behind to hold fast to each other, the intimate physical union takes place by the plan of God and two become one. "They shall be one flesh."

In the New Testament Jesus Christ reinforces the one-flesh concept while explaining the divine viewpoint on marriage to the religious leaders of the day:

> Have you not read that from the beginning the Creator made them male and female, and said, For this reason a man shall leave his father and his mother, and shall cleave to his wife, and the two shall be one flesh? It follows that no longer are they two but one flesh. What therefore God has joined together, let not man separate [Matthew 19:4–6].

In other words, if the Pharisees were acquainted with Genesis 1:27 they should know that even though Adam was created before Eve, he was at once created male, designed for intimate physical union with Eve who was created later as a female. Each, Jesus reminds them, was made for the other with the definite purpose of joining together *one* man to *one* woman. He then quotes Genesis 2:24 (and it is clear that he viewed this passage in combination with 1:27 as a divine ordinance, and not as a mere description of what takes place on earth). In fact, he goes a step beyond to articulate the permanence principle: "What therefore God has joined together, let not man separate." The divine institution is not to be tampered with because, from every angle, it has been God who designed the potential for an intimate sexual union and ordained that it be realized only in the intimate and lasting attachment of marriage.

In the first letter to the Corinthians the one-flesh scripture from Genesis forms the basis of a grave warning against fornication.

What? Know ye not that he which is joined to an harlot is one
body? for two, saith He, shall be one flesh. . . . Flee
fornication. Every sin that a man doeth is without the body;
but he that committeth fornication sinneth against his own
body [1 Corinthians 6:16,18].

Run away from fornication and adultery as you would from a
rattlesnake or the bubonic plague, the Bible counsels. The sins of
sexual lust are deadly to your health and happiness. In fact,
fornication, which includes adultery in its scope of sexual unclean-
ness (porneia in the Greek), stands apart in the catalog of sin
because it is a sin against yourself, destroying your own body,
personality, character, and vigor. The one-flesh principle still
operates when your body is joined to the body of another for
whom there is no caring or lasting commitment. You may not even
have respect for this person, but you will become one in a dreary
imitation of the relationship God designed for blessing. The
gnawing emptiness follows.

Ancient Romans quoted a gloomy proverb that described the
attempt to cure loneliness through the temporary joining of two
bodies without a union of whole persons: *Post coitum omnis animal
triste.* "Every creature is sad following sexual intercourse." Afterward (outside of marriage) one is alone again. Men and women
may try to smother their loneliness and anxiety with casual sexual
encounters, but are left with even more loneliness when the
encounter is finished. Sex can only fulfill its primary purpose as the
healer of loneliness when it functions within marriage as the
Creator designed it. As one young man told me,

The big difference can be felt in the moments after orgasm.
When it's casual sex, you have no feeling for your partner
afterward. You want to move away. When it's your wife you
are making love to, the half hour afterward is just great.
You're drawn even closer to each other. The feelings you share
cannot be described.

Again quoting the Genesis 2:24 passage, the book of Ephesians
offers the most compelling of all evidence that the one-flesh
relationship was designed exclusively for the permanent commitment environment of marriage. In what at first may seem a radical,
unconventional use of human sexuality, the Bible chooses the one-
flesh union of husband and wife to picture the intimate closeness,

total commitment, and permanent love relationship of Jesus Christ for the church (see Ephesians 5:23–32). One can find Old Testament precedence in the fact that the sexual bond of husband and wife is used again and again to portray the relationship between God and his people, Israel.

The Semitic expression "one flesh" indicates a merger of two complete personalities, not just two physical bodies engaging in sex acts such as animals do. This expression opens the door to what Paul called "a great mystery." It is not by happenstance that human beings have intercourse while looking at each other, that only humans enjoy the face to face position of coitus. As May observes, this posture represents the ultimate vulnerability, the greatest exposure of one's very self (1969: 311).

Even the biblical expression for sexual intercourse between husband and wife — to *know*— suggests this mystery. "Adam *knew* Eve his wife; and she conceived" (Genesis 4:1). "Then Joseph . . . took unto him his wife: and knew her not until she had brought forth her firstborn son" (Matthew 1:24–25). The Hebrew word *yadha* of the Old Testament and the Greek word *ginosko* of the New Testament have the connotation of experiential knowledge through entering into relationship with that which is known. The choice of this particular word to denote sexual intercourse infers that sexuality provides the opportunity for the most complete and fulfilling knowledge of one another available in this life. But the knowing can only happen in the lifetime context of marriage.

White calls sex the

> physical girder which two people whose flesh has become one use to help build the house of a solid relationship. Behind the sexual feelings lies a longing to know and to be known, to love and to be loved. . . . Acceptance and mutual disclosure are not the activities of a moment but the delicate fabric of a lifetime's weaving [1977: 36, 19].

And so, the origin, nature, and stated purpose of human sexuality have already shaped its function. The biblical perspective is that human sexuality can function normally only when it is expressed within the commitment structure of marriage. Premarital and extramarital sex are viewed biblically as a dysfunction, an abnormal or impaired use of this most precious gift. Such dysfunction results in a loss of efficacy: Sex can no longer solve mankind's loneliness problem; it can no longer unite two people in an ever-growing relationship of multidimensioned pleasures.

When sex functions properly, pleasure will result. The Bible specifies sexual delight as an integral part of marriage. One book, "The song of songs, which is Solomon's," is wholly devoted to this theme. Herein can be found some of the most beautiful, erotic, yet holy, love poetry in all of literature; and the work celebrates not a sexual fling such as the television "soaps" might consider diverting, but a love relationship between bride and bridegroom that is replete with exquisite sexual pleasures. This comes forth clearly in modern translations or in the vivid interpretive paraphrase *A Song for Lovers* by S. Craig Glickman.

The Old Testament law reflects the strong biblical emphasis on sexual pleasure in marriage. In Deuteronomy 24:5 the new husband is relieved of all other responsibilities to "be free at home one year." The reason? "To cheer up his wife which he hath taken." The Hebrew phrase "to cheer up" meant to delight one's wife, to know her in order to discover what is sexually pleasing to her.

The practical book of Proverbs shows cause and effect concerning the richest sexual pleasures available to the married couple. If you remain deeply in love with your marriage partner, these delights will be yours, the Bible says. But if you turn to adultery instead, some unpleasant things will inevitably occur. Verses 9 through 14 of Proverbs 5 explain the sexual, spiritual, and social destruction that come when sex is misused. Verses 18 and 19 offer the rewards of the sex relationship within marriage:

> Let thy fountain be blessed; and rejoice with the wife of thy youth. Let her be as the loving hind and pleasant roe, let her breasts satisfy thee at all times; and be thou ravished always with her love.

The wife is pictured, both here and in the Song of Solomon, as a cistern, a well, a spring shut up, a fountain sealed for her husband, whose waters will satisfy to the fullest. Even this may be an inadequate statement. To be "ravished" in the Hebrew language means to reel and stagger as if intoxicated, to be enraptured and exhilarated. To be "satisfied" is to have your thirst slaked, to take your fill, to be satiated and abundantly saturated with that which pleases. The verse speaks literally of the wife's nipples and then describes them metaphorically as fountains of wine that will keep the husband intoxicated with her love. Observe that this passionate relationship is with "the wife of thy youth," indicating the permanence of the love affair.

But these delicious pleasures are promised only within marriage. Many plain words are spoken about sex outside of marriage. For example, the following:

> Lust not after her beauty in thine heart. . . . Can a man take fire in his bosom, and his clothes not be burned? Can one go upon hot coals, and his feet not be burned? So he that goeth in to his neighbor's wife; whosoever toucheth her shall not be innocent. . . . Whoso committeth adultery with a woman lacketh understanding; he that doeth it destroyeth his own soul [Proverbs 6:25,27–29,32].

The function of sexuality in a marriage assumes such importance that the Bible issues definite guidelines in 1 Corinthians 7. These provisions are included: Each is to provide the sexual satisfaction the other spouse needs. (To fail to do so would be to defraud one's partner.) The bodies of both belong to one another, and sexual relations are to be equal and reciprocal; each has the right to initiate sex, and neither has the right to use it as a bargaining point. The pleasures of sex are to be regular and continuous in the marriage with abstinence forbidden except for a brief time by mutual agreement.

These guidelines point to two other aspects of normal sexual functioning. First, sex is to function as a vehicle for loving, not using. Second, sex is to be an expression of the total person — the body becoming a symbol of the inner self; expressing what can be expressed in no other way, so that sexuality and personality are fully integrated in the act of love. When sex functions in this way the keenest pleasure will come from giving the partner pleasure in a recurring unity of body, and spirit, in a sharing of feelings so deep, they could only be communicated in the safety of lifetime commitment.

A science fiction novel a few years ago chillingly portrayed a futuristic society growing out of our own in which couples were not called lovers, but *users*. This comes uncomfortably close to reality in certain segments of of our culture today. A 1978 survey of American television reported that 88 percent of all sex presented on television was sex outside of marriage — people using other people for momentary gratification. This is the sexual choice that leads to meaninglessness.

But for those who ask if there is a place for the occurrence of sex outside of marriage, the biblical answer is an unqualified *no*. Not to limit our enjoyment of sex — we have seen that the Creator is concerned about our continuing pleasure, that pleasure is God's invention — but to enhance it. Not to restrict our freedom, but to give us the freedom to find the real meaning of our sexuality in the union of persons, not just bodies. The ecstasies of sex reach their fully liberated expression only in the one — flesh union of marriage. New dimensions of satisfaction as lovers unite physically, emotionally, and spiritually, can be experienced only by the couple who make their sexual choices according to biblical criteria. Only for them is the promise, "That your joy may be full" (John 15:11).

Marriage is the ultimate expression of love and personal commitment as two lovers covenant to spend their lives together; while sexual intercourse becomes the ultimate physical and emotional expression of that love and commitment. In the plan of God, they come together literally at the same time!

REFERENCES

MAY, R. (1969) Love and Will. New York: Norton.
Newsweek (1973) "Games singles play." July 16: 57–58.
SAPP, S. (1977) Sexuality, the Bible, and Science. Philadelphia: Fortress Press.
SMALL, D. H. (1974) Christian: Celebrate your Sensuality. Old Tappan, NJ: Fleming H. Revell.
SINGER, D. and J. SINGER (1982) "Sex on TV: How to protect your child." TV Guide 30, 32: 33.
WHEAT, E. (1980) Love Life. Grand Rapids, MI: Zondervan.
WHITE, J. (1977) Eros Defiled. Downer's Grove, IL: Inter-Varsity Press.

Sexual Relations within and outside of Marriage Can Be Equally Acceptable

CATHERINE S. CHILMAN

This chapter reviews and critiques research and theories regarding nonmarital heterosexual intercourse (coitus). The term nonmarital, rather than premarital or extramarital, intercourse is used because it is more accurate in that it fails to assume that all adults eventually marry (although the vast majority of them do). The term extramarital intercourse, which is one kind of nonmarital coitus, refers to sexual intercourse between married persons outside of the marital relationship.

NONMARITAL COITUS

INCIDENCE

Little is definitively known about the incidence of nonmarital intercourse among single people over the age of 22 or so. Also, reliable information about male sexual behaviors tends to be somewhat lacking because the only adequate national, recent studies on this topic have been carried out with young women ages 15–19 (Zelnik et al., 1982). I has also reviewed virtually all research on the topic of adolescent sexual behaviors; this review included many smaller studies of high school and college youth in various parts of the country (Chilman, 1978, 1983).

The following major findings in respect to trends are revealed by these studies and research analyses. There was a marked and increasing shift toward far greater freedom and permissiveness in the sexual attitudes of adolescents and youth, starting in about 1967 and continuing through at least 1979. This shift was similar to other social movements of the 1960s and 1970s toward far greater equality between the sexes and rejection of traditional patterns of thought and behavior, as discussed later in further detail. As of 1979, almost half of the young women in the United States had, reportedly, experienced intercourse by age 19 (as compared to about one-fourth in 1971). Intercourse becomes more prevalent as young women grow older, with about one-fifth reporting intercourse by age 15, two-thirds by age 19, and three-fourths by age 22 in 1979.

It appears that by the late 1970s, the rates of nonmarital coitus among young women were about equal to those among young men: a far different situation for whites (data for blacks are not available) than that of the 1920s through the early 1960s. It seems that, in terms of behaviors and expressed attitudes, the double standard of sex behavior (permissiveness for men, restrictiveness for women) has been sharply reduced, at least for about half or more of the youth population.

Older members of the population have also become more liberal in sex attitudes (and, presumable, sexual behaviors) since the mid-1960s. For instance, national survey data for 1972 and 1978 show that each 10-year age group, 26 through 65 (plus) years was more apt to express permissive sex attitudes in 1978 than in 1972.

Differences are also found by age, gender, race and other demographic characteristics. In 1978, males were in general, more apt than females to have permissive sex attitudes. Similar trends are found for blacks compared to whites (with blacks more apt to be permissive). Higher levels of permissiveness were also found for city dwellers and the never-married, divorced, or separated. People with higher levels of education and persons who were low in religious affiliation and church attendance also tended to be more permissive than other groups (Singh, 1980).

Interestingly, the youngest age group in the national surveys analyzed by Singh showed a slight drop in permissiveness between 1972 and 1978, with 84 percent in 1972 expressing approval of coitus among the nonmarried but "only" 82 percent expressing this in 1978. The politically conservative climate of the early 1980s has also included elements of sexual conservativism, but it is too early to tell whether the population is moving toward more traditional sexual attitudes. According to an analysis by Yankelovich (1981), a number of surveys show that people yearn for the stability of the "good old days" but are not willing to give up their sexual freedoms.

POTENTIAL COSTS AND BENEFITS OF NONMARITAL COITUS AMONG SINGLES

The following presentation of possible costs and benefits of nonmarital coitus pertains especially, but not exclusively, to adolescents (particularly females) because this is the group for which the most information is available. As potential benefits one can list such possible gains as psychological and sexual fulfillment; reduced tendency to repress sexual drives and interests; development of increased independence from the family of origin; consolidation of gender and sexual identity; increased intimacy and bonding with the partner; and enhanced self-awareness (see, also, Chilman, 1983).

On the potential costs side, one can list such possibilities as pregnancy; unplanned parenthood; venereal diseases; over-involvement with partner before (or without) psychological readiness for intense pair-bonding and partner intimacy; being sexually exploited and/or sexually exploiting another person; guilt and anxiety if personal values do not accept nonmarital intercourse at all or during the adolescent years or before a commitment to marry; fear of being discovered; lack of privacy; and conflict with family members and "meaningful" others.

PROBLEMS OF UNPLANNED PREGNANCIES

An unplanned, nonmarital pregnancy usually creates serious problems, especially for women. There is no easy solution to such a pregnancy. Pregnancy resolution through abortion has become increasingly common with over half of young pregnant women under age 18, along with large numbers of older women resorting to this procedure in recent years. Although abortions in the first three months of pregnancy are usually physically safe if performed by qualified medical personnel, abortion is apt to be stressful in terms of psychological, social, and financial costs. Emotional costs are especially apt to be high if the woman believes that abortions are morally wrong and if she feels she must keep the matter a secret from others, including her sex partner, family members, employers, and friends. They are also high if she is more or less forced to have an abortion against her will through pressure from other people. (For instance, see, Luker, 1975; Klerman et al., 1982; Evans et al., 1976; Chilman, 1983).

White people are more likely than low-income, black people to marry if pregnant in order to prevent an illegitimate birth. This is not to say that poor blacks readily accept births outside of marriage but, rather, high fertility values plus high unemployment rates (especially among young people) plus the frequent availability of welfare assistance for single (but not married) mothers may often combine to make parenthood without marriage seem a better choice than either abortion or marriage. In fact, various studies of low income black adolescents show that a forced marriage (especially youthful) to legitimate a pregnancy often has more adverse results than bearing a child outside of marriage. Such marriages are apt to fail; moreover, adolescent (and, perhaps, older unmarried) mothers who remain single often live with their parents and are more apt than young married women to finish high school, obtain employment and not have another early pregnancy (Furstenberg, 1976; Moore and Burt, 1982). It has become much easier than formerly for unmarried pregnant women and mothers to complete high school (and, to some extent, college). As of 1972, federal legislation prohibited discrimination in the public schools against pregnant students or mothers.

A large number of adolescents today carry their pregnancies to term as single parents. Of black adolescent mothers 80 percent and twenty percent of white ones are not married. Although the great majority of young, white, unmarried mothers formerly placed their babies for adoption, few do so in today's more tolerant climate.

Many people predict universally dire long-lasting consequences of nonmarital (especially adolescent) childbearing. It is now recognized by research specialists in this field that adverse physical consequences for adolescent mothers and babies are not apt to occur because of the mother's youth, per se, but are largely, if not completely, associated with the frequent failure of pregnant adolescents to seek and obtain adequate prenatal care and to follow basic rules of health and nutrition during pregnancy (Baldwin and Cain, 1980).

In general, claims of severe negative consequences of adolescent childbearing tend to confuse the concept of consequences with factors often associated with early parenthood, but not necessarily the *result* of this parenthood. In brief, leaving school early, unemployment, welfare dependency, failed marriages, higher rates of later childbearing may not always result from nonmarital adolescent pregnancy and parenthood per se. Rather, young people whose lives have been damaged by such stresses as poverty, racism, disorganized or conflicted family life may be more likely than others to become unmarried parents. Far less is known about the results of nonmarital childbearing among older groups but it is likely that many of the principles discussed above would apply. There is growing and alarmed recognition that female-headed families with children are especially apt to be poor, particularly if the mothers are black or Hispanic-American. This applies fairly equally to the never-married, separated, and divorced. Reasons for the higher rates of poverty for female-headed families include the failure of most absent fathers to provide child support, racism, poor jobs and low wages for women, and lack of free or low cost, high quality childcare facilities. (See, for example, Cherlin, 1982.)

CONTRACEPTIVE USE

About half of the teenagers who take part in intercourse do not use contraceptives during the first year of this sexual activity (Zelnik et al., 1982). There are many reasons for their failure to do so including a risk-taking attitude, the hope that "I'll be lucky and won't get pregnant," low motivation to prevent a pregnancy, poor communication with partner, problems in long-range planning, little hope for one's future as a student or employee, fear of contraceptive side-effects, and letting intercourse "just happen" whether or not contraceptives are available at the moment (Chilman, 1983).

The poor contraceptive behaviors of adolescents will probably be increased with current (January, 1983) federal government mandates that when family planning clinics have federal funding, they must inform the parents of young adolescents if contraceptive supplies are provided. Although surveys show that over half of the adolescents who feel a need for contraceptives confide in their parents, another group of young people say they would continue to have intercourse but would not get contraceptives if there were requirements of parental notification. They believe that they would be in an impossible family situation if their parents knew about their sexual activities and contraceptive use.

Advocates of parental notification tend to think that adolescents will refrain from intercourse if they cannot get contraceptives without parental knowledge. However, the increase in sexually permissive behaviors on the part of teenagers (as well as adults) stems mainly from profound changes in the larger society rather than from contraceptive availability per se.

SOCIAL CHANGE AND INCREASED SEXUAL PERMISSIVENESS

Shifts toward freer sexual behavior, equality between the sexes, a departure from traditional religious beliefs and from rigid patriarchal, familial attitudes spring from profound societal changes. These include industrialization and its evolution towards a "high tech" society; reduced infant and maternal death rates leading to a resulting population "explosion" and the needs then for a lower number of births; worldwide mass communication and transportation; a global "revolution of rising expectations" for the "good life" of equality, prosperity, and personal fullfillment; increased job opportunities for women; and the spread of household technologies that reduce the time and energy required for homemaking.

Traditional moralities that called for sexual abstinence outside of marriage (especially for women) were based on an entirely different set of social and economic conditions of a rural past. Attempts to turn back the attitudes and behavioral clock to an earlier, largely imagined-as-happier period of time are bound to fail unless, of course, our economy is regressed to the conditions of the early 1800s or so — a movement that few would applaud even if it were possible.

COITUS AMONG YOUNG TEENAGERS

All in all it seems probable that in light of the above changes, a large and equal number of men and women, including adolescents, will continue to have nonmarital intercourse. This seems especially true for adolescents over age 17 or 18, particularly when one considers the early age of puberty for today's adolescents (age about 12.5 years for girls) and the later average age at marriage (about age 25) for women.

Arguments today about the acceptability of nonmarital intercourse for teenagers swirl mainly around younger age groups: teenagers who are still in high school and are alleged to lack the social and psychological maturity (or economic resources) to take part in potentially dangerous, as well as possibly rewarding, coital partnerships. We have already seen that nonmarital pregnancies are not easily resolved. This is apt to be especially true for younger teenagers. Although pertinent research is lacking, it seems probable that coitus in an immature, uncommitted relationship might to psychologically damaging to the persons involved. Thus, it may well be advisable for young adolescents (those under age 17 or so) to refrain from coitus. However, of course, individuals vary in their level of development and any general principle has its exceptions — especially if it is a tentative principle with inadequate research foundations.

Be that as it may, programs that make contraceptives available to sexually active youth should also recognize and support the (probably) sound decision of many teenagers to refrain from intercourse while they are so young and, for some whose values so dictate, before they are married.

PROBLEMS AND SUGGESTIONS REGARDING CONTRACEPTIVE USE

For those who are having coitus or planning to do so, safe, effective, readily available contraceptives are essential. However, besides the possible barriers mentioned above, completely safe, immediately available and highly effective contraceptives do not exist at this time. The orals generally prescribed for sexually active adolescent (and, often, older) women, have a number of problems. These include possible unpleasant side effects such as weight gain and bleeding, potential health dangers (especially if used over the entire fertile life-span), the need for medical examination and prescription and difficulty in taking continuing medication when sex activity tends to be sporadic, unplanned, infrequent — typical of younger teenagers. There are also apt to be psychological costs that may include guilt, fear, anxiety, loss of self-esteem, estrangement from parents, and so on. On the economic side, one must consider the financial costs of many contraceptives (see below).

The most nearly perfect contraceptive for persons who have intercourse sporadically is the condom. Anti-condom attitudes often held by males and, hence their partners, require rexamination. Along with their desirability in being safe and highly effective (if used correctly) goes the further advantage of affording protection for both partners against venereal disease. In general, increased male responsibility for contraception, both within and outside of marriage, seems to be a "must" even if this responsibility is only the male's understanding and support of his female partner in her acquisition and use of contraceptives.

COHABITATION

DEMOGRAPHIC TRENDS

According to 1978 U.S. Census figures, about 2.3 percent of the U.S. adult population reported themselves as living in unmarried cohabiting relationships (Glick and Spanier, 1980). This was a sharp increase over the preceding decade and probably represents underreporting of the true state of affairs for a large number of people. Half of the men and two-thirds of the women reporting themselves in this status had been married before. This previously married group included a wide age-range of people. However, most of the never-married were in their late teens or early twenties. Cohabiting couples were more apt to live in cities, to have no children, to have relatively low incomes, to have high rates of unemployment, and to be black. Newcomb (1979) writes that cohabitation has existed for a long time, particularly among "lower class persons." The recent increase has been mainly in the middle class. As most of the research has involved college student samples, there is a false impression that cohabitation is mainly a trend among highly educated youth. However, even for the under age 25 group only a small percentage have a college education.

Most of the members of the young, college student group have never been married but do not think of cohabitation as replacing marriage. Rather, they tend to think of it as a prelude to later marriage but not necessarily with their present partners (Macklin, 1980; Bower and Christensen, 1972). Yllo (1978), in her survey of a national sample of the general population, concluded that about 18 percent of the men and women had experienced cohabitation. Arafat and Yorburg (1973) found that almost 80 percent of their respondents said they would enter a cohabiting relationship if they had the opportunity to do so; somewhat similar findings are given by Henze and Hudson (1974).

Young people along with older persons in the population show a growing tendency to accept cohabitation as a viable life-style, especially if it is combined with affection and exclusivity. Although there is only a small proportion of cohabiting couples in the population at any one time, it is estimated that about one-fourth of college students are involved in such relationships at some point in their academic careers (Macklin, 1980).

OUTCOMES OF COHABITATION

Research with small samples in various colleges (as reviewed by Macklin, 1980) shows that when cohabiting couples are compared to those who are not in this status, few differences appear in respect to personal "adjustment," academic achievement, and marital status of parents. When cohabiting college student couples are compared to married ones, no significant differences are found in a number of studies between the two groups in respect to self-reported emotional satisfaction, sex satisfaction, division of labor, and level of communication. When married persons who lived in a cohabiting premarital relationship are compared to those who did not, very few differences are found in respect to marital satisfactions and marital stability.

Cohabiting, never-married couples are lower than married ones in respect to level of commitment to partner. They are also more likely, in general, to be liberal and equalitarian in respect to sex roles and low in religiosity (Macklin, 1980, 1981).

Research in a state university in New England revealed findings fairly similar to those summarized by Macklin. Risman, Hill, Rubin, and Peplau (1981) in a two-year study of 231 undergraduates found that there were no significant differences between cohabiting couples and those who were just "going steady" in respect to rates of marriage and rates of breaking off the relationship. Although the cohabiting men in this study were more apt to have nontraditional sex and sex role attitudes, this difference was not found for the women. Both groups of women were "avant garde" in their expressed attitudes.

Cohabiting women were more apt than the "going steady" women to report male dominance in their relationship and were more apt to see themselves at a power disadvantage. However, they were also more apt to express emotional satisfaction and to believe they would marry their partners — however, the latter was not differentially true for the male cohabitors compared to males in a "going steady" dating relationship. Cohabiting males were more apt to express a high level of sex satisfaction. On the other hand, both groups of women expressed high sex satisfaction. The researchers raise a logical question in wondering whether the cohabiting women see themselves as both more dominated by their partners and more emotionally satisfied with them as a result of cohabiting or as a preexisting condition conducive to the woman's participation is this status.

All in all, research to date — albeit fragmentary and lacking in adequate random samples — seems to indicate that cohabitation has neither markedly positive nor markedly negative effects on the college undergraduates involved and who have been studied most frequently.

Research with other groups of cohabiting couples appears to be almost nonexistent. However, Newcomb (1979) points out that, unlike marriage, there is no legal tradition with regard to cohabitation. This results in a lack of protection of legal rights of all parties involved. However, since 1973 there has been a trend through court decisions for statute law to develop a more precise definition of the legal rights and obligations of cohabitants. There has also been a growing tendency toward greater legal protection for illegitimate children, including those of cohabitants. However, there is considerable variation in state laws and most states have not adequately defined these rights.

About 20 percent of all cohabiting couples had one or more children in their households in 1977 (Glick and Norton, 1977). Almost no research exists regarding the effects of cohabitation on children. This is an important area of further study.

In general, much more research is needed regarding the effects of cohabitation on noncollege populations, including its effects on people in varying age groups, including the elderly who may cohabit to avoid the reduction of social security payments. Then, too, we need to know more about the impact of cohabitation on people who are separated, divorced, or widowed. In a further consideration of the possible costs and benefits of this form of nonmarital sex behavior also see the more general points made earlier in this chapter concerning the possible costs and benefits of nonmarital coitus.

EXTRAMARITAL INTERCOURSE

TRENDS

NORC survey data and other national studies show that over 80 percent of American adults think that extramarital coitus is wrong (Singh, 1980; Yankelovich, 1981). Risman et al. (1981) found that only 15 percent of undergraduates studied in a New England state university were accepting of extramarital coitus. Thus, this behavior is viewed much less permissively than nonmarital coitus.

The few (but generally small and unsatisfactory) studies that are available concerning extramarital coitus indicate that its incidence has increased markedly in the past 15 years or so (Hunt, 1974; Bell et al. 1975: Levin, 1975; Maykovich, 1976). The known trends in the behavior of adolescent women and of the larger society lends credence to the above findings. It appears that this behavior has particularly increased for middle class women (Macklin, 1981). However, it is probable that the majority of married people in the United States do not engage in extramarital affairs or if they do, such behavior is infrequent during their marital careers.

Peabody (1982) proposes that the main causes of the above trends are to be found in the kinds of social change factors that were discussed earlier in respect to social change and nonmarital coitus.

CHARACTERISTICS OF PERSONS INVOLVED

Research about the characteristics of people involved in extramarital coitus tends to be limited to small middle class groups. According to these studies, people who participate in extramarital coitus tend to be individualistic, nonconformist, academics, creative, willing to take risks, complex, and concerned about developing their own ethical systems (Whitehurst, 1978). Whitehurst concludes further that marriages in which the partners agree to extramarital sex relationships are most apt to occur in a liberal political climate and among affluent groups who have a situational opportunity for such behaviors as well as the support of like-minded peers.

The available studies often quoted in today's literature concerning the "causes and consequences" of extramarital coitus show factors usually more characteristic of relatively privileged white groups. According to the few published, fairly recent studies of sex behaviors of low income and blue collar families, extramarital coitus on the part of males is common but is frowned upon by peers for white (although less so for black) females (Rainwater, 1970; Rubin, 1978, Ladner, 1971; Furstenberg, 1976). Extramarital intercourse is not so delicately and extensively negotiated by these marital pairs as today's advocates of sexually open marriage espouse in the intellectual, idealized pattern for the relatively privileged people that they apparently study, counsel, and identify with.

A few small studies of middle class samples have failed to reveal that people involved in extramarital affairs are different from other marrieds in respect to neuroticism, level of maturity, and negative attitudes toward the self. Although some of the "extramaritals" said their marriages were unsatisfactory, others did not make this claim.

Some advocates of so-called "open marriage" (O'Neil and O'Neil, 1972) say that such a marriage includes permission by the partners (Ramey, 1976) for extramarital coitus. Others argue that the ideal open marriage does not include this behavior but does promote many other opportunities for individual growth of husband and wife. Allowances are made for close friendships with persons of the same and opposite sex. Some observers write that opposite sex friendships tend to lead to sexual involvement (Banashek, 1978; Gagnon and Greenblatt, 1978). However, Smith and Smith (1974) among others argue that such friendships are "a vehicle for individual development and enhanced marital intimacy." Knapp (1976) finds that people in sexually open marriages put a high value on honesty, personal growth, and complexity of intimate relationships.

Reiss (1982) observes that people who espouse closer opposite sex extramarital relationships are apt to subscribe to the "script" that disassociates sex from love and marriage — a viewpoint also supported by the Risman et al. (1981) study of college student attitudes toward extramarital sex. This study along with others indicates that people who have had coitus with a large number of people before marriage are also apt to have extramarital coitus. On the other hand, people who have premarital coitus only in the context of a loving, exclusive relationship are less likely to have extramarital affairs.

OUTCOME OF EXTRAMARITAL COITUS

The outcomes of extramarital coitus have been investigated in small, methodologically weak studies using volunteers who are mainly middleclass and white. Therefore, the results of this research should be viewed with caution. It shows that extramarital coitus may or may not damage the marital relationship (Johnson, 1970, Hunt, 1974; Bell et al., 1975; Levin, 1975; Ramey, 1976; Glass and Wright, 1977; Atwater, 1979). Moreover, the outcomes of sexually open marital arrangements to which both partners agree appear to depend on the characteristics of all the people involved: those within and those outside the marriage (Knapp and Whitehurst, 1977). According to Macklin (1980), such marriages should include primary fidelity to the spouse.

Mazur (1977) points out that open communication with marital and extramarital partners is essential if sexually open marriages are to succeed. The people involved must be aware of and able to deal with problems of jealousy and possessiveness (a tall order, in my opinion). In discussing her research overview of these marriages, Macklin (1980) states that problems associated with them include the need for constant communication and negotiation, dealing with feelings of loneliness and rejection, and coping with practical difficulties such as the use of time and money. On the other hand, she reports that respondents involved in such relationships tend to be enthusiastic about such benefits as increased self-esteem, self-awareness, and ability to communicate.

However, and most unfortunately, reports are not available from people who have dropped out of extramarital affairs. They might well show considerably less enthusiasm for such arrangements.

In general, researchers suggest that sexually open marriages work only when the primary marital relationship contains a high degree of mutual respect, understanding, affection, and agreement regarding this life-style. The individuals involved would seem to need such personality traits as flexibility and capacity to deal with complexity. The extramarital or so called "satellite partner" needs a high degree of personal security in order to accept his or her position.

Commenting on insights gained from her clinical practice, Peabody (1982) writes that sexually open marriages tend to "work" when the people involved are at an advanced stage of ego development, have equalitarian attitudes, and are low on rigidity, possessiveness, and power-oriented attitudes. Although many clinicians have thought that extramarital affairs indicated personal problems of the individuals involved and should be discontinued, she finds that such behaviors can be supportive of the person's psychological health if the individual has the above-mentioned personal characteristics.

It is important to recognize that the researchers seem not to have considered the possible impact of extramarital affairs on the children and other family members involved. Moreover, they seem not to have studied the impact of these arrangements on the "satellite" female partners who may be single: never-married, separated, divorced, or widowed. Because of the numerical imbalance of men and women in the population with the greater number of women becoming progressively larger after the age of 25 or so, extramarital affairs are very apt to involve single women, especially after age 35. These women may well have experienced many earlier strains in their lives and therefore may be low on financial and psychological reserves. It seems likely that they would be highly dependent on their male lovers. While the sexually open marriage may be gratifying and nondamaging to the marital pair, the extramarital "satellite" may find the situation extremely stressful. However, she may be lacking in viable alternatives if she wants an extramarital heterosexual relationship.

The problem of numerical disparity becomes extreme for people in their sixties or older. It is then compounded by the higher rates of health problems for males, including those that affect their sexual performance. Although recent studies have increased popular understanding and acceptance of the psychological and sexual needs of "senior citizens," there is very little consideration of the needs of the large numbers of widows and the many fewer widowers in their frequently difficult "golden" years. Probably so little attention is paid to this problem because it is an exceptionally difficult one.

IN CONCLUSION

As can be seen, nonmarital coitus both among single and married persons has both its potential costs and potential benefits. On the benefits side, there are the possibilities of enhanced freedom, personal fullfillment, and breadth of experience. The potential costs are such factors as possible guilt and anxiety, problems of contraception and untimely pregnancy, lack of legal protection and, for the married, damage to the marital relationship.

In deciding whether or not one wishes to engage in nonmarital coitus, it is important to weigh the possible costs and benefits to the self and to "significant others" including any children who may be involved. Beyond such a pragmatic process, it is also important to examine one's own values, beliefs, and goals and to discuss them honestly with those "whom it may concern." It is my own belief that "recreational," noncommitted sex is apt to be alienating for the self and one's partners. Further, I see coitus as being uniquely intimate and filled with deep psychological significance as well as physical pleasure (this is quite possibly a particularly feminine view-point). Thus, sex without commitment and affection seems to be a denial of its potential for being an enormous part of achieving full humanity in a total partnership with a cherished other. Nonmarital, including extramarital, sex can fullfill the above conditions; but if it does so there are particular risks of deep, perhaps *temporary*, involvement. In the case of extramarital sex there are also risks of serious damage to the marital relationship.

REFERENCES

ARAFAT, I. and G. YORBURG (1973) "On living together without marriage." Journal of Sex Research 9 (May): 97–106.
ATWATER, L. (1979) "Getting involved: Women's transition to first extra-marital sex." Alternative Life-Styles 2: 38–68.
BALDWIN, W. and V. CAIN (1976) "Adolescent Pregnancy and Childbearing — Growing Concerns for Americans." Population Reference Bureau 31 September) 2 Washington, DC.

BANASHEK, M. (1978) "Infidelity: What it can and can't do for your love life." Mademoiselle (March): 210–219.

BELL, R., S. TURNER and L. ROSEN (1975) "A multi-variate analysis of female extramarital coitus." Journal of Marriage and the Family 37: 375–384.

CHILMAN, C. (1983) Adolescent Sexuality in a Changing American Society: Social and Psychological Perspectives for Human Services Professionals. New York: John Wiley.

———— (1982) Adolescent Sexuality in a Changing Society. New York: John Wiley.

———— (1978) Adolescent Sexuality in a Changing American Society: Social and Psychological Perspectives. Washington, DC: U.S. Government Printing Office.

CHERLIN, A. (1981) Marriage, Divorce, Remarriage. Cambridge, MA: Harvard University Press.

CONSTANTINE, L. and J. CONSTANTINE (1973) Group Marriage. New York: Macmillan.

EVANS, J., G. SELSTAD, and W. WELCHER (1976) "Teenagers: Fertility control behavior and attitudes before and after abortion, childbearing or negative pregnancy test." Family Planning Perspectives 8 (July/August) 4: 192–200.

FRANCOEUR, A. and R. FRANCOEUR (1974) Hot and Cool Sex: Cultures in Conflict. New York: Harcourt Brace Jovanovich.

FURSTENBERG, F., Jr. (1976) Unplanned Parenthood: The Social Consequences of Teenage Childbearing. New York: Free Press.

GAGNON, J. and C. GREENBLATT (1978) Life Designs: Individuals, Marriages, and Families. Glenview, IL: Scott, Foresman and Co.

GLASS, S. and T. WRIGHT (1977) "The Relationship of Extramarital Sex, Length of Marriage, and Sex Differences on Marital Satisfaction and Romanticism." Journal of Marriage and the Family 39: 691–703.

GLENN, N. and C. WEAVER (1979) "Attitudes Toward Premarital, Extramarital and Homosexual Relations in the U.S. in the 1970's." Journal of Sex Research, 15 (May): 108–118.

GLICK, P. and A. NORTON (1977) "Marrying, divorcing and living together in the U.S. today." Population Bulletin. Washington, D.C.: Population Reference Bureau.

———— and G. SPANIER (1980) "Married and unmarried cohabitation in the U.S." Journal of Marriage and the Family 42: 19–30.

HENZE, L. and J. HUDSON (1974) "Personal and family characteristics of cohabiting and non-cohabiting college students." Journal of Marriage and the Family 36 (November): 722–726.

HUNT, M. (1974) Sexual Behavior in the 1970s. Chicago: Playboy Press.

JOHNSON, R. (1970) "Some Correlates of Extramarital Coitus." Journal of Marriage and the Family 32: 449–456.

KLERMAN, L., M. BRACKEN, J. JEKEL, and M. BRACKEN (1982) "The Delivery — Abortion Decisions Among Adolescents," pp. 219–235 in I. Stuart and C. Wells (eds.), Pregnancy in Adolescence. New York: Van Nostrand Reinhold Co.

KNAPP, J. (forthcoming) "Personality and sexually open marriage." Journal of Sex Research.

———— and R. WHITEHURST (1977) "Sexually open marriages and relationships: Issues and prospects," in R. Libby and R. Whitehurst (eds.) Marriage and Alternatives: Exploring Intimate Relationships. Glenview, IL: Scott, Foresman.

LADNER, J. (1971) Tomorrow's Tomorrow: The Black Women. Garden City, NY: Doubleday.

LEVIN, R. (1975) "The Redbook report on premarital and extramarital sex: The end of the double standard. Redbook (October): 38–44, 90–192.

LUKER, K. (1975) Taking Chances: Abortion and the Decision Not to Contracept. Berkeley: University of California Press.

MACKLIN, E. (1981) "Education for choice: Implications of alternatives in lifestyles for family life education." Journal of Marriage and the Family 30 (October) 4: 567–577.

——— (1980) "Nontraditional family forms: A decade of research." Journal of Marriage and the Family 42, 4: 905–922.

MAYKOVICH, M. (1976) "Attitudes vs. behavior in extramarital sexual relations." Journal of Marriage and the Family 38: 693–699.

MAZUR, A. (1977) "Beyond jealousy and possessiveness," in R. Libby and R. Whitehurst (eds.) Marriage and Alternatives: Exploring Intimate Relationships. Glenview, IL: Scott, Foresman.

MOORE, K. and M. BURT (1982) Private Crisis, Public Costs. Washington, DC: Urban Institute.

NEUBECK, G. (1969) Extramarital Relations. Englewood Cliffs, NJ. Prentice-Hall.

NEWCOMB, P. (1979) "Cohabitation in America — Assessment of Consequences," Journal of Marriage and the Family 41: 597–603.

O'NEIL, N. and G. O'NEIL (1972) Open Marriage: A New Life Style for Couples. New York: Evana and Co.

PEABODY, S. (1982) "Alternative life styles to monogamous marriage: Variants of normal behavior in psychotherapy clients." Family Relations 31 (July) 3: 425–434.

RAINWATER, L. (1970) Behind Ghetto Walls: Black Families in a Federal Slum. Chicago: Aldine.

RAMEY, J. (1976) Intimate Friendships. Englewood Cliffs, NJ: Prentice-Hall.

——— (1975) "Intimate groups and networks: Frequent consequences of sexually open marriages." The Family Coordinator 24, 4: 515–530.

REISS, I. (1980) Family Systems in America. New York: Holt, Rinehart and Winston.

RISMAN, B., C. HILL, Z. RUBIN, L. PEPLAU (1981) "Living together in college: Implications for courtship." Journal of Marriage and the Family 43 (February) 1: 77–84.

RUBIN, L. (1976) Worlds of Pain. New York: Basic Books.

SINGH, B. (1980) "Trends in attitudes toward premarital sexual relations." Journal of Marriage and the Family 42 (May) 2: 387–393.

——— B. WALTON, and J. WILLIAMS (1976) "Extramarital sexual permissiveness: Conditions and contingencies." Journal of Marriage and the Family 38, 4: 701–712.

SMITH, J. and L. SMITH [eds.] (1974) Beyond Monogamy. Baltimore: Johns Hopkins University Press.

SPRENKLE, D. and D. WEIS (1978) "Extramarital sexuality: Implications for marital therapists." Journal of Sex and Marital Therapy 4 (Winter): 278–291.

WEIS, D. and M. GLASNERICK (1981) "Attitudes toward sexual and nonsexual extramarital involvements among a sample of college students." Journal of Marriage and the Family 43, (May) 2: 349–356.

WHITEHURST, R. (1970) "Open marriage: Problems and prospects," in B. Murstein (ed.) Exploring Intimate Life Styles, New York: Springer Co.

YANKELOVICH, D. (1981) "A world upside down." Psychology Today (April).

YLLO, K. (1978) "Non-marital cohabitation: Beyond the college campus." Alternative Lifestyles 1: 37-54.

ZELNIK, M., J. KANTNER, and K. FORD (1982) Sex and Pregnancy in Adolescence. Beverly Hills, CA: Sage.

SEX AND MARRIAGE

Questions

1. *What influences a person's decision to engage in premarital sex?*
2. *Are there sex differences in the way people decide on the appropriateness of sexual relationships?*
3. *What are the pros and cons of sexual relationships that involve neither affection nor commitment?*
4. *Should couples test their sexual compatibility before they decide to get married?*
5. *What are the long-term and short-term consequences of sexual relationships in general?*

Social Policies

This section deals with three issues — whether sex education should occur only within the family; whether parenthood is acceptable only within the conventional means; and whether it is acceptable for sex therapists to engage in relations with their clients. Should society be concerned with the issues raised or should consenting adults be allowed to do as they please? Is the family the rightful focus of the questions raised in this section, or are these matters the concern of social policy beyond the family?

SEX EDUCATION

Sex Education Is the Right and Responsibility Only of the Family

JOHN STEINBACHER

In March, 1981, more than 200 parents showed up at a regular board meeting of the Jurupa School District in Riverside County, California, to loudly protest materials being used in a sex education course at Roubidoux High School. To this reporter, viewing the passions on both sides of the issue, it was instant deja vu, a throwback to the early 1970s when this kind of protest was widespread throughout the United States. In those early years of school sex education, no place was the opposition to the course any louder and more organized than it was in the city of Anaheim, California, where for nearly a year, massive and highly vocal attacks were launched against a broad-based sex education and family life course that was brought into the district with the blessings of then superintendent, Paul Cook. In the process, careers were literally destroyed, and people in positions of power were toppled.

The superintendent who brought the program into the district, was forced into an early retirement; the school nurse, Sally

Williams, resigned; a number of school board members lost their positions, and the much advertised family life program was radically altered to conform more to the tastes of the many protesters.

Many of the opinions expressed by parents in the Roubidoux High School controversy sounded uncomfortably familiar to this reporter. Parents were protesting the use of a textbook, *Marriage, The Family and Personal Fulfillment.* "You are exposing children to a value system that says there are no values," said Verne Lauritzen, the spokesman for the family group that called itself Concerned Parents Facing Contemporary Issues. Another parent complained, "We are not opposed to sex education, but it does not have to be so explicit. . . . We feel this book is imposing a different type of morality on us. . . . You do not have the right to force your morality on me." Still another protested, "It is hard enough to raise kids, today . . . we do not need that garbage for our kids to see, to compound that problem." Lauritzen also complained that his group was facing a closed door in attempts to make suggestions on the curriculum and on "more acceptable" materials being used in other districts.

On the other hand, the course was defended by one of the sex education teachers, Annmarie Weaver, who stated that the course was needed because of the alarming statistics in regard to pregnancies, venereal disease, and the breakdown of forced marriages.

In this latest Southern California protest, many of the same factors appear to be present that led to the catastrophic confrontation in the city of Anaheim a decade earlier. In retrospect, it appears obvious that much of the complaint in Anaheim could have been defused if the school district had been more concerned with working out a compromise than with defending itself against attack.

First, the course was put into the district without any public discussion. Parents were suddenly confronted with materials that, in many cases, offended their sensibilities. Later, sorting it all out, it became apparent that the controversy was due to several factors, most of which could have been forseen and perhaps resolved before a full-blown, parents-versus-the-schools issue erupted. First, parents were not told in advance that there was going to be such a course; second, parents had no idea what kinds of course materials were being used; third, there was (from the position of many parents) too much emphasis on a philosophy of relativism. In other words, parents were alarmed that the students were being given the mechanical nuts and bolts of sexuality without any ethical or moral standards on which to base their subsequent behavior. This last was no doubt the most serious charge, and it is perhaps where sex education and family life courses will continue to be attacked in the years ahead. The following question arises: Is it possible for the public schools to teach all about sex without taking any stand in regard to the morality or the immorality of any act? There are those of us who believe that it is not possible for the public schools to take a clear-cut, moral standpoint on the right and wrong of sexual intercourse and other actions under various circumstances for the simple reason that the public system has to please a pluralistic society that supports it. To teach sex education in a Baptist or a Catholic school, on the other hand, would seem to be much easier because those supporting that education system have a more or less common view of what is right and wrong in regard to sexual activity. It is only when those teaching the course in a parochial school system get outside the mainstream thinking of their particular denomination or group that controversy erupts. For instance, there was a great deal of controversy in the early 1970s over materials being used in Catholic schools; but if you look at it closely you will see that the problem was principally that some of those teaching the materials were, in the eyes of the parents, flaunting the very moral precepts on which the school (and the Church) was founded. In most cases, this question was resolved when courses were designed that took into account these particular moral precepts. For instance, it would be insensitive on the part of a Catholic teacher to tell female students that one has the right to decide whether or not to have an abortion. Any teacher who persisted in that view would be courting the wrath of a good part of his or her constituency, and that wrath would not be unexpected when it came.

Unfortunately, the public schools have a much more difficult time trying to decide what is right and wrong in regard to sexual relationships. In any cross-section of public school parents you will find just about every attitude imaginable — all the way from the one who believes that incest is a fine thing to the one who believes that all sex is just plain dirty and every view in between. With such a pluralistic group paying the school bills, is it any wonder that it would be almost impossible to have a sex education course that would be free of controversy?

Ideally, sex education belongs in the home. Practically no one would take issue with that. However, carrying out that seemingly universal belief is something else again. Realistic statistics seem to indicate that most people do a rather poor job of teaching about sex in the home — but this is not to say that they are not capable of doing so. There has not been, over the past decade, enough emphasis placed on parental involvement in helping their own children to view their sexuality in a healthy manner. I do know that there was some talk, in the 1970s, of starting classes for parents — so the parents could better handle their own responsibilities in that area — but it doesn't seem that much came of this. Whether this was due to parental lack of interest or to the inability of the school district to attract their interest is not clear to me. I still think that this is an area that needs to be explored more fully, and I do not accept the common misconception that parents just don't care. I think that many of them do care, and very deeply. It is just that they do not have the personal tools to use in the home; this, it seems to me, desperately needs to be rectified.

Family life and sex education courses have been around now for more than a decade in most of the school districts in the land. Many of these courses are elective so they do not touch the lives of all of the students. However, I do believe that by now enough students have taken these courses that we should be able to get some kind of statistics on what happened to the students who took the courses and to those who did not. Some people are insisting that the current alarming rise in venereal disease and teenage pregnancies (and abortions) is due at least in part to the "permissive" attitudes inculcated in students who take the public school sex courses. Is this true or false? It is not enough for those promoting such courses to simply shriek loudly that current unwholesome behavior is not due to sex education courses. It is also not enough for sex education opponents to claim that all these problems should be laid at the feet of those who promote sex education. We need some precise statistical analyses rather than half-baked personal opinions.

Those opposing public school sex education courses have long protested that their basic underlying philosophy is one of "secular humanism," a philosophy they define as relativistic. Protesters say that their children are being taught that in such delicate areas as sex, there really is no such thing as right and wrong. If these protests are too simplistic, they could, it seems to me, be laid to rest once and for all if the public school administrators would spell out what is right and what is wrong in sexual activity. But that's the Catch 22 of the situation. How do you do that without enraging a lot of parents who have differing views? To be perfectly honest about it, it seems to me that it is just about an impossible situation.

One of the areas that concerned us in the 1970s was the qualifications of the instructors. It did not help when one of the most vocal supporters of the sex education program in Anaheim was arrested and pled guilty to a wide assortment of felonious sexual activities with his own children. To say that this revelation alarmed some of the theretofore uncommitted parents is putting it mildly. When I was a reporter on the story, I always maintained that sex education instructors would have to go Ceasar's Wife one step further when it came to being above reproach. There were, unfortunately, suggestions from some psychiatrists that some people were attracted to sex education as a career because they were hung up on the subject and this was a wonderful way to act out fantasies without getting arrested. I did wonder at the time just what screening processes potential sex educators went through in college or, for that matter, at the school board level. In the old days it was the coach who was saddled with a rather primitive form of "telling about the birds and the bees" which, it always seemed to me, became his or her job more or less by default.

One of the things that sex educators have lacked from the beginning is "good press" — good public relations, if you prefer. In many ways, this is due at least in part to the nature of the subject. In the midst of a sustained attack from outraged parents Anaheim Unified School District, for instance, hired a newspaper reporter to work full-time as a public relations man for the district. He failed miserably in selling the program, however, because he was forced to be an advocate for some concepts that were generally perceived by the public to be amoral at best and immoral at worst. He ended up losing his job when the school board that hired him lost their own positions in an election.

One of the problems with public school sex education is that it is perceived by many parents as an unwanted intrusion on their personal rights. In a society of individualists, this becomes a particularly worrisome problem for the sex education advocates.

When I was reporting on sex education controversies for the Anaheim Bulletin newspaper, I noted that many parents felt that the schools should have some clearly defined parameters within which they should operate. Over and over again the refrain was heard that the public school family life classes were designed to not only change the morals of the young people but also to change the morals of our society. When public education tries to become all things to all people, it runs the risk of becoming nothing to anyone. Unfortunately for the sex education advocates, many of their early spokesmen didn't do much to allay the fears of parents that their own ideas and beliefs were going to be stripped from the minds of their children. People like William Glasser, Mary Calderone, and others made a lot of statements about human sexuality that seemed to be made mostly for shock effect. By the time some of the school boards became aware that they were losing the confidence of their constituents vis-à-vis family life and sex education, they tried to compensate by setting up parent advisory boards to advise on curriculum and so forth. But by the time the board members around the country awoke to the need for parental involvement from the earliest planning stages on, it was almost too late to convince the parents that the schools really didn't mean to destroy the morals of America's youth. In looking back over the turbulent 1970s in regard to family life programs, it seems difficult for us to understand how local school boards and administrators could have been so insensitive as to believe that the rather "square" parents would not be outraged by real or imagined intrusion into a sphere that had always been thought to belong to the parents.

Even worse, in the case of the famous Anaheim program it became obvious that those in charge attempted to "sneak" the program into the school system without any of the parents knowing about it. The theory — as expressed by one of the program advocates — was that once you got the program into the school system it could not be removed again, no matter how loudly some might protest. Historically, these advocates had some evidence on their side as the history of public education is replete with examples of programs that long outlived their valve because nobody ever got around to dismantling them. I suppose that Paul Cook thought this would be the case in Anaheim: He was quoted as stating, at the height of the controversy, "Once you get the program into the system they can't ever get it out again." That remark, coming at the very height of the battle, was like throwing gasoline on top of a conflagration.

There is another aspect to this controversy over sex education in the schools that seems to have passed right over the heads of the leaders in the sex education movement. Most of the leaders appear to many to be rather avant garde and "far out" in some of their views about life-styles. At a time when many parents are virtually panic stricken as to how their own children will turn out, this becomes a serious problem of credibility. This brings us back to the very serious problem of screening those who will become sex educators. I think that is the single most serious problem confronting the sex education advocates. I do not see that they have really come to grips with this problem over the past decade.

Another problem confronting public school sex education is the feeling on the part of some parents that they have lost control of their children. They either blame TV for it, or the state, or the federal government, or the public schools, or just plain "they." They see school sex education as just another major incursion into the parent-child relationship, and in many cases this is literally the straw that breaks the camel's back. I do not see that public education has done much to mollify them in this regard.

The argument also centers around how various people see the classroom. During the 1970s, many of those on the fringes of education were saying that the public school classroom must become a mental health clinic with the teacher serving as a psychotherapist because it was obvious that all of the children were mentally ill in one way or another. Teacher journals started referring to teachers as "psychotherapists," a word that put fear into the hearts of many rather naive and trusting parents who had a totally different perception of the role of the teacher in the classroom. Then, when different perception of the role of the teacher in the classroom. Then, when people like Ashley Montague tell thousands of teachers at a teacher conference in San Diego which I attended as a reporter that "every child in America comes to school at the age of six mentally ill, because he comes to school with certain values he inherits from his parents, from the family unit," it is the equivalent of waving a red flag under the nose of an already angry bull. Parents need read only that kind of a quote in their daily paper — as they did in mine — to come to the conclusion that their long-trusted school system has turned into a personal enemy. Words, after all, are what we live with and by, and sex education advocates should be particularly careful about how they try to voice their ideas. In the 1970s there was altogether too much sensationalizing on too many late night talk shows on the part of people like Mary Calderone and Ashley Montague; instead of preparing a large segment of the public for the forthcoming family life programs, these rather explicit and often sensational kinds of discussions alarmed the parents, causing all sorts of alarm bells to go off in the heads of many of the viewers. This was especially true on the part of viewers who perceived family life programs as perhaps the final, intolerable intrusion on the part of the state or federal governments into the private lives of people. It was, I suppose, inevitable that family life and sex education should become something of a political as well as a moral issue because most opponents of the program perceived it to be yet another grab on the part of statist-minded people of another segment of privacy and individuality. Whether their fears were justified or not is beside the point. If the 1980 elections taught anything, it was that a sizable segment of the electorate — and even, perhaps, a large majority — were opting for less intrusion of government into their lives. And, as sex education and family life programs are seen by many of these same people as perhaps the most intrusive of all, it is not surprising that there was this kind of a backlash against the programs. The liberals who were promoting these programs simply could not comprehend that others would not look favorably upon government employees telling their children what is or is not right in such a personal area as sex. In the minds of the opponents, the fact that virtually all of the public school programs were framed in such a way that no easily identifiable moral precepts could be seen made it even worse. The absence of strict rules of behavior, these people believed, therefore implied no rules of behavior or morals at all. In fact, taking it one step further, they presumed the absence of clear rules of right and wrong proved that the programs were deliberately immoral.

Proponents of family life have made the same mistake as was made by their colleagues in the liberal arena who advocate massive forced busing to achieve racial balance. In both cases, they forgot that parents would see these kinds of programs as attempts by an all-powerful — and therefore frightening — state to "take their children away from them." In fact, some of the more extreme types projected that family life and sex education programs were merely the first step in a clearly defined plan to take all of the children of the United States away from parents and put them into state-run institutions. With that kind of a mind set, it is no wonder that many parents became virtually hysterical when confronted with what they believed to be the first stage in a massive, statist plan to alienate their children from them. Attempts to rationally disprove this concept proved fruitless, as could be expected, because those attempting to do the disproving were merely looked upon as agents of the statists who were trying to pull the wool over the eyes of the parents.

In February, 1981, a debate took place in the courtroom in Sacramento, California, over the issue of creation versus evolution and of whether either or both of these theories should be taught in public schools of the state. The decision in the matter proved disappointing to both sides of the widely publicized debate, heralding the fact that this same issue will no doubt surface again and again in other places and times and that perhaps the issue will never be resolved. The same thing can be said for family life and sex education programs. Those of us who were involved in reporting the great sex education controversies of the 1970s are constantly being reminded that no matter how much things change, they still remain the same. Although not receiving as much media coverage today, those 1970-style battles are still raging here and there around the country — and not always in such hotbeds of conservative political opinion as Orange County, California. For instance, Riverside, California — where a major battle is being fought at the very time of this writing — would generally be considered to be a rather liberal bastion: That is, it is heavily democratic, a "college" town, and has an extremely liberal daily paper. Yet the nature of the controversy is not a wit different from that fought in the city of Anaheim nearly 10 years ago. Only the cast of characters has changed and the name of the parent group doing the protesting. In reading the newspaper accounts of the battle, one is struck with how little has been learned by public school administrators over the past 10 years. Once again they admit that they used rather inept means to choose their textbooks. Even the author of the text announced in the newspaper that he was surprised that his book was being used at the high school level, as it was too explicit and was intended for use among upperclassmen in college. Then there were the same old recalcitrant stances taken by the teachers in the local program — the insistence that *they* really knew what was best for the children after all — and a thinly veiled suggestion that the protesters were a bunch of semiliterate, ultraconservative, behind-the-times people who were simply using this issue as an excuse to attack the whole school system. Belatedly (after the damage has already been done as regards parent-teacher-school relationships) the board now admits that they erred not only in a choice of textbooks but that their entire textbook selection method was deficient in critical ways. Worst of all from their standpoint and from the standpoint of peace in their school district is the fact that the board members insist that they, the administrators, and the teachers know what they are doing and that the parents do not understand what is best for the children.

So, in 1981 there was the largely ignored cry from the parents, "You do not have to feel you can force your new morality on me and my children"—and we will no doubt hear this cry over and over again in the years ahead.

SEX EDUCATION

V–B

Sex Education Should Occur outside the Family in Schools, Youth Groups, and Agencies

ANDREA PARROT

The arguments raised by those who oppose sex education outside the home revolve around the following issues: (1) Imparting sexual knowledge is the right and responsibility of only the family; (2) if sex education is taught in schools or churches, will the morals and values of the parents be upheld or undermined? (3) What type of qualifications, characteristics and training do sex educators have that make them capable of such a task? (4) Examination of the statistics in the past decade since sex education has been taught in some schools indicates that there has not been a decrease in teenage pregnancy or sexually transmitted diseases (formerly known as venereal disease); and (5) does sex information lead to sexual experimentation? Each of these issues will be addressed in order to argue for the need of sex education in schools, churches, youth groups, and agencies.

RIGHT AND RESPONSIBILITY OF FAMILY ONLY

Most sex educators agree that imparting sexual knowledge is the right and responsibility of the family unit. In fact the most important sex learning takes place in the years before schooling when parents teach sexuality verbally and nonverbally by their actions and expectations (Gadpaille, 1970). Realistically the family is not able to prevent their children from learning about sex from other sources; however, Greenberg (1975) in a study of high school students reported that the majority of sexual knowledge and attitude formation is based on information obtained from peers and literature–only 15 percent of sex information is obtained from schools and 21 percent from parents. It is obvious that the media is a pervasive force in all of our lives, but especially in the lives of children and adolescents. One can learn much about sexual behavior and attitudes condoned by society by looking at the Jordache jeans advertisements on television or in the New York Times Magazine section. Movies and other media sources are also providing clear messages about sexual behavior. A sampling of 1980 adolescent sex movies included "Little Darlings" which depicted two 15-year-old girls vying to see which could lose her virginity first; "The Blue Lagoon" which portrayed almost nude sexual experimentation of a teenage boy and girl, resulting in the birth of a child; and "Foxes" which idolized four Los Angeles teenage girls and their exploits with sexual initiation. All of those movies were rated "R." Many songs that teenagers listen to also provide very clear messages about standards and values. Popular songs bombard our teenagers with suggestions such as "do it to me one more time" (by Captain and Tenille); "push, push in the bush" (by Musique); "do you want to make love, or do you just want to fool around?" (by Peter McCann); "I don't want you to cook my bread. I don't want you to make my bed. I don't want you to be true, I just want to make love to you" (by Foghat); and also "And we'd steal away every chance we could, To the back rooms and alley or the trusted woods. I used her and she used me, but neither one cared. We were gettin' our share" ("Night Moves" by Bob Seger).

In addition to the songs and movies, the dime store paperback love stories which adolescents read are filled with explicit premarital and extramarital sexuality and a variety of even more deviant sexual experiences. The worst offender of teaching values and morals contrary to the teaching of strong family values are the television soap operas — a case of sex education that takes place within the home. Although the media provides very clear statements about sexual behavior and morals, they do not also provide the necessary information about the consequences of such behavior.

By the time one reaches adolescence, the major source of sexual information and behavior reinforcement is provided by the peer group (Heisler, 1980; Thornburg, 1974), with the media becoming an increasingly preferred source (Sherreffs and Derelsky, 1979). The information provided by friends and the media, however, is often inaccurate (Reichett and Werley, 1976; Thornburg, 1974). In a study by Thornburg (1974) it was found that students received the most accurate information (on veneral disease, abortion and menstruation, respectively) from school, literature, and their mothers; and the least accurate information (on homosexuality, intercourse, and masturbation) from their peers. Often peers (knowingly and unknowingly) provide inaccurate information to each other about sexual norms, physiology, and standards of our society. Lines that males use on females to get them to cooperate sexually include such inaccuracies as "if you don't have sex by the time you are sixteen, you will become a lesbian," or "everyone is doing it" (Gordon, 1978). It is not possible for parents to know of all the sexual information to which their children are exposed outside the home. It is clear, however, that these sexual messages are everywhere and that our young people may be believing and/or living according to these standards without parental knowledge or approval.

Adolescents of both sexes need help in determining the importance and functions of sexuality in their lives, changing sex roles, patterns of family life-styles, facts about anatomy and physiology, emotional needs at various ages, and responsibility for their own behavior in interpersonal relationships throughout the life cycle (Fohlin, 1971). Adolescents need to establish a sexual and ego identity apart from the family unit. "Sexuality is nurtured first in the family and continues to develop and express itself as the individual reaches beyond the family and relates to people in all walks of life" (Lindquist, 1968).

When asked, most adolescents charge the home, the school, and the church with failing to provide sex information. The adolescents further indict adults for presenting information to adolescents in a negative, unwholesome way. Since adolescents obviously gain so much of their knowledge about sexuality from other youth, it seems vital that the home and the school become involved in the task of disseminating accurate information about human sexual behavior in a positive, wholesome way [Thornburg, 1972: 90].

This problem does not begin in adolescence, however, but exists when the child is quite young as well. Many of our children suffer from chronic lack of sex information (or misinformation) which is perpetuated by adults. The passage below, taken from *Sex Education for Today's Child: A Guide for Modern Parents,* illustrates this problem:

An eleven-year-old boy described the time when he was in first grade and he had wanted to know how a doctor can tell whether a newborn infant is a girl or a body. Incredible as it may sound, no one would give a straightforward answer.

"First, I asked my teacher," the boy said, "but she got sort of red in the face and said I should ask my mother when I got home from school. So I asked my mom, but she got red in the face, too, and said she way busy making dinner, and that I should ask my dad when he got home from work.

"Dad didn't get red in the face, but he didn't answer my question, either. He told me that was a good question and to ask Dr. Brody the next time I had an appointment with him. My dad probably thought I'd forget all about it by the time I saw Dr. Brody, but I didn't. I didn't even care that much about the question any more — I was just mad because no one would answer it.

"When I asked Dr. Brody how he can tell whether a newborn baby is a boy or a girl, he smiled. Then he put his hand on my shoulder and said, 'Danny, you know how I can tell every time? Right after the baby is born, if the nurse wraps it in a pink blanket, it's a girl, and if she wraps it in a blue blanket, it's a boy!" (Uslander et al., 1977: 13).

Sex education which is the responsibility of *only* the family is our goal; but until families are fully knowledgeable about sexual information (including physiology, emotions, peer pressure, non-familial sources of sexual learning) and are comfortable discussing the topic, the aid of sex education professionals may be necessary to assist the parents (reinforce family values and morals) and provide them with the information they need to become more knowledgeable about sexuality. Research consistently indicates that parents generally do not feel adequately prepared or comfortable about teaching sex education to their children (Conley and Haff, 1974; Roberts et al., 1978). It is a tremendously difficult battle for parents to try to counteract the negative effects of peers and media on their own schools, churches, youth groups, and agencies can be helpful in reinforcing the values and morals of the parents.

MORALS AND VALUES OF THE FAMILY

Saxon (1976) suggests that parents be provided with an opportunity to help determine the type of sex education their children receive in school. In order for a school program to be fully effective, it must have parental support; but parents must understand the program and its components in order to support it. Offering the same course to parents is a good way to expose them to its scope and provide them with information at the same time. Parental complaints after taking the course are rare. In five years, only seven out of more than two thousand students were excused due to parental request (Saxons, 1976).

One important question which Libby (1970) asked in light of parental and student concerns was this: Should sex education programs be designed to meet students needs and goals, or to satisfy parental needs and attitudes? In Saxon's study, it was suggested that parents be involved in the initial planning; if this is not possible, their input should be requested after the program is underway. Feedback has been primarily positive in these cases; Saxon reports only two exceptions. Parent input should serve as guidance to develop a program to address student concerns.

Numerous studies nationwide have addressed the question of whether parents support schools teaching sex education. Results ranged from 77 percent who fully supported sex education (1977 Gallup Poll, released in 1978) to 97 percent who elected to keep their children in sex education programs already existing in schools (Kirby et al., 1979; Gendel and Green, 1971).

A study by Roger Libby in 1970 examined parental attitudes toward both general and specific aspects of high school sex education programs. Of the parents 82 percent, regardless of age, approved of integrating high school sex education into the curriculum as well as requiring a course in family life and sex education. This overwhelming support for sex education may be due in part to the fact that a large percent (72 percent) of both parents and students felt that parents did not provide sufficient sex information for their children (Conley and Haff, 1974). Parents generally do not feel adequately prepared or comfortable teaching sex education to their children. In a Cleveland study, although most parents said they wanted their children to know about erotic activity by their teens, less than 12 percent had ever discussed premarital intercourse, venereal disease, or contraception with their children (Project on Human Sexual Development, 1978).

Parents and students should be involved in the planning of sex education programs. Parental resistance will be minimized, and the course will reflect students needs and parental concerns (Saxon, 1976; Gendel and Green, 1971). Parents become doubly annoyed if they are ignored in the decision-making process or if their morals and values are undermined (Scales, 1980). Student participation in the program itself should be optional, as both parents and students have the right to avoid sex education (Saxon, 1976).

In the 1970 Position Paper on Family Life Education, the National Council on Family Relations included the following passage:

> The NCFR recommends that comprehensive and sequential family life programs, which include sex education, should be a planned portion of the regular curriculum from pre-school through college. It further recommends that these programs should actively involve parents and that adult family life programs should also be developed.

Programs often are conducted through health agencies, youth-servicing organizations, parent and community organizations, religious institutions, public media, and other organizations as well as the public school system. Common objectives of these programs should be determined, intertwined, and coordinated closely (Select Committee on Population, 1978).

Education programs also must be provided for parents to provide them with information they never received, assure them that their children are not learning pornography, inform them of their children's unspoken needs, and indicate how parents can best help their children in sexual discussions and with sex-related problems (Alan Guttmacher Institute, 1976; Lindquist, 1968). "It is desirable, if not necessary, for parents to become involved in the program itself, not just to give permission for their youngsters to participate but to participate themselves" (Carton and Carton, 1971). Gendel and Green (1971) suggest that adult sex education should be a consistent segment of every developing program of "sex education" at any level.

Many researchers recommend programs in elementary school because of the importance of attitude formation and the evidence of sexual exploration and experimentation during that time. The specific advantage of teaching sex education at this level is that the children are typically less defensive and less emotionally involved in certain topics of sex than are adolescents. Thus, programs for elementary and middle-school children feasibly could provide primary prevention of mental health problems rather than remedial sex education (Carton and Carton, 1971). In a 1969 survey by Byler of 5000 students, grades K-12, it was found that these students not only wanted sex education to be taught in schools but felt that it should be initiated *no later* than 5th grade.

Schools cannot do the parents' job of providing complete sex education to students, but can serve only as a supplement to what children learn at home (Gadpaille, 1970). Currently, schools do not and *cannot* provide comprehensive education of sexuality. This is due, in part, to the fact that schools are not considered the most important source of sex information. In fact, schools are reported to be the fourth most important source, after peers, literature, and mothers, in that order (Thornburg, 1972).

Szasz (1970) reports that within the school, teachers are viewed as an available source of information. This role includes both formal and informal education inside and outside the classroom. Teachers transmit knowledge in accordance with the available sexually related knowledge in their area of expertise rather than transmitting the opinion of the school board or government. Szasz further indicates that teachers are expected to be able to forecast future trends in the field of sex education and the needs of students. In order to do so, it may be necessary for teachers to develop ties with community groups and obtain current resources and materials. It would be more realistic to assume that these needs would be met if every teacher in the district were trained to deal with sex education issues and discuss them when brought up by concerned or interested students (Szasz, 1970).

Needs assessments must be completed for communities and students, and the program should be tailored to meet the students' needs. Advisory groups should be established to involve the community and reflect community values and morals (Gendel and Green, 1971). While community involvement is likely to yield support, subterfuge is guaranteed to generate community hostility (Fohlin, 1971). Courses should be designed to explore the issues likely to be most beneficial to the students in a given community, and minimize the amount of parental resistance (Angrist et al., 1976; Gendel and Green, 1971; Saxon, 1976; Lindquist, 1968).

A broad range of community support and involvement is essential to the development of a successful sex education program in order to accurately reflect the values and morals of the community (Thomas, 1978; Sex Education Committee, 1975). Advisory groups should be included to determine broad program goals and be involved in the planning and implementation of the program (Hawley et al., 1976). In a study completed by the Department of Health, Education, and Welfare in 1979, model of exemplary sex education programs were examined. All of the exemplary programs stated that special teacher training and community and parental support were major reasons for the successes of the programs (Kirby et al., 1979).

QUALIFICATIONS, CHARACTERISTICS, AND TRAINING OF TEACHERS

Gadpaille believes that "parents should also be informed who the teachers of sex education are and how they are selected" (Gadpaille, 1970: 305). Conley and Haff examined concerns of parents and students about the qualifications of teachers. Conley and Haff also reported that parents did not consider age important but indicated the following areas as very important: the ability to talk freely and maturely without embarrassment; an interest in and a high level of knowledge of family life education; a sensitivity to reactions and feelings of students; an understanding of self and own attitudes; and familiarity with changing family living patterns and practices. Also, parents favored family life education at all grade levels and the inclusion of teaching morals and values as well.

Most experts in the field of sex education agree that sex, age, and marital status have little effect on the quality of sex education instruction (Carerra, 1972; Kirby et al., 1979). Specifications of teacher characteristics are provided by Dr. and Mrs. Wilkie (who disapprove of school sex education) as follows:

> At least 30 and perhaps no more than 45 or 50 at the most, married (for the first and only time) for at least five years and preferably 10 or more, perhaps even a physician-husband and a nurse-wife, physically attractive in build and face. He should be dominant and she should show deference. Finally, in order to teach about children they must have children, probably both sexes and ranging in age from pre-school into the teens or beyond [Wilkie and Wilkie, 1979].

It is clear that given this impossible list of qualifications and characteristics, very few of us would be considered qualified. Certainly priests and nuns would not be appropriate, but most parents would also not be considered qualified. Perhaps demographic characteristics should not be included as part of the teacher selection criteria. More important factors for sex educators to possess have been enumerated by the American Association of Sex Educators, Counselors and Therapists (AASECT, the organization granting certification for sex educators). AASECT qualifications include the ability to communicate effectively a healthy acceptance of sexuality, a high degree of empathy, an inherent respect for others–specifically respect for students' rights, abilities to make intelligent choices and responsible decisions, ability to treat sensitive areas in a consistent manner, and flexibility and knowledgeability.

The areas of knowledge that sex educators must possess were identified in a study completed by Michael Carerra (1971). The following areas were identified as being essential to sex educators: reproductive anatomy and physiology, psychosexual development, language of sexuality, menstruation, pregnancy, birth, sex differences and sex roles, trends and issues in sex education, psychology of adolescence, methods and materials in sex education, human growth and development, the role of sex in marriage, nocturnal emissions, masturbation, petting, premarital coitus, dating, courtship and mate selection, guilt and conflict related to sex behavior, leading discussions of group dynamics, and use of techniques and curriculum aids. A 1980 study of training that New York State sex educators possess indicated that over 90 percent had training in human sexuality, values clarification, adolescent pregnancy prevention; over 70 percent had training in communication techniques and group process and group dynamics (Eggleston, 1981).

If teachers have training to use all the parental, community and school effort in a positive, unified attempt to establish a school, community and home-based sex education program then young people may receive consistent messages about sex from adults. Their peers and media are already giving them inaccurate, exploitive messages about sex which could be contrasted with accurate, positive, consistent information from adults. Such information may provide children and adolescents with some measure of helpful information to be used in the decision-making process which they are forced to use daily in regard to themselves as sexual beings.

EFFECTIVENESS OF PAST EDUCATION PROGRAMS

A fourth argument against nonfamilial sex education is that even though there are qualified, well-trained educators, teenage pregnancy and sexually transmitted disease rates have not decreased since school sex education has existed. Several reasons that account for this follow.

Attitudes and behaviors are developed all through students' lives. In addition, sex education programs are given after many students have already had one or more pregnancies. The sexual behaviors of students are also strongly influenced by the emotional and sexual needs of teenagers. Students are in sex education classes for only about 3.3 percent of their time for *one* semester (five hours per week) while they receive much incorrect information from other sources at the same time (peers, media, parents, etc.). Information about problems such as sexually transmitted diseases may provide students with the necessary initiative to seek diagnosis and a cure if they suspect they may have contracted a sexually transmitted disease. Finally, now that social stigma has been removed from teenage pregnancy, rates of reporting are increasing.

The opponents to school or community sex education point to studies of program effectiveness and state that the programs have not done what they should have (decreased teenage pregnancy and sexually transmitted disease rates). In many of the studies there was no consideration of factors such as extent of teacher training, comprehensive presentation of important topics, length of time presented, which facts presented, or if the program was required (Gordon et al., 1979).

If the effectiveness of sex education programs is to be accurately measured, change in adolescent sexual behavior should not be the only measurement criterion. Sex education for five hours a week for 20 weeks cannot realistically be expected to counter an entire life's worth of sexual learning. It is for this reason that many community agencies and organizations must be enlisted and utilized to aid parents in teaching accurate information and parental values and morals to our youth.

There are many issues which should be addressed in discussing the changes necessary to improve sex education programs. These include needs assessment to plan appropriate programs, program development, jointly sponsored programs, programs for parents, teacher training, classroom environments, teacher training institutions, evaluation, and legislative mandates.

EFFECT OF SEX EDUCATION ON SEXUAL EXPERIMENTATION

The research has consistently indicated that sex education does not lead to sexual experimentation (Gordon et al., 1979). In fact, the opposite is often true. Studies have been done relating to sex education initiated in the home and also in schools. In both cases adolescents are likely to postpone sexual experimentation longer than their peers and, when they do become sexually active, are more likely to use contraceptives to prevent pregnancy (Gordon, et al., 1979; Kirby et al., 1979). In short, by providing adolescents with some information about their sexuality, they are more likely to make decisions that are right for them based on fact, not peer pressure.

CONCLUSION

Youth groups such as 4-H, scouts, and the like may be instrumental in providing youth with accurate information so that the adolescent peer group will pass on less inaccuracies. Religious groups may target both parents and youth to confirm a specific value system delineated by the community. Social service agencies often reach adolescents once they have become pregnant and/or have a sexually transmitted disease; adolescents at such a time are likely to be ready and willing to learn how to prevent such problems in the future. All of the groups mentioned above may be effective; however, they have one problem in common: They reach only a select group, not all parents or adolescents. Schools have the advantage of reaching all students and, therefore, would be an ideal place to teach sex education. Schools alone are not the answer though. Information and values must be reinforced in as many places as necessary to have the greatest effect. Parents are the key to the success of any sex education program and must provide guidance to the other organizations involved.

Children, preadolescents, and adolescents are the groups most likely to benefit from courses presented by teachers who have had training in the areas of community organizing skills and strategies, and teaching techniques in sex education. At this point in time, students are receiving most of their sex information from their peers and the media. This is due, in part, to the fact that parents usually have a very difficult time discussing sexuality with their children although parents want children to have information that reflects parental values and is necessary to make sound decisions. Teachers also are attempting to impart sex information to young people, but usually do so without parental knowledge and support. Parents quite often feel excluded from the decision-making process relating to what should be included in a school-based sex education program, although they feel they should have the right to help determine the content. Teachers are afraid that parents will not allow the teaching of sex education at all and, therefore, keep the program content secret from parents. The resentment and discontent between the two groups grow, and the message to the students from teachers is that sex should be hidden and is sneaky. The message from parents is that sex is bad and one should not react in a positive way to it. One common mixed message children in our society receive is "Sex is dirty and sinful, save it for the one you love."

While considering the controversy over where sex education belongs, Thornburg (1974) points out several important considerations:

Naivete is an expensive price that many of our preadolescent and adolescent youth pay for being thrust into sexual behavioral roles with limited and inaccurate sexual information.

The influence of mass media is powerful and cannot be disregarded by the adult sectors of our society. The excitement, thrills, and naturalness of sexual involvement is made highly attractive to our emerging and vulnerable youth.

No one can legitimately disregard the social impact of the peer group, a phenemonon which begins during preadolescence and extends into young adulthood. Considering that they are the most frequent source of information, and that for the most part, they are inaccurate in what they share, we must consider giving our youth adequate, consistent, and formative information. They need more than just their reference group to emerge with an understanding of human sexuality.

We, as a society, educate about sexuality through inferences and exclusion. We tell our young people that they will feel differently when they are in love. They experience new sensations or feelings when they are sexually aroused. They infer that because they are experiencing this new feeling, they must be "in love;" and if they are "in love," sex is acceptable.

While the schools, churches, and parents are all arguing over who should be educating their children and how such education should be done (thereby excluding themselves from effective sex education), the children are getting sex education from the media and peers. The media and their peers are presenting much more explicit and incorrect information than parents, schools, youth groups, or churches would. The later set of potential sex educators (parents, schools, youth groups, and churches) may be able to counteract some of the negative effects that peers and media are causing in relation to sexual information and development.

In this society as sexual information is everywhere, we assume that adolescents don't need sex education because they have already received the information from their families or somewhere else along the line. In reality our youth are really inadequately informed and are struggling to get some accurate, reliable information. The following passage by R. D. Laing (1972: 56) presents the problem that adolescents face today:

There is something I don't know
    that I am supposed to know.
I don't know what it is I don't know,
    and yet am supposed to know,
and I feel I look stupid
    if I seem both not to know it
    and not know what it is I don't know.
Therefore I pretend I know it.
    This is nerve-racking
    since I don't know what I must pretend
    to know.
Therefore I pretend to know everything.

I feel you know what I am supposed to know
but you can't tell me what it is
because you don't know that I don't know
what it is.

You may know what I don't know, but not
  that I don't know it,
and I can't tell you. So you will have
to tell me everything.

REFERENCES

Alan Guttmacher Institute (1976) 11 Million Teenagers. New York: Planned Parenthood Federation of America.

ANGRIST, S.S., R. MICHELSEN, and A.N. PENNA, (1976) "Variations in adolescent knowledge and attitudes about family life: Implications for curriculum design." Adolescence 11 (Spring) 41: 107–126.

CARRERA, M.A. (1972) "Training the sex educator: Guidelines for teacher training institutions." American Journal of Public Health (February): 233–243.

CARTON, J., and J. CARTON, (1971) "Evaluation of a sex ed program for children and their parents: Attitude and interactional changes." The Family Coordinator (October): 377–386.

CONLEY, J.A., and R.S. HAFF, (1974) "The Generation gap in sex education: Is there one?" Journal of School Health 8 (October) 44: 42–437.

DEARTH, P.B. (1974) "Viable sex education in the schools: Expectation of students, parents, and experts." Journal of School Health (April): 190–193.

EGGLESTON, A.P., (1981) "Effect of teacher training on sex education." Ph. D. dissertation, Cornell University.

FOHLIN, M.B. (1971) "Selection and training of teachers for life education programs." Family Coordinator, 20: 231–240.

GADPAILLE, J. (1970) "Parent-school cooperation in sex education — how can the professionals help?" Family Coordinator: 301–307.

GALLUP, G.H. [ed.] (1978) Gallup Poll: Public Opinion, 1978. Scholarly Research Inc.

GENDEL, E.S., and P.B. GREEN, (1971) "Sex education controversy: A boost to new and better programs." Journal of School Health (January): 24–28.

GORDON S. (1978) You Would If You Loved Me. New York: Bantam.

——— P. SCALES, and K. EVERLY (1979) The Sexual Adolescent. North Scituate, MA: Duxbury Press.

GREENBERG, J.A. (1975) "Study of personality change associated with the conditioning of a high school unit on homosexuality." Journal of School Health: 394–398.

HAWLEY, N., M.A. HASKIN, and H. CLEMES (1976) Project Teen Concern: An Implementation Manual. Rockville, MD: U.S. Department of HEW, Publication HSA 77–5600.

HEISLER, A.B. and S.B. FRIEDMAN (1980) "Adolescence: Psychological and social development." Journal of School Health (September): 381–385.

KIRBY, D., J. ALTER, and P. SCALES (1979) An Analysis of U.S. Sex Education Programs and Evaluation Methods. Atlanta, GA: Center for Disease Control, U.S. Department of HEW.

LAING, R.D. (1972) Knots. New York: Random House.

LIBBY, R.W. (1970) "Parental Attitudes toward high school sex education programs." Family Coordinator (July) 3(19): 234–246.

LINDQUIST, E.B. and J.K. BAIN, (1970) "A follow up study on in-service training in family life education." Family Coordinator (January) 1, 19: 88–94.

LINDQUIST, R. (1968) "Teach sex education as the fourth 'R.'" Whats New in Home Economics 39: 59–62.

National Council on Family Relations (1970) "Position paper on family life education." Family Coordinator (April): 183–186.

ROBERTS, E.J., D. KLUNE, and J. GAGNON (1978) Project on Human Sexual Development: Family Life and Sexual Learning, Population Education Inc.

REICHETT, P.A. and H.H. WERLEY (1976) Sex knowledge of teenagers and the effect of an educational rap session." Journal of Research and Development in Education 1, 10.

SAXON, B. (1976) "Our first five years: Sex education at Lee High School." Journal of Research and Development in Education, 1, 10: 30–35.

Select Committee on Population (1978) Fertility and Contraception in America: Adolescent and Pre-Adolescent Pregnancy. Washington, DC: U.S. Government Printing Office.

Sex Education Committee (1975) Sex Education, A Critical Concern. New York: New York State Coalition for Family Planning.

SZASZ, G. (1970) "Sex education and the teacher." Journal of School Health (March): 150–155.

THOMAS, G.H. (1978) "Community involvement key to sex education success in Falls Church," in P. Scales (ed.) In Search for Alternatives to Teenage Pregnancy. Washington, DC: National Alliance for Optional Parenthood.

THORNBURG, H.D. (1974) "Educating the preadolescent about sex." Family Coordinator, (January): 35–39.

——— (1972) "A comparative study of sex information sources." Journal of School Health (February): 88–90.

USLANDER, A.S., C. WEISS, and J. TELMAN (1977) Sex Education for Today's Child: A Guide for Modern Parents. New York: Association Press.

WILKIE and WILKE (1979) "Good sex educators are." Impact Journal of the Institute for Family Research and Education 6 (October).

SEX EDUCATION

Questions

1. *Is it possible to teach value-free human sexuality? Is there such a thing as "just the facts"?*

2. *Do preteens and teens turn to parents for advice in areas other than human sexuality? If teens learn from peers, would it be sensible and valuable to stress peer education and peer counseling?*

3. *Could the media play a responsible role in sex education? If so, in what way?*

4. *As elementary and secondary schools reach virtually all youngsters, are they the most suitable agents to provide sex education?*

5. *Is a school-parent-church partnership desirable for the design and implementation of a sex education curriculum?*

6. *Is it possible to teach certain basic and simple sexual concepts to preschoolers?*

7. *Should there be a state-mandated sex education curriculum, or should this be left up to the local school district?*

8. *Is there a teaching formula or format that lends itself especially well to this topic?*

VI–A

Any Member of Society Who Wishes to Become a Parent Should Be Allowed to Do So Only through Traditional Means

GRACE KETTERMAN

The traditional means of forming a family have varied as long as mankind has been able to record its history. Much of the Eastern world has planned families through the mutual agreements of two existing families or clans. In some societies families originate through the purchase of a wife by a dowry system.

It is in relatively recent history, in fact, that the idea of a romantic marriage has evolved. The freedom of two individuals to form a family out of mutual attraction and "falling in love" is a cultural newcomer to history.

Yet every culture and age has developed its own family form. In many cultures this form is influenced by their religion. In others, by the economy; and in still others, by the political beliefs of the state. In fact, some authorities believe it is the interference of the

189

state in family customs and behavior that presents the greatest danger to the institution of the family. It is thought that as political entities begin to decline, they reach into the privacy of the family to bolster a declining economy and failing strength of the state. The vicious cycle thus established may account for the fall of a state, or an entire civilization. Certainly the coincidence of the deterioration of family strength with the decay of entire cultures is great.

In today's Western world the traditional means of becoming parents had been clearly defined. First a young woman and man meet and by some mystical attraction begin dating. Until the past decade, this dating was allegedly restricted to a variety of activities, sometimes in groups and sometimes private. There was socially circumscribed display of affection between the couple. Only after a ceremonious wedding, did the couple engage in actual sexual intercourse. It was only a few decades ago that a suitor was expected to ask his prospective father-in-law for his daughter's hand in marriage."

It was fervently hoped by the young couple that a pregnancy should not take place on the wedding night or during the first month of marriage. To have a child before the ninth month of marriage became grist for the local gossip mills who eagerly counted down the months from marriage to childbirth.

Young women who were so indiscreet as to become pregnant outside of wedlock were socially ostracized and even disgraced. During the mid-1940s until about 1970, such young ladies were protected by their parents by sending them to any of several "maternity homes." Older single women who became pregnant often used such institutions as did younger girls. In most such cases, the child was given up for adoption, and the mother, sadder but wiser, returned home to pick up her life and hope no one else was the wiser!

It was during that era that I served as director for such a maternity home. After serving the needs of over 900 such women, we began to see a dramatic change in society. The legalization of abortion gave women a choice regarding the continuation of their pregnancies. The ready availability of contraceptives prevented many pregnancies.

But the most dramatic change of all was the revolution in society's attitude toward unmarried mothers. A major national magazine portrayed an attractive teenager cuddling her new baby in her canopied four-poster bed. Single teenage mothers were pictured showing off their babies to peers between classes, and the widespread acceptance of such attitudes was touted.

One of the last young women to seek the privacy and shelter of our institution was a popular leader in her local high school. Her family, chagrined at her irresponsible actions, went through elaborate measures to hide their daughter and enable her to return home unscathed by potential critics.

After an uneventful pregnancy and delivery, this beautiful young mother decided she simply could not part with her baby. Her devoted parents chose not to argue with her, and the young mother and baby went home with them to do quite well.

Since then, with increasing frequency single women have had their babies, kept them (with varying degrees of success), and the world in which they live has accepted them. In fact, increasing numbers of women of mature ages have elected to become mothers without the ceremony of a marriage and/or a husband. A national news article depicted this as an economic factor and raised an interesting question. "Is is not," the article posed, "the right of every child to have and know its father?"

Whether, indeed, such is the right of every child is relevant. Today's frequent search by adopted children for their biological parents is well recognized; and the need for an established, personal identity is deeply interwoven in the very fiber of being of most people.

Biologically, it is significant to note the mating and family patterns of the higher species of apes and chimpanzees. In several such classifications, a single male and female stay almost exclusively together at least through the maturation of their offspring — as long as six or seven years. In other groups a single male may develop a small harem of five or six females but stays exclusively with them for some years. The male shares in care of the young and provides food and protection for his "family."

The conventional means of becoming parents, then, in the Western world means that a man and woman meet, for a bond of interests and shared ideals, activities and goals. After a period of courtship varying in length they become engaged, and after another variable period of time, they are married. This is a formal ceremony which may be extremely simple or extremely elaborate, and is performed by a civil authority or clergy person.

Subsequent to marriage, the couple will conceive a child and establish a family of one or several children. There is a major argument, however, regarding the definition of a family. Many contend that single persons, a couple, or a person and pets may justifiably be called a family.

Webster's Collegiate Dictionary (1966) defines a family as (1) all the people living in the same household; (2) a group consisting of the two parents — one's husband (or wife) and children. The first definition certainly allows for a more varied composition of a family. The second does not, and it is this second definition that will be used in the discussion of the traditional family unit.

PROBLEMS IN UNCONVENTIONAL PARENTHOOD

The philosophy of the Western civilization at least since World War II and the preceding worldwide depression has been one of growing hedonism. This asserts that pleasure is the principal goal of life and should be pursued at all reasonable costs. Pain and grief, therefore, must be just as carefully avoided.

To want a child and to be unable to conceive and bear one is understandably a painful disappointment. Recently on a radio talk program it was reported that an estimated three million women in the United Stated under 30 have tired and been unable to conceive a child. Their aggregate disappointment is an indescribable quantity. It is small wonder that they will try many things in order to alleviate their pain.

There are many options they may be afforded in an attempt to have babies. None of these options however, is free from serious risks; and the results of several such choices can now be documented to be potentially more painful than childlessness.

Perhaps the least risky and most widely accepted answer to infertility is that of medication to increase the likelihood of pregnancy. A young wife came to me for psychotherapy for depression over her failure to conceive a child. She felt that she was disappointing her parents by failing to give them a grandchild. She also felt that she compared unfavorably with her sister who had two children. She was worried about the possibility of a child with some birth defect. After many agonizing months of doubts, longings, and careful medication, this young woman became pregnant and delivered a perfectly normal child. She went into severe postpartum depression from which she recovered very slowly.

Commonly the fertility medication results in multiple births. Rarely are twins or triplets exactly what parents would choose and the burden of providing for two or more babies all of their needs may create more pain than pleasure!

Currently a major legal battle is being waged over *surrogate* mothering — another option available to childless couples. surrogate mothering has grown from being a shocking rarity only some five years ago to a commonplace means of have a child. In this event, a woman willingly is inseminated by a prospective father who is married to a sterile woman. The legal case concerns a woman who bore a child who was seriously neurologically impaired. The couple who had yearned for a healthy infant could not accept the handicapped baby, and the father denied that it was in fact his child. He insisted that some other man must have been the father. The surrogate mother, in turn, did not want a baby to keep and only agreed to produce a child for the couple. According to her, the contract to bear a child for them was valid and she contended it could only by the child of the man involved. At this writing, the courts have not determined the party responsible for this infant and it is likely it will become a ward of the state. The cost of care for this infant alone could become a sizable tax burden on the citizens of that state for many years to come.

Artificial insemination has been a recognized medical practice for over 30 years. By this technique, sperm from a male is artificially implanted into a fertile womb and a woman may conceive and bear a child by this means. The woman may be married but, of course, this is not biologically necessary. Usually artificial insemination is performed in a currently married woman and only with the fully informed consent of her husband.

Under the duress of the disappointment of a wife at her infertility, a man may consent to such a procedure but later regret it. In fact a recent study showed some increase in divorces in a group of couples who had children born from artificial insemination. Apparently the husbands felt resentment, at first unconsciously but later very openly. Their sense of inadequacy was so severe that it impaired their ability to enjoy a child even though it was conceived by their spouse.

The suggestion of building a super race out of sperm banks from men of unusual giftedness and women who excelled in intelligence or other creative talents has been widely publicized.

Adoption has been practiced for many years. Adopted children have greatly enriched the lives of countless families. Likewise, adopted children have been given opportunities to develop interests and abilities through their adoptive parents' generosity that they otherwise would not have.

Currently, however, statistics indicate that some 45 percent of adopted children have emotional problems that are severe enough to require professional counseling. The unhappiness and dissatisfaction of adopted children is further accented by the growing compulsion to find their biological parents. Television has glamorized the reunions of such adoptes and their birth parents, perhaps further encouraging such searches. In my own considerable experience, however, such reunions are as likely to result in heartache as in joy.

Test-tube babies are a growing phenomenon of modern medical science. The first such baby born to a couple in england is now several years old and, according to reports, is a healthy child. This procedure has been duplicated in other countries with successful pregnancies resulting.

Test-tube babies are conceived entirely in a laboratory. On ovum is placed in a carefully prepared solution simulating the secretions of the female reproductive tract during the cycle of fertility. Semen from a male is introduced into that solution, and penetration of the ovum by a sperm can even be observed under a microscope. At a carefully chosen time, the fertilized ovum is implanted in a prospective mother's uterus. The time of implantation must coincide with the exactly appropriate period of her menstrual cycle in order for the uterine lining to "accept" the tiny embryo. Any ovum and or sperm from any two people may result in such an embryo although usually the sperm and/or ovum from one or both of the spouses is used.

While this procedure is new and experimental great care and attention are given to its exacting techniques. The tendencies are, however, for human beings to become careless as experience brings familiarity to any process. What monstrosities could result from such a circumstance one can only imagine. It is, in fact, a miracle of modern medical science that such an event is possible at all.

PHILOSOPHICAL ISSUES

NATURE'S SELECTIVITY

It is possible that nature has her own ways of dealing with the world's overpopulation problems. As the complexities of the civilized world increase, stress factors arise that may prevent the conception and birth of babies. The selective processes of nature may well be intended to limit the children born who would add to the already heavy burdens of overpopulation. The natural balances in our world are remarkable, and over a period of time they can take care of most of the problems of plant life and the lower animals. It is mankind's ingenuity and inevitable shortsightedness that tends to distort nature's fine balances.

It is wise, therefore, to learn from the animal world. The examples of the gibbons that are mostly monogamous and who mate at least for the time of the maturation of their young, seems to be a successful pattern. But if overcrowding and food shortages occur, their mating pattern changes along with their "family" composition.

Being able to accept infertility may be a major strength. Submitting to the wisdom of nature may be an important means of helping that balance in systems to become a positive one.

PROCESSES OF FORMING A FAMILY

As one considers the basic functions of biologic creatures, the rituals of mating, conceiving, pregnancy, and delivery are remarkably similar although unique in certain details. The processes of preparation for the birth of a baby are parts of the parenting "instinct." It is possible, then, that some, at least, of the problems of the families of adopted children, may be influenced by the failure of the parents to live through those prenatal influences. This idea is in no way to be taken as a denouncement of those wonderful adoptive families who have shared love that has enriched each life within the group! It is quite likely that the reasons for adopting children and the basic strength of the parents may be determining factors in successful adjustment of the children as well as the parenting instincts.

ULTIMATE RECOGNITION OF LIMITS

The human race has surmounted incredible odds. Knowledge has accumulated with ever-increasing rapidity. There are, indeed, few hurdles that are insurmountable by people or the machines we have created. With each new surge of knowledge and the vistas each opens, we feel more and more powerful. Although no one says so aloud, there is a growing sense that we are omnipotent. Therefore, we may get anything and everything we want.

This sense of limitless power is, furthermore, present in all children. Perhaps this is instinctive, but I see it as the natural outgrowth of child-bearing techniques. When baby cries, someone comes quickly in response. When cutting a tooth, pictures are taken to capture the great event. When taking his or her first steps, movies capture the great moment. Much of babies' first two years of life is spent being the center of their universe.

Such omnipotence reemerges as adolescents move into adulthood with all of the physical, social, and growth changes that this involves. Much of it remains, perhaps unconsciously, in most of us.

But eventually, we must each face our ultimate limits. Our finiteness is real; and there are, after all, some things we will never do. We must sooner or later, face old age, death, and the ubiquitous taxes! And also, over the long periods of time, we will learn (and can even now from history) that we have assumed more power and controls than we should have. Knowing where those limits are and need to be is wisdom. Finding out where they are not and exploring those areas to the maximum, is marvellous adventure. This philosophy is perhaps no where more important than in decisions regarding the forming of families.

Choosing to satisfy one's own desires, no matter what the risk or possible damage to a larger system, is selfish, extremely shortsighted, and eventually dangerous!

THE FAMILY'S STRUGGLE IN SOCIETY

Divorce has increased with alarming rapidity in the Western world. Divorce in England from 1931 to 1961 increased nearly seven times, and doubled from 1961 to 1968. By liberalizing laws permitting divorces, the state encourages divorce. In the United States "four out of ten marriages today [1981] end in the divorce courts" (Vogue, 1982).

Problems of the children of divorce have been widely studied. Few families, in fact, have failed to feel the painful edge of the division that rends hearts as well as families. In a psychiatric treatment center serving some 130 children from 5 to 18 years of age, some 80 percent of the patients come from broken homes.

As the rates of divorce have risen, so have many social problems. A major concern to the United States if that of *teenage pregnancies*. The pregnancy rate among 14-year-olds is 6.7 per 1000. Among 15-year-olds it is 18.2 per 1000. The cost to the taxpayers of helping these young people approximates six billion dollars annually (USA Today, 1982).

I personally have worked with some 900 unwed mothers as director of a maternity home in the Midwest. In an unpublished study of these young women, we discovered some significant facts. They overwhelmingly admired their fathers and yet had extremely remote relationships with them. They had conflicts with their mothers, but yearned for a closeness they did not feel with them. They had low self-esteem despite measurable success in school, jobs, and even interpersonal areas. They needed to feel secure, significant, and desirable. And they needed, in many cases, a baby to love — and most of all, to love them.

One young lady of 13 (going on 31) said to me as I gave her a physical examination, "I sure do hope you'll find I'm pregnant!" Since few 13-year-olds really want to be pregnant, I questioned her reason for this hope. Her reply is unforgettable: "Well, you see, my parents made me give away my dog because I didn't take care of him. But if I had a baby, they couldn't make me give that away!" The irresponsibility, loneliness, unmet needs, and confused feelings of this girl are a representative of those of many of her generation. What sort of families can such troubled young people create?

The increase in child abuse has been alarming to many of us. When such lonely, love-starved young mothers find that their babies drain them of more energy than a baby's budding love can replace, some of them displace their frustration on their children. Certainly there are many other studied causes of child abuse, but the immature unmarried mothers are of grave concern to those of us who strive to understand and help them.

Another social factor of immeasurable impact on families is that of the women's liberation movement. Undoubtedly women have the real power to make or break the spirit and significance of marriage and the family. In my experience with this movement from its inception, I have seen much good effected. I have been troubled, however by the anger and stubborn rebelliousness against men. In attempting to analyze these feelings, I have been astonished to find that few of the angry women have really understood that the things they dislike so intensely in the men had been instilled into those males by women — their mothers!

One such woman, in desperate outrage at her husband, divorced him. Then she discovered that her own anger was forming in her son the very traits she despised in her husband. Such anger, even though it is stimulated by pain of one sort or another, begets more anger — and more pain. Again, what sort of family can such a vicious cycle create?

Some writers feel that the extremists in womens's liberation forces are so great a divergence from human behavior patterns that they will remain a minority. They believe this movement will fade away once its objectives of equality in work, law, and the economy are achieved.

Fatherless families have already become the norm in wide areas of society. Either by original choice or by divorce, many women are electing to bear and raise one or more children alone. The reverse situation is also being seen more frequently as fathers are gaining custody of their children and raising them alone.

Single-parent families, with father or mother, raise significant questions regarding a child's identity as a total person. If all men are mean or all women are selfish, who is a child to be like? Much has been written about the maleness and femaleness of all of us. Some balance of these traits as unique to everyone and is one measure of personal health. What is to be the source of such a balance in the life of a child raised by one parent?

The unisex movement is another factor to be considered. This was of some concern in the 1970s. Currently (at least in the Midwest) it is my impression that this movement is subsiding. The tendency was for such people to collect in communes and to live informally, communally. Whether communes will revive or grow remains to be seen, but it seems doubtful.

One authority has predicted that the family of the future will be serial in nature, and that changes will take place as children come and go and as age progresses. They predict there will be a trial marriage period. (This seems to be present already in the now-common "live-in arrangement.) There may be several, serial marriages before entering into the main marriage for the purpose of having and raising children. After the children are grown, a final marriage will be contracted that is likely to last until death. Older, single adults, it is predicted will then enter into group marriage that is mainly for companionship and convenience.

To my Midwestern conservative thinking, these family styles of the future (emerging even in the present) lack warmth, completeness, and stability. They seem devoid of the maturity of commitment and empty of the stimuli to character development through the struggles of the difficulties of marriage.

I propose, therefore, the maintenance of the traditional family. Its inception certainly needs a great deal more rational thinking and planning and could do with much less romantic-idealizing. Perhaps a modification of the Eastern arranged marriage in which parental advice and counsel would be part of the choice of a spouse makes some sense.

The planning for and conception of children by the spouses should be ideal. Each child should be anticipated with loving joy. The sharing of both joys and responsibilities by the extended family or near friends will provide security for children and pleasure for childless relatives and friends.

My family was composed of seven children, a grandmother who lived with us, and our parents. But we all relied greatly on our Aunt Helena who moved in to help all of us during periods of stress. A new baby, an illness, or any unusually intense work could prompt her arrival. She rocked my parents' grandchildren, baby-sat when needed, and sewed doll clothes that were treasures. Her life added immeasurably to all of ours, and so, I hope, did our young lives enrich hers.

Many exceptionally fine teachers of mine have never married, or if married, they had no children. Their maternal instincts surely were subliminated in the marvelous care they provided for us, their students. These people have influenced more lives, more profoundly, than they may ever have done as parents. It is not the end of the world to be unable to bear children. In fact, it may be that coping with the grief over such an inability mellows and matures one.

The needs of children are profound, widespread, and increasing. I would conclude with a plea for those who may be unable to bear children by conventional means to consider accepting natures verdict. Turn those creative yearnings into channels of love and service to the needy lives around you.

Serving as Big Brothers, Big Sisters, or supportive people to children who need supplemental parenting can be of inestimable value to the children and the volunteer. The avenues for such service are endless. Hospitals are in constant need of volunteers. Working with children's organizations such as Scouts or Camp Fire will draw on every ounce of your ingenuity! (I've done it for years!) Serving as a volunteer in your local school system offers an endless variety of tasks. One lady placed and tended hanging plants through her local grade school. The children swarmed about her as she tended plants and taught horticulture to them.

Men, especially, seem to be at a premium in the lives of children. Service clubs offer an organized manner of reaching out to both little or older children. A professional photographer who is a friend of mine, spends at least one evening a week teaching photography to emotionally troubled children.

The purpose of families are multiple — creating life, nurturing, protecting, training and educating, playing with, and finally releasing the products. The traditional family should be strengthened and kept — until a better plan can be conceived.

REFERENCES

American Journal of Psychiatry (1979) "Battered Parents." October.
BERGER, D. M. (1980) "Couples' reaction to male infertility and donor insemination." American Journal of Psychiatry (September).
BLISTER, D. (1963) The World of the Family. New York: Random House.
Ebony (1982) October.
KAY, F. G. (1972) The Family in Transition. New York: Halsted.
USA Today (1981) Teenage pregnancy." May.
US News & World Report (1981) June 22: 90:12.
Vogue (1982) "The divorce report." October.

PARENTHOOD

Any Member of Society Has a Right to Become a Parent through Natural or Artificial Means

NOEL P. KEANE

The decision by any member of society to become a parent, regardless of fertility capacity, has constitutional protection. Legally, there exists a private realm of family life which the government cannot enter and which has been accorded both substantive and procedural protection. (Smith v. Organization of Foster Families, 431 U.S. 816, 842, 1977). This private realm includes freedom of choice in certain family matters. Among the decisions that an individual may make without unjustified interference are personal decisions relating to marriage, contraception, family relationships, and child rearing and education (Carey v. Population Services Int'l, 431 u.s. 678, 684–85 1977; Roe v. Wade, 410 U.S. 438, 453 1972).

Author's Note: I wish to acknowledge gratefully the assistance of Nancy A. Pirslin and Carol S. Chadwick.

This zone of decision making is accorded the constitutional right of privacy. This right is the right of an individual, married or single, to be free from unwarranted governmental intrusion into matters that fundamentally affect a person, such as the decision whether to bear or beget a child (Planned Parenthood v. Danforth, 405 U.S. 438, 453, 1972).

SURROGATE PARENTING

Surrogate motherhood is an arrangement between a married couple unable to have a child because of the wife's infertility, and a fertile woman who agrees to conceive the husband's child through artificial insemination, carry it to term, then surrender all parental rights in the child (see, Comment, Contracts to Bear a Child, 66 Cal. L.Rev. 611, 1978). Where allowable, under the laws of the particular state, the natural mother terminates her parental rights and the infertile woman adopts the child to become the legal mother.

In some states, when a surrogate mother is not married and is paid $10,000 to carry a child, the biological father may appear at the hospital and acknowledge the fact of his paternity. By doing so, he becomes the legal father whose name is placed on the birth certificate. There is no adoption process involved. However, the adoption laws in these same states may prohibit the acknowledgement and determination of his wife as the legal mother. In that case, the child becomes part of a family where only the father is legally related to that child. Hence, the surrogate mother remains the legal mother while the father's wife has no legal connection with the baby. What is being asked of the courts by surrogate mother arrangements is that the biological mother terminates her parental rights and the infertile woman be allowed to adopt the child.

In almost every state, there are "black-market-baby" laws which prohibit the buying and selling of babies and which seem to be the main obstacle in the surrogate mother process. These laws were enacted before the practice of surrogate motherhood emerged and therefore they do not directly address this particular situation. Surrogate parenting is not the same as buying and selling a child, the principal distinction being that the issue of a surrogate birth goes back to its biological father and becomes a part of the father's family. If there is an exchange of money, it is merely to defray expenses — not to profit the surrogate mother.

Another difficulty in applying these statutes to surrogate motherhood arrangements is that they relate only to the final phase — the adoption — of an agreement which has other important provisions. The surrogate mother is not paid primarily for consenting to the adoption of the child. Rather, those services which justify substantial compensation are pregnancy and parturition and their ensuing risks and limitations. These statutes do not purport to make it a crime to pay someone for becoming pregnant or having a baby. This omission clearly confirms that surrogate motherhood was never the intended target of the anti-black-market statutes. What the surrogate mother has to offer is what the sterile wife of the biological father unfortunately lacks: the biological capacity to reproduce. The essence of the surrogate motherhood agreement is to redress the injustice of nature in conferring this capacity on certain individuals who are able but unwilling to assume parental responsibilities while denying it to others who are willing but unable to do so.

The laws of this country should allow payment of a fee to a surrogate. It is the recognized constitutional right of a man and woman to procreate. Insofar as the black-market-baby statutes invalidate surrogate motherhood contracts by which individuals effect their rights of procreation and familial self-determination, the anti-black-market statutes and equivalent judicial decisions appear to invade the protected realm of privacy in the most direct and devastating way. In cases where the wife is infertile, the only way the couple can have a child is to arrange for another woman to carry the husband's child. I submit that the statutes are invalid because they affect decision making relative to procreation and the family — rights of privacy that are protected under the constitution. Moreover, where these regulations impose a burden on a fundamental decision, such as whether to bear or beget a child, they are justified only by compelling state interests and must be narrowly drawn so as not to affect more than is necessary (Roe v. Wade, 410 U.S. 113, 155–56, 1973). The means must be no more restrictive than is necessary to accomplish the purpose.

There are several purposes of the anti-black-market statutes — namely, the promotion of the family and the prevention of commercialization of adoption decisions. The statutes are not narrowly drawn to accomplish either of these purposes. As applied to the compensation received by a surrogate mother from a childless married couple, the statutes actually prevent a family from alleviating the childlessness which may endanger its viability. Generally, an otherwise constitutionally protected activity cannot be deprived of protection simply because it is the subject of commerce. Statutes that make it a crime to pay a physician for delivering a baby or performing an abortion would unquestionably be held unconstitutional. Yet to say that a surrogate mother has the right to conceive and bear a child but not be compensated is to make essentially the same argument. What the state cannot overtly prohibit, it cannot indirectly outlaw either. A state-created obstacle need not be absolute to be impermissible (Carey v. Population Services Int'l, 431 U.S. 678, 688–90, 1977). Thus requirements that unduly burden the right to abortion are unconstitutional (Planned Parenthood v. Danforth, 438 U.S. 52, 1976).

The right of privacy is the constitutionally protected interest most obviously implicated by anti-black-market legislation, but other constitutional questions may also be raised. The disparate treatment accorded payment of "surrogate fathers" or sperm donors involved in AID (artifical insemination as a donor) as opposed to surrogate mothers is a type of discrimination by sex that may violate the equal protection clause. If a husband is sterile, he can purchase semen from a sperm bank for insemination of his wife. Surrogate fatherhood is apparently lawful in all jurisdictions, enjoying explicit legislative recognition in some, despite the fact that the semen is usually paid for and the sperm donor assumes none of the risk and burdens of that of an "ovum donor." Some might contend that purchasing the reproductive capacity of semen for use in artificial insemination is not the same thing as paying a woman for her reproductive capacity to carry a child. But, in such a case the child is genetically related to only the mother or the father of the couple who have arranged for the child's conception. If there is no payment involved and if the surrogate mother is unmarried, the process can be completed easily. The issue of paying a fee is what has caused the major difficulty.

The Equal Protection Clause of the Fourteenth Amendment to the U.S. Constitution requires the government to treat similarly situated individuals in a similar manner. The aim of the equal protection clause is to prevent arbitrary classifications that are discriminatory. I submit that the sperm donor who is paid to be a surrogate father and the ovum donor who is paid to be a surrogate mother are similarly situated and that the differing treatment accorded the them is unconstitutionally discriminatory. If, by law, people are put into different classes, the U.S. Supreme Court will review the basis of the classifications to determine their validity. When a discriminatory scheme affects a fundamental interest, such as the right of privacy, the State must show a compelling reason for creating the classification and that the classification is necessary to serve that interest. Also, the classification must be drawn narrowly to achieve only the compelling interest and not more.

If the classification is based upon gender, but no fundamental right is affected, the Supreme Court will review the classification to determine if it substantially serves a legitimate state interest. The standard of review for a gender-based classification is less strict for that of a classification affecting a fundamental right.

There is uncertainty as to whether payments to a surrogate mother for various purposes (the use of her reproductive capacity, foregone, income, medical expenses, consent to adoption, etc.) are in fact forbidden. This may also render such statutes void for vagueness as applied to surrogate motherhood. Enactments, like the Michigan statute, that prohibit paying consideration in connection with adoption except for charges and fees approved by the court, without specifying the criteria for approval or disapproval, may well constitute a denial of due process in that no standards are provided to guide the decision maker's discretion. Additionally, insofar as surrogate motherhood arrangements among consenting and competent adults represent an exercise of personal liberty that is not detrimental to third parties or society, state interference with these arrangement on moralistic grounds may be unconstitutional simply because it exceeds the scope and proper purposes of state action under our constitutional system. As surrogate motherhood becomes more common, inevitably these and other constitutional questions will have to be litigated unless the statutory and decisional law is modified to accommodate the unique features of the surrogate motherhood situation.

If the surrogate mother is married, additional difficulties arise at the adoption stage. In some states, adoption by the donor and his wife may be blocked by an irrebuttable presumption that a child born to a married couple is the legitimate offspring of that couple. The statutory objective of treating the husband as the father is to assure support to all children (People v. Sorensen, 68 Cal. 2d 280,

437, P.2d 495, 1968). In such states, the biological father in a surrogate parenting arrangement cannot assert his parental rights over his natural child. Parental rights over that child automatically vest in the surrogate's husband. The donor-husband and his wife would be unable to adopt the child in such a state unless direct, private adoption is available. However, other states regard this presumption as rebuttable if there is clear evidence that another is the biological father. These states offer a friendlier forum for the adoption proceedings.

Under Michigan law, when a child is born to a married couple there is a legal, but rebuttable, presumption of paternity in the husband (Mich. Comp. Laws Ann. Sec. 710.54, Supp. 1981). In a Michigan case, a circuit court refused to recognize the biological father of a child conceived by a married woman through surrogate motherhood. The child was born, but there is no father entered on that child's birth certificate. The biological father has custody of the child under a probate power of attorney. But, if something were to happen to the biological father, it is indefinite who would gain custody of the child. The case is presently before the state appeals court. I am asking that the county circuit court be ordered to allow the biological father to assert his paternity under Michigan's Paternity Act.

The courts cannot stop surrogate motherhood arrangements. They can stop the adoption process by which the legal status of the child is changed. However, there is no change in the legal status of the child through the payment of the fee and the father receiving the child. But, unless surrogate mothers can be offered meaningful compensation for their services, very few children will be brought legally into the world in this manner. Pregnancy and childbirth are hazardous, time-consuming, painful conditions which few women can be expected to experience for the sake of someone else unless they receive meaningful compensation. By using the surrogate procedure without the adoption process, there are two drawbacks. First, the child would remain in a home where only the father is legally connected to that child. Almost every couple will take that over the other choice that they have, which is no child whatsoever. Second, there is a possibility that the surrogate will carry the child and then not give the child to its father. This situation demonstrates the need for courts to recognize surrogate motherhood arrangements so that these issues may be resolved within the legal system.

ARTIFICIAL INSEMINATION OF A DONOR

When a married couple is unable to have a child because the husband is sterile, the couple can go to a sperm bank and draw on semen sold by a medical student. The semen is purchased by the couple for insemination of the infertile husband's wife. In that case, then, the child will be biologically related only to the wife. A number of states have enacted statutes legitimizing children conceived through AID if the husband consented to such an insemination. There is no adoption process; the husband's parental status arises by presumption of the law. Simply by the fact that the mother of the child is married to the husband at the time of conception or birth, the husband is legally presumed to be the father of that child. The infertile husband's name is automatically entered on the child's birth certificate as the legal father of that child.

As the right to bear a child is fundamental, the state cannot discriminate between married and unmarried women in access to AID. The state's concern is in the best interests of the child, but that is not in conflict with the single woman's fundamental right to bear a child nor does it outweigh that right. It is not just the traditional nuclear family that can claim the protection of the right of privacy (Moore v. City of East Cleveland, 431 U.S. 494, 503–04, 1977). Additionally, by making this distinction, the state would be creating an irrebuttable presumption that single women were less capable of rearing children than married women. Such classifications would not be drawn narrowly enough to serve the best interests of the child. The right to bear a child is a fundamental right and the state cannot bar single women from access to AID to exercise that right while allowing married women that option. Many single women have found that some infertility clinics refuse to allow single women access to their services. If a single woman were to take such an infertility clinic to court, the clinic would most likely be barred from continuing such a discriminatory practice. In at least one case in Michigan, the infertility clinic settled the matter out of court and no longer forbids single women access to their facilities.

ADOPTION

Adoption, which was unknown at common law, is a purely statutory process. Ordinarily, adoption statutes must be strictly complied with in order to consummate a valid adoption. Nonetheless, the argument misses that point that whether or not the state is obliged to authorize adoption, once it has done so its activity in that area is subject to constitutional limitations (cf. Maher v. Roe, 432 U.S. 464, 469–70, 1977). Thus a state is not constitutionally compelled to provide for appeals in criminal cases; but if it does so, due process and equal protection forbid the state from requiring indigent appellants to pay for transcripts if they cannot afford to do so (Griffin v. Illinois, 351 U.S. 12, 18 1956). A state need not maintain public schools and may allow them to be closed, but not if the object is to circumvent a racial desegregation order (Griffin v. County School Board, 377 U.S. 218, 231, 1964). A city may prohibit the posting of flyers on utility poles, but if it opens the forum by allowing any such use of utility poles it cannot condition such use on the prior permission of city officials unguided by explicit and nondiscriminatory standards (Dulaney v. Municipal Court, 11 Cal. 3d 77, 82, 112 Cal. Rptr. 777, 781 520 P.2d 1, 5, 1974).

Where the state monopolizes the means of implementing certain fundamental decisions protected by the right of privacy, it may not impose conditions that effectively exclude some individuals from resorting to the only means provided. In Boddie v. Connecticut, 401 U.S. 371 (1971), the Supreme Court held that as a matter of due process a state cannot constitutionally impose court fees and costs on indigents that restrict their access to the courts for the purpose of seeking a divorce. Due process is implicated because resort to state courts is the only avenue to dissolution of a marriage. A statute may be held constitutionally invalid as applied when it operates to deprive an individual of a protected right even if its general validity as a legitimate exercise of state power is beyond question.

The right to go to court "is the exclusive precondition to the adjudication of a fundamental human relationship. The requirement that these appellants resort to the judicial process is entirely a state-created matter" (Boddie, at 383). The holding in Boddie with respect to divorce is equally valid with respect to adoption.

Once a state provides for divorce or adoption, the procedures to be followed and the conditions to be compiled with are subject to constitutional limitations. Adoption, like divorce, is a method of effectuating basic decisions about family affiliation — a method monopolized by the state. The state's general authority to impose fees on divorce petitioners or prohibit payment for consent to adoption may be well established; but if the application of these conditions effectively prevent particular classes of people from exercising their familial privacy rights, then as to those classes the requirements are unconstitutional. It is irrelevant that the state is not to blame for the sterility of certain married women who desire children, just as it is irrelevant that the state is not to blame for the poverty of certain married persons who desire a divorce. The point is that the state has provided the only means to implement their respective marital decisions. Consequently the state cannot enforce requirements which in practice prevent access to state-created and state-monopolized procedure.

CONCLUSION

Surrogate motherhood is a recently developed solution to childlessness caused by female infertility. The fact that it has always been a technically possible process but that it has just emerged as a feasible option indicates that changing social attitudes have lead to an acceptance of the practice of surrogate motherhood. Artifical insemination as a solution to childlessness due to male infertility was techinically possible many years prior to its accepted and frequent use. Again, changing social attitudes were a major factor in it becoming a solution to the problems of human infertility. With these changing attitudes, the legislation concerning procreation and adoption have also changed. Legislation governing artificial insemination as an answer to a husband's infertility had been enacted in many states with little problem. However, legislation has not yet been enacted to fit the unique features of surrogate parenting. As more and more couples form alliances with surrogate mothers, the legal implications of such relationships are being clarified.

Current reexamination of parenthood, marriage, and sexuality has led people to experiment with new solutions to old problems. Until recently, a married couple with an infertile wife had but one option if they both wanted a child and wanted to stay married to one another — adoption. Sometimes this involved a frustrating 10-year wait. Furthermore, the adopted child would have no biological relation to either of the adoptive parents. Surrogate motherhood offers a new alternative. Once the surrogate mother is chosen and impregnated, the couple need wait only nine months before the child can become a member of the family. During the surrogate's pregnancy, the infertile wife and her husband can share in the growth, development, and birth of the infant. The couple brings into their family an infant who is — partially — the biological offspring of the couple. As time goes by, more and more childless couples are opting for surrogate motherhood, Hopefully, changing societal values will be reflected in relevant and enlightened legislation.

REFERENCE

KEANE, N.P. and D.L. BREO (1981) The Surrogate Mother. New York: Everest House.

PARENTHOOD

Questions

1. *Should there be laws to govern who can have children?*
2. *What alternatives exist for couples who are unable to have children because of infertility in either partner?*
3. *What are some problems associated with single parenthood?*
4. *What rights should a surrogate mother have with respect to the child after it is born?*
5. *Should a sperm donor's name be placed on the birth certificate of a child conceived with his sperm?*
6. *Should adopted children have the right to seek out their natural parents?*
7. *Should people be allowed to pay surrogate mother's compensation above and beyond the amount necessary to cover medical expenses related to the pregnancy?*
8. *Is purchasing the reproductive capacity of semen for use in artificial insemination the same thing as paying a woman for her reproductive capacity to carry a child?*
9. *What laws should exist that protect a retarded child born to a surrogate mother and then unwanted by her or the couple who commissioned her services?*

Therapists or Surrogates Should Not Have Sexual Contact with Clients

LAURA J. SINGER
JO ANN M. MAGDOFF

Erotic contact between psychotherapist and patient[1] has been talked about, written about, and generally considered morally incorrect. Therapists who write about the negative consequences and implications of erotic behavior approach it from diverse starting points, among which are the following: (1) descriptions of expectable personality configurations of (generally) female patients and (generally) male therapists; (2) discussions of the ethics

Authors' Note: We would like to thank Jean Holroyd for sending us a copy of her unpublished paper. This feminist analysis of erotic behavior has added an important dimension to the problem. We would also like to thank Patricia Keith-Spiegel for making her work available to us, and Schoener, Milgrom and Grance of the Walk-In Counseling Center, Inc., Minneapolis, Minnesota. In addition, we wish to acknowledge Rosemay Rochester and Eunah Bader who completed preliminary research for this chapter.

involved, including implicit sexism; (3) recourses available for patients (and lack of recourse available to offending therapists; and (4) from a Freudian perspective, analyses of how erotic contact between patient and therapist interferes with the development and interpretation of the transference. For us, the most significant questions for treatment emerge from the analysis of transference and countertransference.[2]

In this chapter we will assume the importance of the transference in the therapeutic process, thus seeing erotic contact between therapist and patient as destructive to each and to the treatment. We will introduce a new dimension to the problem raised by such erotic contact by situating and understanding the treatment in terms of everyday life. We will then outline the history of the problem, discuss psychological characteristics as described in the literature of female patients and male therapists, review some implications and recourses — therapeutic and other — available to the patient, and conclude with specific suggestions as to how therapists can be helped and how they can help themselves to avoid such actions. Our conclusions will be situated within the theoretical framework outlined in our introduction.

> The professional attitude is rather like symbolism, in that it assumes a *distance between analyst and patient.* The symbol is in the gap between the subjective object and the object that is perceived objectively [Winnicott, cited in Dahlberg, 1970: 121].[3]

In this chapter we are dealing with two themes suggested by Winnicott. Therapist and patient as both subject and object reflect differing ontological perspectives. In other words, during the process of therapy, what is experienced as real for the therapist and what is experienced as real for the patient is overlapping but not identical. Each participant approaches the situation from his or her own perspective; and each walks away with a unique reading of what has transpired. "Symbolism," particularly metaphor, expresses the "gap" between therapist's and patient's realities.[4] We will argue that erotic contact between therapist and patient confounds the various realities of therapy by mistaking metaphor for everyday life. This is detrimental to patient and therapist, and points to a basic misconstrual of the underpinnings of psychotherapy.

DIFFERENCES BETWEEN PATIENT'S REALITY AND THERAPIST'S REALITY

What some therapists treat as everyday material for their patients is, in fact, not. It is metaphoric discourse *about* the everyday. Therapy is a part of the patient's everyday life in that it occurs within the everyday. Yet it is a special time, demarcated and set apart from the ongoing flux of unremarked upon, "unremarkable" daily life. We are concerned with how metaphoric usage in the sessions relates to ontological considerations for therapist and patient. What is real for the patient? For the therapist? To understand the differences and congruities, we need to situate the experience of both patient and therapist within the context of their necessarily distinct everyday lives.[5]

WHAT IS THE THERAPIST'S EVERYDAY REALITY?

There are many differences between the reality of the treatment situation for the therapist and for the patient. What is special time for the patient is everyday work life for the therapist. Doing therapy as everyday work may be somewhat like doing any type of work. Relationships and social behavior outside the work setting may resemble relations at work. Critical theorists have pointed out links between the quality and content of work relations and of other social relations.

At the end of a day of being treated like a nonperson, giving very little information about oneself, and mastering the benign mask that seems to come with the practice, it may be difficult for the therapist to let the mask slip and become a "regular" person at home or with friends.

The isolation imposed by therapeutic neutrality, the fostering of the transference and a day's work devoted to providing a non-threatening atmosphere in which patients' intimacies, associations, and interpretations can be revealed comfortably, is predicated upon the strength of the therapist to put the patient's needs before his or her own. Feelings elicited in the therapist during a session (countertransference), become, according to the theory, one more piece of data to be used as a diagnostic tool. Countertransferences elicited by the patient often require immediate, if unspoken, interpretation. It is assumed that the therapist can later integrate countertransferential materials that relate to himself or herself at leisure. The therapist as a real person with desires, irritabilities, and likes, drops out of the exchange: He or she functions as an interpretive vessel who must not take things personally. It can be extremely difficult, as any practitioner knows, not to take things personally when they are personally addressed and resonate with one's own self-perception or ego ideal.[6]

We argue that the verbal and nonverbal disclosures of the patient provide much of the therapist's everyday life. What is a special time for the patient is ordinary work time for the therapist. Material brought in for the session has a metaphoric relation to the everyday — it is *about* daily life, it is not the everyday. This distinction can become fuzzy for the therapist for whom metaphor takes on the trappings and functions of reality. The sessions are, after all, his or her work life. A tendency for therapists to distinguish between dream material which they see as "symbolic" and everyday material which they take to be "real" often reinforces the move whereby therapists treat metaphor as concrete.

For therapists who experience the metaphorical aspects of the session as ontologically ambiguous — confounding the distinction between what "is" their everyday life and what "is about" their patients' everyday lives — the session assumes a misplaced concreteness. Therapists may extend their theoretical blind spot behaviorally into erotic contact with the patient.

As metaphor in the session takes on the status of reality, the "as if" qualities of transference-love and countertransference response gain status as being *real*, and the demarcation between the idea and the act blurs. The problem we are faced with when therapists have sex with their patients is thus ontological as well as ethical.

For the therapist, the work situation is alienating in a manner not usually associated with the psychoanalytic meaning of the term. He or she is alienated from himself or herself, being a controlled and nonspontaneous actor in a daily work situation in which inattentiveness and self-involvement are prohibited. It is extremely difficult to "turn off" a stance of "therapeutic neutrality" after a full day's work; it may be extremely difficult to maintain the requisite distance during that work as well. We see erotic behavior between therapist and patient as one manifestation of a larger problem. For therapists, much of their daily lives is lived in an "as if" situation. Therapists most often refrain from acting upon their desires. Sometimes they don't and the result or their attempt to turn "as if" into "is" may be sexual behavior between therapist and patient.

Erotic behavior between therapist and patient has been aptly called "as if intimacy" (Keith-Spiegel, 1981b: 2). We argue that the process whereby "as if" becomes "is" is one in which metaphor, a relation of analogy, is transformed into metonymy, a relation of contiguity. Boundaries constructed within the session between everyday relationships and the interactions of therapy — the patient's transference, and the analysis of that transference; the therapist's countertransference — are blurred if not destroyed in an attempt to transform the metaphor of transference/counter-transference-love into the "real thing." But the "is" of the transference cannot escape the strictures of the therapeutic setting. The patient is still a patient, with the everyday aspects that implies (e.g., payment for sessions); the therapist is still a therapist and this session is part of a work day. By erotic behavior, the therapist is attempting to alter the quality of his or her everyday life and the daily life of the patient. The result is spillage and isolation: Metaphor is confounded with everyday life.[7]

> I assume that sexual feelings are inevitable in intense psychotherapy but these feelings must be seen as metaphor. Acting literally upon them is at best irrelevant [Dahlberg, 1970: 114].

HISTORICAL OVERVIEW

Erotic contact between psychotherapists and their patients and former patients is currently the subject of much concerned discourse. It is, however, nothing new. Reich, Bernfield, Fenichel, Rado — among Freud's colleagues and contemporaries — married former patients. Others had affairs with women who had been patients (see Chesler, 1972). Freud did not approve. Distressed by Ferenczi who claimed to be acting as a "loving" parent would act, Freud told him the following:

What one does in one's technique one has to defend
openly . . . why stop at a kiss? . . . soon we shall have
accepted in the techniques of analysis the whole repertoire of
demivergerie and petting parties, resulting in an enormous
interest in psychoanalysis among both analysts and patients
[Marmor, 1972: 4].[8]

Unlike Ferenczi whose ideas he both extended and modified,
Wilhelm Reich maintained a strict distinction between talking and
other behavior. He recommended *verbal* sexual behavior as the
means for patients to explore therapist/patient sexuality and
eschewed sexual *actions* between therapist and patient. In 1966
James McCartney published a paper entitled "Overt Transference"
in which he reconstituted Reich's theories to rationalize, as
Marmor (1972) put it, "the most extreme form of sexual acting out
with patients that has ever, to my knowledge, been reported in the
psychiatric literature" (p. 9). McCartney, subsequently ousted from
the American Psychiatric Association, echoed Ferenczi's statement
to Freud when he wrote that "in working through overt transference the analyst should allow himself to be reacted to as though he
were a parent" (in McCartney, 1966: 236).

Writing on McCartney (1970), Dahlberg says McCartney claims
that some patients (10–30 percent he estimates) need to do more
than just talk about their feelings toward their therapist. They need
to caress, fondle, observe, and examine the body of the therapist
and have all or some of these activities reciprocated and, in some
instances, have sexual intercourse with him in order for the
immature person to come to full maturity (p. 108). A fallacy in
McCartney's logic is the basis of Marmor's (1972) critique: "Since
when is it necessary for a parent to have sexual intercourse with his
children in order to enable them to achieve sexual and emotional
maturity?" (p. 6).

Barnhouse (1978) adds a further dimension to the problem of
erotic contact when she generalizes that "every therapeutic encounter involves parent/child transference reactions, and therefore, any sexual encounter between patient and therapist, regardless of the sex of the participants, is incestuous in character" (p.
535).[9]

Recently, a certain ambiguity toward erotic contact with patients
has been expressed by some practitioners. For example, in an
interview with Gaines (1972) Shepard remarks that an erotic

therapist can "hurt his patient badly" while claiming that "there *are* people who've benefited from this kind of sex therapy" (p. 13).[10] We have not found presumed "positive" effects to be clearly defined or substantiated.[11]

SOME STATISTICS

Reports of erotic contact between patient and therapist are increasing, but the statistics appear to skim the surface.[12] In a nationwide survey of 1000 Ph.D. psychologists conducted in 1977 by Holroyd and Brodsky with a 70 percent return rate, 5.5 percent of males and .6 percent of females reported having had sexual intercourse with patients; an additional 2.6 percent of the males and .3 percent of the females reported having had sexual intercourse with patients within three months after the termination of the therapy. Perhaps the most surprising figure is the recidivism rate: 80 percent (p. 843). These percentages agree with those of Kardener et al. (1973): Approximately 10 percent of psychiatrists report erotic contact and 5–7 percent specify sexual intercourse.

Jacqueline C. Bouhoutsos (Sobel, 1981), chairwoman of a study group under the auspices of the California State Psychological Association, has recently communicated the results of a statewide questionnaire sent to mental health practitioners. As only 16 percent were returned, the figures are not statistically significant. However, they appear to corroborate the results of the studies mentioned above.

Barnhouse (1978) suggests that the impact of feminism may account for an increase in the number of cases being reported. She argues that today's sexual climate may also facilitate discussion of hitherto unmentionable topics and, perhaps, make sexual activities between therapists and their patients appear more permissible.[13] In addition, we see feminist court battles against sexual harassment in work settings and feminist support networks as helping to encourage women to assert themselves.

Jean Holroyd (forthcoming) sees erotic contact as an instance of sex-biased therapy, noting its prevalence among male therapists and female patients:

Conservative estimates indicate one in twenty male therapists and one in two hundred female therapists have had intercourse with patients during treatment. A much higher percentage have had erotic contact with patients, and again it is primarily female patients who are involved [p. 1].

The very nature of the therapeutic setting lends itself to seduction. Patient and therapist are closeted in a softly lit, small space. They are uninterrupted while the patient is the recipient of the sort of undivided attention one gets as a tiny infant, accompanied by what Kohut (1977) calls "the therapeutic reinstatement . . . [of] the gleam in the mother's eye" (p. 116). In some therapies power imbalance is physically accented, as the patient reclines, unseeing, while the therapist sits watching in patient control. In all therapies, power is unequally distributed. Taylor and Wagner (1976) describe this built in imbalance:

Not only is the therapist in a higher status position by having the client come to him or her, but by virtue of being a therapist he or she is assumed to be more powerful and more competent than the client. . . . In the therapeutic situation the therapist is free to ask about any aspect of the client's life, and the client assumes that only a therapeutic purpose is involved. The relationship is simply not fair when the therapist turns it into a sexual relationship [p. 597].

Real power differences between the patient and therapist are enhanced by the incestuous aspect of "transference-love" (see above, Barnhouse, 1978; and Marmor, 1972). We would argue "countertransference-love" has incestuous aspects as well. Because of culture-specific attitudes towards incestuous parents — father-daughter is bad, mother-son is worst — some authors have argued that the small number of female therapists reporting erotic contact with male patients reflects the negative sanctions towards mother-son incest and/or a cultural assumption that "maternal" is nonsexual (Barnhouse, 1978; Marmor, 1972).[14]

There are other, social reasons for the apparent relative scarcity of women therapists engaging in erotic contact with male patients. These reflect differences between male/female gender identity in this culture, and the differences in how men and women are socially constrained regarding sexuality. As Holroyd (forthcoming) compellingly points out, mutual erotic attraction between patient and therapist is not restricted by gender — some female therapists may be expected to be just as attracted to some male patients as some male therapists are to some female patients. The point is that male therapists more often act out their attraction sexually than do female therapists.[15] Holroyd (forthcoming) argues, and we concur, dissimilar behaviors of male and female therapists that have been reported need to be understood in light of social, cultural assumptions about men and women (e.g., differential access to power) that resonate with cultural expectations. Even without erotic contact, "the status difference between males and females in society at large is reproduced in the male-therapist/female-client relationship" (p. 15).

PSYCHOLOGICAL CHARACTERISTICS

Much has been written attempting to draw a diagnostic picture of the female patient most likely to participate in sexual relations with her male therapist. An analysis of the composite picture corroborated by our clinical data shows a portrait that is so broad that it would include most of the women who come for treatment, whatever the presenting problem.[17] However, Stone (1976) adds a dimension that we consider critical: "Impulsivity in these women," he writes, "was a regular feature. Many of the women are of borderline personality organization, with an *ever-present desire to actualize rather than verbalize transference*" (p. 15, emphasis added). The metaphoric, in other words, strives to become the real.

Male therapists who engage in sex with their patients have been characterized as falling into a nearly equally wide range of types, including young practitioners, older men, men in the throes of separation and divorce, fearing impotence or homosexuality (Butler and Zelen, 1977; Kardener et al., 1973; Stone, 1976; Dahlberg, 1970; Holroyd, forthcoming).[17] We have observed a pattern among therapists who marry patients (occasionally serially). These men begin by acting out a rescue fantasy. The new wife is adoring and totally dependent. After some time, the qualities of dependency he found so attractive seem cloying, clinging: When does his turn come to be rescued? He tries to "help her grow up" usually by sending her to another therapist. When she becomes more independent and assertive, he cannot tolerate it and so leaves her.

Male therapists engaging in erotic behavior with patients can also be placed among a continuum we might call from "public" to "private." Chesler (1972) has described one segment — "patriarchal," charismatic leaders of cult-like groups. These men we would place on the "public" end of the spectrum. They engage their patients in many if not all aspects of their lives. They often make little distinction between working relationships and everyday life — in effect, living the metaphor. Near the "private" end of the continuum we would place psychoanalysts and other psychotherapists who have erotic contact with patients, often limiting their involvement temporally (the time of the sessions), and spatially (the office).[18]

THERAPEUTIC IMPLICATIONS

Patients may turn to a female therapist once they are no longer erotically involved with their male therapist. Singer reports several patients who have come to her with this as the presenting problem. They exhibit symptoms described by the Minneapolis Walk-In Counseling Center (Schoener et al., 1976). Under the rubric of "common experiences of the woman client sexually involved with a male therapist," the Minnesota group mentions "guilt," "shame," "grief," "anger," "fear," "depression," "loss of self-esteem," "ambivalence and confusion" (pp. 2–4; see Cordrey, 1971, as well).

Several discussions in the literature focus on the patient's experience of sexual contact with his or her therapist as inducing guilt reactions resembling those that emerge with incestuous behavior. The termination of the affair and of treatment may result in separation and grief reported to be similar to that elicited by the death of a parent (Cordrey, 1971; Schoener et al., 1976).

Patients report negative responses to erotic involvement with their therapists ranging from comparatively mild expressions of anger and resentment to extremely painful and damaging consequences — for example, difficulties in subsequently establishing trusting relationships. It has been hypothesized that erotic involvement between therapist and patient may be implicated in some suicides (Dahlberg, 1970; Stone, 1976; Barnhouse, 1978). Very bad consequences to the therapists are rare. One possibility — censure by professional organizations — usually involves little more than the expulsion of offending members.[19]

Legal recourse for patients is scant and is complicated by each state's diverse legislation. It is extremely difficult, as Stone (1976) notes, for a patient who has been sexually involved with her or his therapist to find suitable redress: Ethics committees are hamstrung in many ways; the law is costly financially and often emotionally.

Within the literature, advice to patients covers a wide range of possible courses of action which, admittedly, are not often effectual.[20] Barnhouse (1978) makes some suggestions to therapists required to "pickup the pieces" after patients have been sexually involved with a former therapist. She mentions the rebuilding of trust, to which we would add taking care not to join the patient in collusion against the former therapist; not aggravating her feelings of helplessness while dealing with the factors that led to sexual contact; and distinguishing the manifestations of the original problem from symptoms arising out of the unprofessional sexual incidents. If the patient plans to prosecute, it is very likely that she will need additional support from the new therapist while dealing with the grievance (pp. 545–546; also Schoener et al., 1976: 5).

Sexual contact between patient and therapist is expressly forbidden in the ethics guidelines issued in 1980 by the American Psychiatric Association, as it had been in 1977. As practitioners, we are taught to regard the welfare of our patients as of paramount concern. In treatment, our own feelings are not to be acted upon but determine the nexus of countertransference to be interpreted and discussed with our patients where appropriate.[21]

CONCLUSIONS

The theoretical underpinnings discussed in our introduction have concrete, practical ramifications. We see two areas in which direct action is indicated. They are both educative, in a broad sense. The first involves training programs: We would like to see training programs incorporate as a matter of course ontological issues that underlie the therapeutic process in their curricula.

To successfully perform as a professional therapist entails a degree of isolation and control that may take a high personal toll on the therapist. His or her desire to mitigate the experience of being completely alone can have many different results. Erotic contact with patients is one extreme form this behavior may take. We contend that in addition to personal psychological motivations it is impelled by the desire to break the boundaries of metaphor. By engaging in erotic contact the therapist attempts to transform the relationship with the patient into a "real" one, to change the nature of everyday work for the therapist. If we are correct, then it is one example of this more generalized problem.

Erotic contact between patient and therapist raises ethical concerns as well — and the problem of ethics in therapy is a complex one. We agree with Barnhouse (1978) that there is a certain ambiguity attached to "ethical" treatment which is, at the same time, putatively "value-free": Implicit moral judgments underlie a number of aspects of treatment.[22] We further maintain that the acknowledgement, and explication of ethical assumptions underlying treatment should be a part of training programs.[23]

Positions taken on the rightness or wrongness of a particular therapeutic behavior — in this case, sexual behavior — need to be further situated philosophically. It is possible to regard ethics in terms of systems of preference or belief as generally shared consensual values: acts of faith, sociability, or law. To approach the problem as a purely ethical one bypasses the theoretical importance of the nature of the different realities operating for patient and therapist. An insistence that sexual contact between therapist and patient is primarily a pragmatic issue — what percentage of patients are harmed, what percentage helped — fails to address underlying ontological problems.

Any treatment that uses interpretation tacitly (if not explicitly) assumes the primacy of verbal interactions. Certainly all psychoanalytic training programs as well as many training programs in psychotherapy share a framework object relations theorists have clearly expressed: There is a distinction between the object as it exists and the various internalizations of the object — the psychological object (see Winnicott quote above, p. 224).

The object in a session is perceived in more than one way. It is a psychological object — it exists in someone's mind — while it also has ontological status — it exists in the world. People make sense out of the world by utilizing certain symbolic formations. These operate psychologically, transforming an object in the world into an internalized psychological object and projecting an internalized psychological object out into the world. This is nothing new. We suggest that a further move is in order. Our conclusions lead us to stress the importance of different experiences of daily life — of what is "out there" — for patient and therapist.

We would like to see attention paid to ontological considerations. These are variously expressed by therapist and patient, undergrid the symbolic processes whereby the psychological object is constructed and maintained, and need to be understood as they relate to the realities of everyday life. Through such an analysis, we believe an important aspect of the problems engendered by such actions as erotic contact between therapist and patient will be avoided: The attempt to render "as if love" into "real love" would be understood immediately by the therapist-in-training to be a real as well as an ethical impossibility.

Our second recommendation deals with therapists already in practice for whom continuing peer supervisory sessions in groups which share a common theoretical base could enrich their work. We feel these groups might function most effectively if they included both experienced therapists and beginning therapists as beginning therapists raise issues that are often taken-for-granted by those who have been in for a long time. Ideally, within any group there would be a skilled diagnostician, someone skilled in transference and countertransference processes, and someone concerned with the exploration of ontological issues. Perhaps with participation in such groups we can begin to avoid erotic contact between therapist and patient by dealing effectively with some of its shared causes.

NOTES

1. As senior author, Singer prefers to use the term "patient" to refer to people in therapy; Magdoff prefers "client."

2. We would like to point out immediately that we assume transference and its analysis to be fundamental to treatment, and also to indicate that we are not objecting to nonerotic physical contact between patient and therapist per se in

other treatment modalities (Virginia Satir's "healing hands" come immediately to mind as an example of therapeutic touching).

3. The quotation above was cited in Dahlberg (1970) whose work on erotic contact between patient and therapist has been an important resource for us.

4. The importance of metaphor in treatment has been discussed by Lacan (1977). Towards the conclusion of writing this chapter, Jacques Lacan died. We would like to take this opportunity to express our regrets that such an outstandingly provocative thinker is no longer with us.

5. For the purposes of our inquiry, we are not treating social, everyday reality as "the average expectable environment" of ego psychology.

6. The therapist's subjective reactions are often like a psychological, personal hermeneutic.

7. For a discussion of this process, see Levi-Strauss (1967).

8. Freud's 1931 quotation appeared in Jones' Life and Work of Sigmund Freud, vol. III.

9. Negative effects of therapist/patient sexuality on aspects of transference and countertransference have been explored by many writers (Fromm-Reichmann, 1950; Saul, 1962; Thompson, 1964; Van Emde Boas, 1966; Kardener et al., 1974).

10. Taylor and Wagner (1976) interpret their data to show that 21 percent of 34 cases had positive effects; 32 percent had mixed effects, while 47 percent were negative experiences for the patient and/or therapist (p. 594).

11. Nor has the California Study Group whose findings of a four-year study were reported in the August 19, 1981, issue of the New York Times. Holroyd (forthcoming) in her discussion of the problem suggests that whatever "positive" effects there may be, they seem to be felt and reported more by the therapists than by the patients.

12. Based on the 1973 survey by Kardener, Fuller, and Mensh, Stone (1976) projects the total figure of 10 percent to imply that perhaps two or three thousand psychiatrists across the country have "an ethical value system shaky enough to permit this sort of erotic activity" (p. 19). In addition, this figure excludes nonmedical psychotherapists.

13. Patricia Keith-Spiegal (1981b) concurs.

14. See the excellent article, "Maternal Sexuality and Asexual Motherhood" by Susan Weisskopf Contratto (1980) refuting the asexuality of maternity.

15. Although it is rare, the phenomenon of female therapists engaging patients in erotic contact does exist. As a therapist, teacher, and supervisor, Singer among others reports data on eroticism between female therapists and patients.

16. Women presenting paranoid symptoms are excluded from the composite portrait. For descriptions of female patients see Stone, 1976; Dahlberg, 1970; Chesler, 1972.

17. Discussions of the characteristics of male therapists engaging in erotic behavior with patients corroborates our point. According to Butler and Zelen (1977: 142) and Dahlberg (1970: 118–120), they are most often forlorn in crisis, sometimes questioning the value of therapy itself. It would be valuable to analyze sexual action between patient and therapist as it develops within treatment. Unfortunately, such data are scanty and, where available, unreliable.

18. See page 218 of this chapter for statistics of psychotherapists in California who have sexual intercourse with patients in their offices.

19. On the other hand, Patricia Keith-Spiegel in an unpublished paper (1981a) entitled "Sex with Clients: Ten Reasons Why It Is a Very Stupid Thing to Do" argues the devastating professional and personal effects even an accusation of erotic contact between client and therapist can have for the therapist.

20. These are enumerated by Stone, 1976; Dahlberg, 1970; Hare-Mustin, 1979; Taylor and Wagner, 1976; and succintly summerized by Holroyd, forthcoming.

21. Existential psychoanalysts often articulate the feelings brought up by the patient in the therapist, as do some Gestalt therapists. However, these techniques clearly specify the limits of behavior appropriate to the therapist, eschewing sexual relations as do more traditional psychotherapies.

22. That is, "adaptation" is often seen as "good"; practitioners perforce make judgments on what is "healthy" or "normal." (See particularly the work of Szaz and Laing on some implications of these assumptions.)

23. Since trainees are, in many ways, in as vulnerable a position vis-à-vis their teachers and supervisors as are patients with their therapists, we feel that sanctions against supervisor or teacher-trainee sexuality should be delineated (see also Pope et al., 1980).

REFERENCES

BARNHOUSE, R. T. (1978) "Sex between patient and therapist." Journal of the American Academy of Psychoanalysis 6, 4: 533–546.

BUTLER, S. and S.E. ZELEN (1977) "Sexual intimacies between therapists and patients." Psychotherapy: Theory, Research and Practice 14, 2: 139–145.

CHESLER, P. (1972) Women and Madness, New York: Doubleday.

CONTRATTO, S. W. (1980) "Maternal sexuality and asexual motherhood," pp. 224–240 in Catherine R. Stimpson and Ethel Spector Person (eds.) Women: Sex and Sexuality. Chicago: University of chicago Press.

CORDREY, L. J. (1971) "Therapeutic eroticism, who does what to whom?" The Marriage and Family Counselors Quarterly 8, 1: 39–49.

DAHLBERG, C. C. (1970) "Sexual contact between patient and therapist." Contemporary Psychoanalysis 6: 107–124.

GAINES, B. (1972) "Sex on the couch: Analysts and their patients." Cosmopolitan (September): 152–155.

HARE-MUSTIN, R. T., J. MARECEK, A. C. KAPLAN, and N. LISS-LEVINSON (1979) "Rights of clients, responsibilities of therapists." American Psychologist 34, 1: 3–16.

HOLROYD, J. C. (forthcoming) "Erotic contact as an instance of sex-biased therapy," in J. Murray and P. R. Abramson (eds.) The Handbook of Bias in Psychotherapy. New York: Holt, Rinehart and Winston.

——— and A. M. BRODSKY, (1977) "Psychologists' attitudes and practices regarding erotic and noneritic physical contact with patients." American Psychologist 2, 10: 843–849.

KARDENER, S. H., M. FULLER, and I. N. MENSH (1973) "A survey of physicians' attitudes and practices regarding erotic and nonerotic contact with patients." American Journal of Psychiatry, 130, 10: 1077–1081.

KEITH-SPIEGEL, P. (1981a) "Sex with clients: Ten reasons why it is a very stupid thing to do." California State University, Northridge. (unpublished)

——— (1981b) "Sex and love between therapist and client." Prepared for a meeting of the Western Psychological Association, April.

KOHUT, H. (1977) The Restoration of the Self, New York: International Universities Press.

LACAN, J. (1977) Ecrits: A Selection, New York: Norton.

LEVI-STRAUSS, C. (1967) Structural Anthropology. Chicago: University of Chicago Press.

——— (1965) The Savage Mind. New York: Doubleday.

McCARTNEY, J. L. (1966) "Overt transference." Journal of Sex Research 2, 3: 227–237.

MARMOR, J. (1972) "Sexual acting-out in psychotherapy." American Journal of Psychoanalysis 22: 3–8.

POPE, K. S., L. R. SCHOVER, and H. LEVENSON (1980) "Sexual Behavior between clinical supervisors and trainees: implications for professional standards." Professional Psychology (February): 157–162.

SCHOENER, G., J. MILGROM, and J. GRACE "Dealing therapeutically with women who have been sexually involved with their psychotherapists." Minneapolis: Walk-In Counseling Center, Inc., 2421 Chicago Ave. S., Minneapolis, MI 55404.

SIMON, B. and R. APFEL (1981). "Overt sex between patient and therapist: A caricature of genitality and generativity," prècis, 190–191, J. Nevis-Olesen and P. Borns (eds.) The Development of the Therapist: Challenges to Theory and Practice. Cambridge, MA: Harvard Medical School.

SPECTOR, B. (1971) "The sexual feelings of the therapist." American Journal of Psychoanalysis, 31, 2: 220–221.

STONE, M. H. (1976) "Boundary violations between therapist and patient." Psychiatric Annals 6, 12: 670–677.

TAYLOR, J. B. and N. N. WAGNER (1976) "Sex between therapists and clients: A review and analysis." Professional Psychology 7: 593–601.

WINNICOTT, D. W. (1965) The Maturational Processes and the Facilitating Environment. New York: International Universities Press.

Touch as a Therapeutic Technique between a Therapist and Client May Be Beneficial to the Client

DAVID MARCOTTE
BRUCE RAU

At a time when the popular press is taking notice of physician-patient sexual relationships and abuses, the professions themselves are becoming more aware of this problem. Some authors are finding increasing evidence that therapist-patient sex may be more prevalent than had been previously thought (Medical World News, 1976). In an attempt to focus on the actual incidence of physician's sexual activities, Kardener et al. surveyed physician attitudes and practices regarding erotic and non erotic contact with their patients (1976). Kardener collected a sample of 460 physician responders out of 1000 questionnaires. Although incidence of patient-doctor sexuality is difficult to estimate, in Kardener's sample of 460 responders, 59 indicated personal sexual contact with patient. This figure of 59 per 1000 is probably conservative.

When one examines physician's specialization and incidence of sexual activity with patients, 18 percent of OB/GYN specialists reported some sexual contact, followed by general practitioners who reported 13 percent; while surgeons and psychiatrists both reported approximately 10 percent of incidence. Although the overwhelming majority of doctors condemn such behaviors, a minority condoning such behavior thought such erotic contact "demonstrates the doctors effectiveness to his patients," "supports and reinforces the patient's sexual appeal," and that "stimulating the clitoris helps the patient relax." In Kardeners subsequent study (Kardener et al., 1976) there were no differences between those physicians who engaged in sexual activity versus nonengagers on demographic variables. However, Kardener found that the erotic practitioners — that is ones who engage in sexual behaviors with their patients — tended to have decreased sanctions about nonerotic contact between physician and patient as well. Of interest is that Dr. Kardener was attacked for performing this study (Marmor, 1979) which began to study an area of behavior some thought best not to explore.

Although every professional group, such as law, psychology, and other helping professionals, share a similar prohibition of therapist-patient or client sexuality, there has and continues to be an increasing incidence of patient-client sexual activity by physicians and members of other professions. This is certainly not due to the lack of potential risk for the practitioner in such relationships. Three types of legal sanctions exist including (1) prosecution under criminal law including rape, fraud, or coersion; (2) malpractice actions; and (3) revocation of license. In reference to prosecution under criminal law, William Masters has publicly suggested that indulgences in sexual relations with a client should be considered as rape (Medical World News, 1976). Sex with a patient recently cost a psychiatrist $350,000 according to a report in Medical World News (1975). Revocation of license on ethical grounds, while always a possibility, has occured infrequently and then only in the most blatant cases. Local medical societies are poorly equipped to investigate complaints and attempt to do so only when multiple complaints exist (Greenbaum, 1976). Because patients view the physician as an authority, complaints may be withheld even when considerable psychological trauma is experienced by a patient (Greenbaum, 1976). Even if such claims are substantiated by a number of patients, the physician engaging in sexual activity with patients can easily distort and confuse the nature of the therapeutic relationship to serve his purpose. There exists reluctance on the part of the professional to interfere with the confidential contract of another professional. There is fear of lawsuit to the person reporting another professional combined with the difficulty of substantiating the abuse of a therapeutic relationship. The more secretive the therapeutic relationship, the more difficult it is to control sexual activity (Greenbaum, 1976).

Although interest in the frequency of doctor-patient sex increased in the 1960s and 1970s, doubts regarding the "appropriateness" of doctor-patient sexual activity have been ever-present. Ferenczi, in writing a letter to Freud (Marmor, 1979), said that he had kissed a patient. Freud, in his response, warned Ferenczi about engaging on such behavior and expressed concern that once you begin to have physical interactions between patients is difficult to know when to stop. Condoning such behavior will then unleash more daring and provocative behavior. The question of what limits are to be set raises very important concerns.

If the incidence of patient-therapist contact is becoming more frequent than originally thought, one source of the change may be changing societal values. Both physicians and patients may be entering treatment relationships with relaxed values about sexual behavior. With touch being more and more appreciated for it treatment value, what is therapeutic and what is sexual may be becoming increasingly cloudy to practitioners.

Beginning in the late 1960s, medical sex-education blossomed because of a profound need for education of physicians in the field of sexual therapy and dysfunction (Lief, 1973; Woods and Natterson, 1967; Holden, 1974). Coincident with the increases of mandatory sex education for physicians was the development of rapid short-term treatment for sexual dysfunctional couples grew at a similar pace stimulated by the work of Masters and Johnsons (1966, 1970) as well as others (Barbach, 1975; Annon, 1974). At the same time some therapists began to examine the actual relationship between patient and physician and to call for alteration of well-established rules of conduct to include sexual activity between patient and therapist (McCartney, 1966; Shepard, 1971).

McCormick (1973) suggests that the current therapeutic scene exaggerates the physical. "Touch," "encounter," "interaction," "love," "massage," "togetherness," and so on are suggestions of contact used with the therapeutic inflection. He states that therapeutic satisfactions come legitimately only from applying our knowledge to our clients' or patients' requirements for help. This means that we cease to serve at the moment we regard our client/ patient as owing us anything or as soon as we contemplate him or her as a source of our own pleasure.

Sexual activity (such as intercourse) *is only part of ones human sexuality*. Dress, appearance, and words can be just as powerful in seduction as touch. Yet these same behaviors in a different setting can be extrordinarily beneficial. The following case example illustrates the profound impact of touch:

> A 28-year-old single male with a college education had been unemployed and living with his elderly parents. Following graduation from college he held only one position, that of a paper boy, for several months. He regressed to avoid social contact with others and would terrify visitors to his home by threatening to harm them. His parents eventually confronted him and demanded that he be hospitalized. After admission to the hospital he remained aloof and detached from others, preferring to isolate himself. At meetings, when forced to interact with others, he would stand menacingly over others shouting abuses of harm. His physician therapist, after considerable patience, eventually intervened by physically restraining the patient, forcing the patient to the floor, holding the patient during one of these tirades. The patient began weeping and described how no one had physically touched him before. His very behavior precluded others from getting close enough to him to touch him, yet he yearned for physical touch. Following this episode, the patient's behavior dramatically changed to more cordial interaction with others and the process of therapy could begin.

As mentioned above, a polar dicotomy can exist with respect to doctor-patient relationships in which some will view all physical contact as inappropriate. The opposite stance expressed by others will label doctors who do not touch as cold, detached, and reserved — a position which has been attributed frequently to analytic therapists. Yet somewhere in between these extremes real relationships do exist. As Gitelson (1952) states, "Even experienced analysts do not adhere to theoretically prescribed conduct." Sometimes with intention and sometimes for their own psychological reasons they change their behaviors and violate strict orthodoxy. Forbidden interaction is inevitably engaged in and effected by some analytic therapists. Systems theory recently has amplified the view of a dyad to include the real relationship of the analyst or therapist and patient. Is a hug or embrace or a touch of a shoulder mean ipsofacto that inappropriate activity is being engaged in? Such an argument can be countered by anyone in medicine who has experienced the profound effect of touch. An example of how beneficial touch can be can be found in any general hospital ward in which patients suffering from pain or confronting serious illness or death can be reassured by just the simple touch of another person. Anyone will be touched by the power of affection who has seen the movie "Looking For Me" which portrays a poignant interaction between a dance therapist and a schizophrenic child in which a great deal of hugging, touching, and affection occurs, leading the child to a much more productive and spontaneous interpersonal relationship with both the therapist and others.

The evaluation of physicians and psychiatrists training background emphasize that the physician occupies a parent/healer role with patients. He or she is to be trusted by patients and not be seen as victimizer. Physicians are trained and agree to accept the hypocratic oath. The hypocratic oath states that "In every house where I come, I enter only for the good of my patients, keeping myself from all intentional ill-doing, all seduction, and especially from the pleasure of love from men and women" (Stedman's Medical Dictionary, 1972). Does this mean that physicians must not use the healing power of touching the patient — not touch as an erotic act but touch as an indication of understanding of one human for another?

Many group therapists encourage the sharing of feelings of compassion between patients in an open group setting. The patients can and do maintain their independence and are able to decide whether or not they want to continue sharing more intimate feelings outside of the therapeutic setting. With other patients in the private patient-therapist enclosed setting more caution and restraint is necessary, but does this mean that there should be no physical contact between patient and therapist? Does it mean that there is no place for nonsexual touching? The line may be difficult to draw, but what about shaking hands? This seems innocuous enough. At the other extreme is any contact with the primary sex parts of the body. We need to think through and set more specific standards. Is a hand on the shoulder for a moment the same as a handshake? We are not proposing that the body be mapped and that zoning regulations be promulgated, but only that we understand the meaning of touch to each particular patient. We should not reject the advantages of positive human interactions because of the fear of being unable to manage the therapeutic situation.

This part of the hypocratic oath was never questioned prior to the 1960s. It was clearly demonstrated to one of the authors during medical training by a case example whereby two medical students were expelled from medical school for engaging in sexual activity with a former patient for which they previously held a minor degree of responsibility. The impression of swift expulsion from medical school had a strong impact on reinforcing the sanction against patient-doctor sex.

In a recent article, Burgess (1981) cited 16 women involved in sexual manipulation by an obstetrician/gynecologist representing a different view of the same activity described by physicians. The majority did not stop the doctor and disbelieved what was actually going on. They felt powerless to interrupt and frequently trusted the doctor. Women in Burgess's study recognized something was wrong. Four women thought something was wrong with them, regardless of their physical response. Eight of the women were orgasmic and most had strong negative emotional responses, including feelings of being unclean, embarrassed, ashamed, or dirty. All of the reactions of the women are similar to the psychology of victimization where one person exerts force over another person by way of position, power, or status. Advantage is therefore taken by the physician over someone who has less power or who appears to be helpless. Kardener et al. (1976) explores the concept of the physician as parent surrogate and the physician's position of power over the patient. Kardener feels that the physician is traditionally seen as a source of support, healing, and succor who becomes lost to his patient when he or she changes roles and becomes lover. In discussing the dynamics of sexual exploitation, Burgess (1981) mentions that this type of adult sexual exploitation is similar to incest exploitation in which a child is repeatedly pressured for sexual activity by a family member. The authors find it interesting that some physicians remain loyal to the accused physician much in the same manner a mother sides with an incestuous father against a child and refuses to believe such a complaint.

SOCIAL POLICIES

Physicians are not immune to the development of strong
emotional reactions that characterize all intense relationships;
sometimes the physician may become enmeshed in an eroticized
transference and lose objectivity. The process of becoming friends,
advisors, lovers, or parents to our patients will contaminate and
destroy the essentially adult contract called for in all therapies
(McCormick, 1973). "Acting on ones' own sexual impulses is no
more appropriate than acting with disgust and anger or any other
feelings which may be part of a physician's behavior while treating
a patient." Our major concern regarding the topic of doctor-
patient sex is the question of whose needs are being satisfied. Any
and all relationships have the potential for abuse and exploitation
no matter where they are — whether in a singles' bar or in a
doctor's office. The world is filled with exploitation which frequently is addressed in the courts. Examination of doctor-patient
interactions can uncover the possible distortion of the relationship
for power, money, success, or parenting. One does not have to
search hard to find examples of exploitation. A recently well-
publicized treatment of a rock star with medications that contributed to his demise brought into serious question whether the
physician maintained objectivity in face of fame and money. The
following case example illustrates how an illicit agreement can
influence therapeutic outcome:

A 46-year-old white married male was referred to one of the
authors by another physician. The patient had a successful
career at an aeronautical design company. Starting at the age
of 40 he began treatment with a number of physicians, each of
whom described his pain as psychosomatic. The patient had an
extraordinarily conflicted hostile relationship with his wife which
was thought to be the genesis of his psychosomatic pain. He
was referred to a therapist, and because of his expertise and
construction design, he volunteered to help the therapist design
several bookcases and change substantially several rooms of the
therapist's home. The therapist welcomed the patient's
assistance and throughout the course of the therapy, a time
which was stormy and difficult, no relief was obtained by the
patient. The therapist felt obligated to continue to pursue all
avenues of interventions with the use of analgesic medications
to which the patient became readily addicted. After the course
of therapy lasting several years, the physician felt unable to
confront the patient regarding his pain. The patient was

hospitalized and transferred to the care of another physician. Subsequently, the relationship with the wife was explored and found to be similar to the relationship the patient had established with his physician. Confrontation with the patient resulted in anger directed at the physician and subsequent termination of his symptoms of pain.

UNDERSTANDING WHY SEXUAL RELATIONS IN PHYSICIAN/PATIENT RELATIONSHIPS EXIST: THE CONCEPTS OF COUNTERTRANSFERENCE/ TRANSFERENCE

In the mental health professions transference (Gitelson, 1952) refers to strong emotional reactions brought to therapy by a patient in which the patient distorts motivations and behaviors of the therapist because experience of others such as friends, parents, or peers. Distortion of the physician can be used in the process of intervention to change a patient's life by correcting the patient's emotional experiences which have been maladaptive. Gitelson (1952) describes countertransference as "strong feelings which arise in the physician as a result of the patient's influence on his unconscious feelings." The term countertransference was originally used to designate the emotional reactions of the therapist to a patient's transference.

Under ideal circumstances, the physician is free of distortion and therefore can act as a sounding board to correct distortions the patient brings to therapy. Frequently, patients are not able to make observations of their own behavior long enough to recognize that their responses are unreasonable or generated from other unresolved relationships, and therefore are untreatable. Development of overt transference (cited by McCartney, 1966) is an example of this. The physician becomes an integral part of the patient's transference in an attempt to alter the behavior of the patient instead of acting as an agent of change in the patient's behavior with others.

A rather dramatic account of a therapists struggle with counter-transference is published by Michael Eigen (1973). During the treatment of a very difficult patient, Dr. Eigen reports that "rarely did he find qualities in a woman like his patient." "She addressed a gap in my life." "She had spent the night with another male therapist but nothing ever came of it." Eigen reported the struggles that confront most therapists when they begin to develop real human interactions with a patient with whom they share a strong private intimate relationship. His quotations are signs of his loss of objectivity when a patient becomes "special" and provides "meaning" to his life, and the therapeutic relationship will be severely disrupted. Transference/countertransference is and will be a part of any intimate relationship. It will be subject to distortion on both the part of the physician as well as the patient. No where is distortion more likely to occur than in settings and situations where strong emotional areas are being discussed or experienced. Such topics that make strong emotional responses and may be taboo to discuss are love, death, erotic thoughts, and even violence. Such events or experiences provoke strong emotional reactions in both patients as well as therapists. Sex is but one of these strong emotional topics.

Kennedy (1977) points out that to engage in sexual relations with a patient is not simply a question of taking advantage of a vulnerable person in therapy. The fundamental failure lies in the lack of appreciation of the transference/countertransference in a relationship. The author states that erotic satisfaction only seems to be what the client wants due to transference feelings towards the helper. In fact, the outcome is frequently to defeat the therapist when he supplies what he thinks the other person wants. This destroys the relationship and compounds the difficulties of the person coming for help.

SAFEGUARDS AND RECOMMENDATIONS FOR THE FUTURE

Of paramount concern to us is that the therapists capacity for distortion of patient interaction is much higher in topics which are highly charged for both the patient and physician. The capacity to judge others behavior or to defend ones own behavior in the area of sexual activity is higher than in other less charged interactions. Safeguards must be exerted to protect both the patient and the therapist from inappropriate distortion of therapeutic relationship. The fact that the vast majority of sexual activity between patient and therapist involves male therapist with the victim largely being attractive, younger, sexually appealing females (Hare-Musten, 1974) reinforces the view that distortion based on the therapist's own need is operating. This question can then be raised: Are male therapists licensed to choose from their female patients which ones they prefer as marital or sexual partners? In her article, Rachel Hare-Musten (1974) theorizes that in order to ethically justify use of sexual relations as therapy a practitioner must first of all able to show special competence in this area and must be able to offer this service in the light of professional standards accepted within his community. If a therapist does feel competent to provide sexual contact to a patient (although it is difficult to see how one can reasonably claim therapeutic competence in this area) the next question would be does the "competent" therapist offer sexual relations to all patients who could benefit from his services rather than just young, attractive patients of the opposite sex? The authors state that even the most liberal communities which grant considerable sexual freedom to their members are unlikely to be accepting of arrangements that include payment for sexual activities or that make sexual activity a "public" part of licensed practice. Acceptable ethical practice also requires that the practitioner inform the perspective patient/client of the important aspects of the potential relationship that might effect the client's decision to enter into the relationship. One such aspect would be the possible use of genital intercourse as a therapeutic technique.

Marmor (1979) points out that it is possible for a therapist to genuinely fall in love with a patient. If and when such an event does take place, he feels that there is a primary obligation on the part of the therapist to discontinue the therapy immediately, thereafter relating to the patient simply as one human being to another.

In order to deal with potential distortion of the doctor-patient relationship, perspective research with controlled populations physicians had engaged in sexual behavior with patients has been proposed by Katz (1977). Williams (1978) begins to outline some of the safeguards imposed by his recommended treatment. Williams report results of 246 males involved in individualized sex therapy over a five-year period with no outcome study. Male patients who had conflicts with partners were assigned a female "body-work therapist" and were supervised by a male cotherapist. Unlike a surrogate procedure which is not under the control of a therapist, thoughts and reactions toward the female cotherapist were dealt with by the therapist. Such time-limited treatment encourages a crisis to occur related to specific sexual fears of males. It is applicable to only 5 percent of males and deals with the relationship, not specific sexual events. Such treatment is based on a tennent that a therapeutic relationship can exist primarily for the benefit of the patient. Williams (1978) states that the treatment perspective of the therapist and coworker are not compromised by such safeguards. Serious questions are raised by such treatment as the procedure can be a substitute for real-life experiences. The success of such treatment can be judged only on whether changes are made in the real behaviors of the patient subsequent to treatment by outcome studies. Williams treatment (1978) team concept is designed similar to the protective mechanism used with nuclear weapons in which two people hold separate codes for the firing of a nuclear weapon. The analogy here is that two people such as therapists and cotherapists are unlikely to share a mutual distortion of a patient thus team work would decrease the possibility of abuse. It is our contention that working alone and picking ones patients for selective treatment leads to abuse and increases the chance that ones own needs will be served. If a disfigured, unwashed, unkept person of a nonpreferred gender is in need of sexual treatment, it is less likely that the therapist's own needs will be satisfied by distortion. Distortion and rationalization of the needs of the physician and/or therapist increase when a patient is younger, attractive, and of the preferred gender. Distortion is minimized by removing the choice of the surrogate or therapist from the decision of who engages in sexual activity with which patient.

Our last concern about sexual activity is its relationship to intimacy in general. Something very important is lost in treatment of sexual concerns when the focus is on mechanical performance/sexual activity rather than the relationship the patient has with the real world. The majority of persons who seek sexual therapy have ongoing relationships and partners. An effective therapist will capitalize on his skill and utilize the patient and current partners to assist in treatment rather than becoming personally involved or involve others for mechanistic success which may or may not affect the relationships that are essential to the patient. When that is not possible — when a therapist utilizes him or herself or a substitute — one must be aware of fostering dependency in the patient, exposing the patient to unrealistic expectations, and exerting power and control over the patient that are the very antithesis of productive goals of therapy.

We have discussed some of the problems that can result from sexual relationships between patients and therapists. We feel that this activity is harmful to both. However, there are some patients for whom having the therapist touch the patient in a nonerogenous zone may be beneficial. More study of this phenomenon should be done to clarify the place of therapeutic touch in sex therapy.

REFERENCES

ANNON, J. S. (1974) The Behavioral Treatment of Sexual Problems. Honolulu, HI: Kapioloni Publishers.

BARBACH, L. G. (1975) For Yourself: The Fulfillment of Female Sexuality. Garden City: Doubleday.

BURGESS, A. W. (1981) "Physician sexual misconduct and patient's responses." American Journal of Psychiatry 138, 10: 1335–1342.

EIGEN, M. (1973) "The call and the lure." Psychotherapy: Theory, Research and Practice 10: 194–197.

GITELSON, M. (1952) "The emotional position of the analyst in the psychoanalytic situation." International Journal of Psychoanalysis 33: 1–10.

GREENBAUM, H., C. NADELSON, and L. MACHT (1976) "Sexual activity with the psychiatrist: A district branch dilemma." Presented at the American Psychiatric Association Meeting, May.

HARE-MUSTEN, R. T. (1974) "Ethical consideration in the use of sexual contact in psychotherapy." Psychotherapy: Theory, Research and Practice 11.

HOLDEN, C. (1974) "Sex therapy: Making it as a science and industry." Science 186: 330–334.

KARDENER, S. H., M. FULLER, and I. N. MENSCH (1976) "Characteristics of erotic practitioners." American Journal of Psychiatry 131, 11: 1324–1325.

——— (1973) "A survey of physician attitudes and practices regarding erotic and nonerotic contact with patients." American Journal of Psychiatry 130: 1077–1080.

KATZ, J. (1977) "Ethical issues in sex therapy and research: Reproductive research conference." Boston: Little, Brown.

KENNEDY, E. (1977) Sexual Counseling: A Continuum Look. New York: Seabury Press.

LEIF, H. I. (1973) "Obstacles to the ideal and complete sex education of the medical student and physician," pp. 441–453 in J. Zubin et al. (eds.

240   SOCIAL POLICIES

Contemporary Sexual Behavior: Critical Issues of the 1970s. Baltimore: Johns Hopkins Press.

MARMORE, J. (1979) "The seductive psychotherapist." Psychiatry Digest (October): 10–16.

MASTERS, W. and V. JOHNSON (1970) Human Sexual Inadequacy. Boston: Little, Brown.

——— (1966) Human Sexual Response. Boston: Little, Brown.

McCARTNEY, J. (1966) "Overt transference." Journal of Sex Research 32: 227–232.

McCORMICK, C. G. (1973) "If you touch, don't take." Psychotherapy: Theory, Research and Practice 10: 199–200.

Medical World News (1976) "The ethics of therapist-patient sex." July: 34–35.

——— (1975) "Sex malpractice costs MD $350,000." May: 37–40.

SHEPARD, M. (1971) The Love Treatment: Sexual Intimacy Between Patient and Psychotherapist. New York: Wyden Books.

Stedman's Medical Dictionary (1972) Baltimore: Williams and Wilkins.

WILLIAMS, M. H. (1978) "Sex therapy," in J. LoPiccolo and L. LoPiccolo (eds.) Handbook of Sex Therapy. New York: Plenum.

WOODS, S. and J. NATTERSON (1967) "Sexual attitudes of medical students: Some implications for medical education." American Journal of Psychiatry 124: 323–332.

ETHICS FOR SEX THERAPISTS

Questions

1. What are the ethical issues involved in sexual relations between patient and client? Under what circumstances are sexual relations between therapist and client acceptable?

2. Who has the right to determine if sexual relations between client and therapist are wrong (state, therapist, client, professional organization)?

3. Are sexual relations between client and patient ever helpful? What is the value of physical touching in a therapeutic relationship?

4. Why don't more clients report having had sexual relations with therapists if such behavior is so harmful?

5. If sexual/sensual behaviors between therapist and client are valuable, where does one draw the line — touching, hugging, kissing, caressing, petting, intercourse?

6. If the intent is for instruction of client or diagnosis of a dysfunction, rather than pleasure of the therapist, is intercourse ever acceptable?

7. If both therapist and client are consenting adults, or if the client initiates, is intercourse wrong?

Politics and Legislation

This section deals with three controversies: whether the state or the family should have control over issues involving the family; whether the federal government should promote legislation relating to family issues; and whether certain forms of sexuality should be encouraged or prohibited by legislation. At issue here is whether any public agency has a proper role in dealing with such private matters as human sexuality, even if one family member's well-being may be injured by other family members. Should these issues be dealt with only by family members themselves or with some help, if requested, by a family member or by the private sector? Is government already too intrusive, or is the government lax in protecting people who need help?

The State Has No Right to Interfere with Sexual Expression within the Family

MICHAEL A. CAMPION

It would be impossible for a community of people to live together without some type of corporate system of laws and rules, formal or informal, to establish limits on sexual aggressive behavior. The reason we need to even consider limits on human sexual behavior is because the nature of humankind is self-centered and sinful (Romans 3:23).

The question is not whether or not to have legislation to control sexually aggressive behavior, but to what extent, by whom, and for what desired outcome. The focus should not be on the exceptions, but rather on what occurs in the majority of sexual problematic areas. The exceptions must be dealt with on a case by case basis which are, hopefully, disposed within the broad legal guidelines.

The extent of state intervention should be limited by whether or not it violates the rights of the individual as established in the First Amendment of the Bill of Rights. "The law by itself, is simply a grouping of words and phrases, innocuous in and of themselves. A law must have the backing of the community for which it is passed"

(Hemmons, 1981). Any law must be in the framework of the Constitution of the United States as well as be supported by the local community in order to be effective. Unfortunately, what appears to be happening many times today is that laws — particularly within the areas of sexual offenses — have become an overinterpretation of the Constitution outside of the context or the intent of the Constitution and without much community support. This can be noted particularly in the area of homosexual legislation that appears to be sweeping the country. The legislation of sexual morality must also be discussed in the context of the American cultural heritage, as well as the philosophical basis for human sexuality.

Sexual expression in the United States has historically been based on the Judeo-Christian ethic. Traditionally, the Bible has not permitted adultery (Exodus 20:14), fornication (I Corinthians 6:9), divorce (Matthew 10:4,6,7), child abuse (Matthew 16:6), the withholding of the rights of one's body to the other in the marriage relationship (I Corinthians 7:4), the physical abuse or harm of the other in the marriage relationship (Ephesians 5:28–30), and that this should all be done under the law of love (I Corinthians 13).

Any fundamental laws with regard to marriage must not lose sight of the fact that marriage has two primary objectives: (1) "to provide a legitimate, descent, and respectable outlet for the sexual passions of men and women," and (2) "to provide a means whereby stable family units can be created so that children can be brought into the world and furnished with the care, attention, education, and nurture which is their due" (Ploslowe, 1951). Without the establishment of stable family units, a society crumbles; and without some legitimate outlet for the sexual passion of men and women, moral decay becomes the rule rather than the exception. However, no system of marital laws of administration can guarantee marriages that are free from discord or conflict or which guarantee morality. Therefore, it is important to develop a workable legal system to deal with interpersonal sexual abuse that takes into account the cultural and moral heritage of the country, as well as the prevailing desires of the community.

The law, however, has been moving away from the rights of the family to make decisions with regard to sexual matters and also moving away from basic Judeo-Christian value systems which are the heritage of our country. The United States Supreme Court has progressively legislated away from Judeo-Christian ethical systems.

In Roe v. Wade (1973), the court struck down laws prohibiting abortion as a violation of the constitutional right to privacy. In Eisenstadt v. Baird (1972), the Court ruled that statutes proscribing the sale of contraceptives to unmarried persons violates the right of privacy and, therefore, any person of any age can purchase contraceptives. Carey v. Population Service International (1977) further defined the contraceptive ruling by expressly permitting minors to procure contraceptives without parental consent.

Doe v. Commonwealth's attorney (1976) effectively invalidated statutes prohibiting both sodomy and fornication stating that consenting adults have a fundamental right to engage in private sexual activity. The recent surge of laws that legitimize sodomy, homosexuality, and other sexual acts indicate a trend by the Supreme Court to move away from the biblical value system. It, of course, is hopeless to legislate morals, but equally inappropriate to condone sexual behavior that violates general societal norms through legislation. It seems that the higher courts in the land tend to operate under a pure law concept that does not take into account the prevailing morals or the traditional moral values of the country. Legal decisions that operate in a vacuum negate the attempt and wishes of the general population, as well as historical value system of the country.

However, there is some residual effort by the United States Supreme Court to try to maintain the privacy of the individual when it comes to sexual matters. Griswold v. Connecticut (1965) insures the right of privacy that emanates from several fundamental constitutional guarantees which protect certain personal decisions and activities from unwarranted governmental interference. The Court decided that rights to family privacy are included in the First, Third, Fourth, Fifth, and Ninth Amendments to the Constitution. The Court acknowledged the right of marital privacy exists and told the government to stay out of the marital bedroom.

The most controversial of all sexual laws, of course involves homosexuality. The trend is definitely toward legislating homosexuality into a realm of normal and acceptable behavior. A key decision by the California Supreme Court in the case of Morrison v. Board of Education (1969) exemplifies the movement toward legitimizing homosexuality. In that decision the California Supreme Court found that the Board of Education was illegal in its decision to fire a teacher because of his homosexuality and that basically being a homosexual does not mean the person would be an unfit teacher.

There are five questions to be considered in any discussion of legislation regarding sexual behavior:

(1) What is the greater good for the most people? Developing legislation to cover the exceptional behavior and to guarantee "rights" to sexual behavior that violates the general traditional and current community value system tends to disrupt the good of all.

(2) What should be the primary area of emphasis: the symptoms or the root cause? Whether it be incest, spouse abuse, or marital rape, for example, the behaviors are really a symptom of the root cause. Society's emphasis, therefore, should not be on the symptoms but on what causes the problem. The cause of the problem is the selfishness and self-centered nature of the individual. Or, as the Bible states it, the sin that is a result of the separation of the human race from God's love. The focus, therefore, should be on how to encourage the spread of the biblical principles that deal with sin and the redemptive power of Christ.

(3) Who is best equipped to treat the root cause of sexual abusiveness? The church is the best equipped because it deals with the basic issues of the human race when it comes to self-centered sin. Rather than emphasize the legislation of morals the government should focus on encouraging the freedom of religion rather than banning prayer in school, Christmas programs, and the distribution of free Bibles. The court should encourage free choice rather than taking away the individual's ability to choose exposure to biblical principles by removing biblical Christianity as an option in society. Unless the child is exposed to sound moral values in the school and other areas of life — in addition to church — they tend to see these values as relating to only a small part of one's life: their church involvement.

(4) Are our current laws adequate without the addition of more legislation that violates more of our personal freedoms? It seems that there are a number of laws on the books to make assault and battery illegal as well as incest and rape. The problem comes when the court begins to legislate away family responsibility in an effort to protect the rights of the individual. A good example of this is giving children the right to decide whether they want an abortion or not without parental consent (Planned Parenthood of Central Missouri v. Danforth, 1976). No longer are the parents responsible for making the decisions of a minor child, the law having decreed

that even a child of 13 years old can decide apart from her parents whether or not to have an abortion.

(5) In any sexual legislation, is it possible to legislate the full range of personal sexual conduct? What constitutes spouse abuse? A shove against the sofa or two broken bones? What constitutes marital rape? Wanting sex twice a week, forcing the wife to have it the second time, or having sex ten times a week and forcing the wife to have it on the tenth occasion? Legislation sometimes is clear on overt behavior at the end of any continuum, but it is very difficult sometimes to discriminate and define variations along the way.

In terms of our culture, there are two basic issues that must be considered in any discussion of sexual behavior. First of all, sexual behavior must be mutually agreeable and mutually pleasurable in order to be acceptable. Second, the sexual conduct should not violate the traditional American value system that was built on the Judeo-Christian tradition. Taking these two principles into consideration, sexual incest and spouse abuse in marriage would not be tolerated because it would be neither mutually agreeable nor mutually pleasurable. Fornication, adultery, homosexuality, then, for example, would not be tolerated because it violates the Judeo-Christian value system on which America was founded.

The principle that sexual behavior must be mutually agreeable and mutually pleasurable as well as not violate the Judeo-Christian tradition would be impossible to legislate and would violate the the personal freedoms of the individual if legislation were attempted. The only way to change basic sexual behavior is by developing a personal value system that respects the individual rights of the other person, and Christianity is the only value system that is based on loving another person through the power of Christ. Every effort of the government, therefore, should be pressed into the service of making true freedom of religion available in America, not to cut off the option of Christianity under the guise of religious freedom. Government resources should be put into encouraging local churches to function and to educate the population toward the importance of a meaningful value system.

Some of the most difficult issues to deal with in the sexual area are the issues of spouse abuse, marital rape, and incest. The annual Uniform Crime Report by the FBI did not list domestic violence as a separate category (Federal Bureau of Investigation, 1978). In fact, statistics on domestic violence have to be ferreted out of a conglomerate of other crimes such as assault, battery, menacing, disorderly conduct, disturbing the peace and, even more tragically, homicide.

Domestic violence is blamed on the male dominant structure of our society and of the family according to Straus (1976). Straus claims that, among other things, economic constraints and discrimination of women, women's burdens of childcare, the negative self-image often held by women, the conception of women as children, and the male orientation of the criminal justice system contribute heavily to domestic violence.

Bowker (1978) states that such values and norms put women into positions where they are easily victimized, while simultaneously encouraging men to exercise their dominance. Bowker, Straus, and others relate the problem of spouse abuse to a number of factors involving society and interpersonal problems. But the question is whether or not the government should or even can step in and legislate away interpersonal problems that may lead to spouse abuse.

There may be sufficient laws on the books at this time to deal with assault and battery; we may not need to instigate new laws that ultimately only infringe on personal freedoms. Many states are instituting domestic violence laws that may actually do this. In Minnesota, (629, 34, 1978, 1979, 1981) for example, the law allows a police officer to make a probable cause arrest on a misdemeanor that involves domestic assault.

On any other misdemeanor assault there must be a formal complaint or citizens arrest. This means that if a police officer is called to a home and if, in the judgment of the police officer, there has been abuse, he can arrest any family member, relative, or child who is residing in that house and take that individual to jail. The person is then finger-printed, booked, and is not even allowed to post bail until he appears before the judge. In all other misdemeanor cases, the individual is able to post bail immediately.

In addition, the police officer may go anywhere to arrest the individual if the officer believes that the person *may* assault someone in the family. A family member may also secure a restraining order to keep a spouse out of the house on a temporary basis just by filling out a petition in Minnesota (518 B.01, 1979).

Legislating against personal violence by taking away individual basic freedoms does not appear to be the best way to deal with domestic violence. Enforcing the laws that already are on the books is sufficient to protect an individual against the violence of someone else.

The emphasis should be to revise our educational system which teaches our children everything except moral behavior. Children should be taught in school how to recognize interpersonal problems and nonviolent alternatives to dealing with frustrations. Rather than spending money in court to possibly abort civil rights, the government should spend money in the schools and through the educational process.

Marital rape is a "five-hundred-pound marshmallow" in that it is a topic that is very hard to define and get hold of. What should be remembered is that making love is not a legal matter, but an intimate, private affair between a husband and wife.

The most difficult aspect of marital rape when one tries to legislate it is the whole process of defining rape in marriage. Is it rape if a husband demands sex with his wife more than twice a week, three times a week, four times a week, or five times a week, and so on? Where is the line drawn between the normal expectations of sexual relationship and rape? It is impossible for the law to set an arbitrary figure with regard to sexual relationship in marriage.

The basic issues with marital rape are the following: How frequently does a husband have a legal right to sex, what constitutes legal grounds for refusal, what does the law recognize as normal sexual relationships between husband and wife, can a husband legally insist on having sexual relationship during his wife's pregnancy, or can a husband legally refuse to have coitus with his wife during the change of life? These and many other sexual issues become very controversial when you try to find answers through judicial process.

Can a husband legally force his wife to have intercourse? According to King (1965) the answer is no. While the husband cannot rape his wife, he can commit assault and battery by forcing his attentions on a reluctant spouse. The concept of rape is not the issue, but the evidence if the wife has been bruised or beaten would lay the foundation for the husband's conviction of assault and battery.

In Minnesota, however, a spouse can be charged with rape of their mate (609, 364, 1981). Marital rape, according to Minnesota law, is when a spouse does not consent to intercourse and the mate forces sexual relations. When the spouse is accused of rape the investigation of the charges is handled like any rape case.

The emphasis should be on education and an emotional caring for each other's needs through a meaningful value system. The wife, for her part, should understand that sex play of any kind with her husband is not morally wrong unless it results in physical injury or actual emotional shock. Emphasis should not be on defining marital rape as a legal issue, but on education that builds open, honest communication between a husband and wife directed toward understanding the sexual needs of each other.

Incest is really not an issue among rational individuals. Incest is contrary to the mores of almost all societies. There are laws currently in effect in America that forbid sexual relationships between parents and their children so there is no need for the government to intrude into the privacy of the family and, in a sense, to ferret out any suspected incest victims. Even though such an action may, in fact, discover some abused children, the consequences for the greater good of society in terms of individual freedoms would far outweigh any government interference in the family.

The government's attention should be spent not on legislation, but on education at the elementary school level to help children recognize the problems of incest and learn how to report it to the authorities. Educational programs should be available through the churches to provide an opportunity for abused children to contact their ministers or rabbis in order to begin the process of dealing with the problem of incest through a family orientation toward the basic values that consider the rights and feelings of others. If the law has been violated, then the parent who commits incest should be incarcerated or dealt with through some acceptable therapeutic means. The due process of law should pertain to the incest victim as with any other crime, but new and additional laws that invade the privacy of the home should not be encouraged as they may violate the personal freedoms guaranteed by the Constitution.

The state has no right to interfere with the sexual expressions within the family if the family does not violate the established laws of the land. The problem comes when laws are established that go outside the bounds of personal freedom in order to legislate morals. Legislation of morals is an impossible task and not within the realm of the judicial system.

It is far more valuable to deal with sexual problems within the family through an educational and spiritual process. There should be courses available in the public schools on parenting, marital communication, and value clarification. The courses should begin on a simple level, and should be taught from junior high throughout the educational process, even into the college level.

Continuing education courses could be available through the junior college for adults. The courses there could be designed to help parents who are under stress to work out the stress that contributes to problems in their lives that may lead to sexual abuses.

Justice (1979) recommends family service centers as a means of reducing sexual problems in the family. If family members, through a free choice process, could make themselves available to such community service areas that would provide counseling, it could help the family work through sexual misunderstandings in the family.

The second and equally important area that should be mobilized to deal with sexual problems within the family is the church. The value system taught in the Bible is essential to breaking down self-centered sexuality and beginning to understand the needs of the other person as an individual. If each member of the family truly integrated the principles of the Bible into their lives, there would be very little maladaptive behavior within the family. The Bible emphasizes love through the redemptive power of Christ. That love is stated in a very straightforward manner in I Corinthians 13:4–7 and is the summary of interpersonal relationships according to the Bible:

> Love is very patient and kind, never jealous or envious, never boastful or proud, never haughty of selfish, or rude. Love does not demand its own way. It is not irritable or touchy. It does not hold grudges and will hardly ever notice when others do it wrong. It is never glad about injustice, but rejoices whenever truth wins out. If you love someone you will be loyal to him no matter what the cost. You will always believe in him, always expect the best of him, and always stand your ground defending him [I Corinthians 13:4–7, Living Bible].

The government should not interfere in sanctity of the family by attempting to legislate morals. There is no way that morals can effectively be legislated without legislating away the personal freedoms of the individual American citizen. The emphasis should, therefore, be placed on education and spiritual value systems rather than legislation to deal with sexual problems within the family. It is hoped that this emphasis could bring the current moral values of our culture back to our traditional Judeo-Christian ethics.

REFERENCES

BOWKER, L. H. (1978) Women, Crime, and the Criminal Justice System. Lexington, MA: Lexington Books.

Carey v. Population Services International, 431 U.S. 678 (1977).

Doe v. Commonwealth's Attorney, 425 U.S. 901 (1976).

Federal Bureau of Investigation (1978) Uniform Crime Report. Washington, DC: U.S. Government Printing Office.

HEMMONS, M. W. (1981) "The need for domestic violence laws with adequate legal and social support services." Journal of Divorce 4, (Spring) 3.

Intrafamilial Sexual Abuse Act 609.364 Minn. Statute, 1981.

JUSTICE, B. and R. JUSTICE (1979) The Broken Taboo: Sex and the Family, New York: Human Resource Press.

KING, G. S. (1965) Sexual Behavior and the Law, New York: Bernard Geis Associates.

Living Bible Paraphrase (1971) I Corinthians. Wheaton, IL.

Minnesota Statute 518B.01, 1979.

Minnesota Statute 629.34, 1978, 1979, 1981.

Morrison v. Board of Education, 461 P. 2d, 375, 82 Cal. R. ptr. 175 (1969).

PLOSLOWE, M. (1951) Sex and the Law, New York: Prentice-Hall.

Roe v. Wade, 410 U.S. 113, 153 (1973) Griswold v. Connecticut, 381 U.S. 479 (1965).

STRAUS, M. A. (1976) "Sexual inequality, cultural norms, and wife beating." Victimology 1 (Spring): 62–63, 66.

It Is the Federal Government's Obligation to Protect Family Members from Exploitation of Each Other

HAROLD FELDMAN

This chapter has three parts. The first describes the pertinence of family crimes. The second presents a continuum of interventions by government and relates these interventions to three classes of theories. The third is an examination of the Family Protection Act as it relates to the topic.

PERTINENCE OF FAMILY CRIMES

One perspective is that the incidence of abuse within the family is so low that the question is moot and there is no need for intervention by anyone. The facts are that the incidence of family abuse is greater than the incidence of similar crimes in the community. In other words, it is safer to be outside in the streets than to be at home in terms of the likelihood of being assaulted?

There are several problems with getting accurate reports on abuse within the family such as unwillingness to report the incident, different criteria used to define a family crime, different data-gathering sources such as court cases, retrospective accounts, unverified reports, persons receiving counseling, newspaper advice columns and national random sample studies.

According to Strauss, et al. (1980) if physical punishment of children by their parents is a form of abuse, then most parents are sometimes violent. Mulligan (1977) found that half of the students reported that their parents had used or threatened to use violence on them when they were high school seniors, and 8 percent of them reported that they had been physically injured by their parents during the last year they had lived at home as high school seniors. About four million children have been kicked, bitten, or punched at some time in their life by their parents while nearly. 1.5 million had this happen to them during the study year. This means that about 30 percent of children had this experience. Last year two thousand children were killed by their parents, one every 15 minutes.

Sibling violence is the most frequent. Four out of five children who had a sibling reported an instance of sibling violence during the year. It has been reported that 40 out of 100 siblings were hit by a sibling with an object, kicked, punched, bitten, or had something thrown at them during the last year.

According to a nationwide study by Strauss et al. (1980) 16 percent of married couples admitted to having engaged in at least one violent act during the last year with each other and 28 percent at least once in their marriage. The authors suggest that their figures may be an underestimate of the number of actual violent acts.

The high rate for spouse abuse takes on even greater meaning when compared with the rate for a similar crime committed by a stranger. The rate for this crime in 190 in 100,000 — less than 1 percent. In other words, one is safer in the streets that in one's home.

The rate of marital rape is less well known as most persons do not consider a wife's being forced to have sex with her husband even if the couple is legally separate to be rape. The assumption is that if she is married that the woman's body belongs to her husband.

According to Kinsey (Kinsey et al., 1948) about 4 percent of those he studied reported that they had been approached by a relative in a sexual manner. Meiselman (1979) estimates that about one or two percent of the population, have been involved in incest.

A number of bills related to family abuse are currently being considered by legislative bodies. In New York State alone in 1982 there were four bills introduced in the assembly relating to domestic violence and 10 bills about sex offenses. A number of studies have been done indicating that witnessing abuse and being abused have negative consequences to the person and result in even more important consequences by having the abuse repeated in the next generation.

The conclusion is that violence in the family is sufficiently frequent to warrant concern and public discussion. There is a good deal of pending legislation about the issues indicating that it is current and is a harmful practice to the welfare of the persons and to the nation.

TYPES OF STATE INTERVENTION

In one sense the state has no right to interfere within the family in terms of adults choosing a mode of child rearing or sexual expression that is agreeable to themselves and in which there is no undue coercion. The main focus of this paper however is on those activities within the family where there is undue coercion due to unequal power and strength between the persons. The clear case of this is incest where the child is forced to have sex with a parent without the child's consent. The other instances are equally germane — child and spouse abuse and marital rape.

The case of child abuse might shed some light on this question. Both the states and the federal government have a significant role in child abuse cases. Yet section 104 of the Family Protection Act prohibits the federal government from interfering with the state statutes on child abuse. A state could then ignore the problem and not take any part in dealing with the parents who abuse the child, and the federal government could not take any part in protecting the children's constitutional rights.

Over all, there is a continuum of functions available to the federal government for dealing with abuses of power, from minimal reporting to direct intervention within the family and changing the social climate of violence in our country. These alternatives are presented so we can choose which types of intervention are desirable rather than accept or reject the proposition of government participation in the family in its entirety.

INFORMATION GATHERING

(1) Central reporting by states to the federal government and dissemination of information to the states provides information that would be useful in helping states check on their reporting facilities. Also, they could compare the extent of these crimes as they relate to the incidence in other states. If the federal government were to mandate this reporting, each state would have a minimum amount of information and increased consciousness on the topic.

(2) Another level of information gathering is to have the states gather information beyond that of the overall incidence of events and develop information about the epidemiology of these crimes. Do they occur with differing frequency among those living in certain housing types such as public housing or trailers? Does crowded living or do isolated settings encourage abuse? What kinds of personal background experiences promotes these crimes? What kinds of treatment programs have been successful both for persons and for groups (e.g., changing housing, providing employment, using family counseling or force? Does confrontation help abusers change or does verbal catharsis have better results? Does removal of the offended person or the threat of it cause the offender to change? These are some examples of the kinds of questions that could be asked in nationwide studies.

(3) The federal government could allocate a set amount of money to disseminate research results. The focus could be on research that would have direct or indirect implications for policy. The dissemination of results would be as important a federal function as the gathering of data. Very little good research is

written for the consumer of the information — the lay and professional persons who are directly involved.

TRAINING PROGRAMS FOR WORKERS AND COMMUNITIES

(1) At the next level, states and the federal government could sponsor educational conferences on these topics. The hearing by the U.S. Civil Rights Commission in 1978 was a landmark conference for those working in prevention and treatment of spouse abuse. This conference brought together research experts, professional workers, and interested citizens and was in large measure responsible for the establishment of a national coalition on spouse abuse. There is a need for greater dissemination of information about successful programs. The federal program could take on the task of disseminating this information.

(2) As the success of programs agains crimes within the family is dependent on community awareness, there could be national programs focusing on increasing awareness of these issues. Especially important would be mobilization of community agencies such as the church and social agencies to have campaigns against intrafamily brutality. This would be an important function of a federal program since many of the significant agencies are national in scope.

DEVELOPING MODEL PROGRAMS

(1) This is a conventional federal function whereby innovative programs can be tried out before huge amounts of money and effort are expended on them. Once a program has been funded by the federal establishment it is very difficult to change or to stop the program even if it is not being effective. Imaginative and practical programs can be selected for short-term funding and then be externally assessed to determine their effectiveness.

(2) The research funding program could occur at two stages — carefully designed but small-scale feasibility studies, followed by larger-scale studies focusing on the public policy issues involved. Both of these methods are important: the first to determine whether there seems to be some potential for a program under

small-scale or laboratory conditions; the second to test the idea under conditions closer to the actual field situation. If an idea passes these two preliminary steps it could then be used in a programmatic fashion.

FEDERAL LEGISLATION ON FAMILY CRIMES

(1) At a preliminary level the federal government could establish model legislation for the states which would bring national standards to the problem. At present, the penalty for the same family crime varies widely between states. In some states the family crime is brought before the family court while in others the victim has a choice of family or criminal court. Some states (Oregon and Pennsylvania) provide for mandatory arrest if there is probable cause, while in other states the crime must be witnessed. In Hawaii, the officer may make a warrantless arrest if the officer has observed the crime. Kentucky provides protective services to adults who agree to prosecute while most states do not. Florida collects $5.00 extra from the marriage license and uses this extra money for family shelters. Some states allow compensation for victims of violent crimes (Indiana) but exclude family crimes. The federal government could not only disseminate this information to the states but could also work toward having model legislation applicable to all of the states.

(2) The next level would be to have these crimes declared federal offenses and have federal laws passed to deal with them. This legislation would focus on the fact that family crimes are serious to the welfare on the nation and must be dealt with at a national level. The family alone is not capable of dealing with these crimes. It would be like putting the fox in the chicken coop to ask the abusing parent to deal with child abuse within the family. On the other hand, a visiting professional from Ghana, Hannah Koomson, was shocked that the extended family was not centrally involved in the resolution of family crimes. In Ghana, if the husband was abusing the wife, she would notify her parents who would call on the husband's parents who would then straighten out the offending husband. This is excellent idea but is perhaps less feasible in this context where independence of the nuclear family is the norm.

The federal government could set minimum standards of punishment or rehabilitation for the offender. There is a schizophrenic condition within our legal system: Rehabilitation of the offender is the rule for family offenses, and punishment of the offender is the rule for the same crime when it does not occur within the family. For example, if a man beats the woman next door, he is considered a criminal and is punished; but if he beats his own wife he is brought to family court and either let go or sent to a counseling center for rehabilitation. After all, the argument is made, who would support the family if the man were placed in prison? This same argument is not made if he had robbed a bank or had beaten the woman next door. In the one case, he had broken the law while in the other he had abused his property — not very prudent but nevertheless a private matter.

The federal government needs to steps in and treat these two kinds of crimes the same way. Strauss et al. (1980) state in this regard that a marriage license is a hitting license.

MODIFY THE SOCIAL CLIMATE

We are a violence loving and promoting society. Our sports are violence prone. We cheer the basketball player who is ejected from the game for having too many personal fouls, the baseball player who is ejected because he complained too loudly and persistently, the boxer who violently knocks out his opponent, the wrestler who acts out cruelty, the hockey players who violently abuse each other and so on. All of these (and more) are examples where the passions of cruelty, violence, and aggressiveness are rewarded. They demonstrate that being violent is desirable. The best-paid boxers are those who can destroy other boxers. They do not show compassion for their opponent but try to inflict as much punishment as possible. They show no emotion or personal feeling — aggressiveness is a business.

The media focus primarily on violence as news. Good news, where someone helps another or where a group organizes to perform a good deed, is ignored. If a group wants to get some publicity about a meeting it will more likely be noticed by the media if there is conflict or opposition expressed. At the 1978 meeting in Houston for women's rights there was little attention paid to the many proposals that were adopted with strong support by most of the delegates, but attention was paid to conflict about a few issues. Conflict, violence, and disaster are considered news but cooperation, collaboration, and sacrifice for the benefit of others is ignored. We need to change this climate so that less attention is paid to violence and more to cooperation.

A minimal amount of time could be mandated for the media to include instances of cooperation in reporting about the events of the day. A person reading the daily newspaper or watching television news would conclude that there is only violence and disaster in the world, and that no one is cooperative. No wonder Robinson Crusoe decided to return to his native "uncivilized" land after hearing the news. Was his "primitive" existence more civilized than ours? Is there less family crime in societies that focus on cooperation?

Perhaps the most significant societal factor is the prevalence of sexism in our society. The norm is that the father is the head of the household and so is obligated to take control over the other members. This attitude is harmful not only to the other members of the family but to the father as well. As a macho male he owns the family. Family sexism is of long standing and is very persistent. An example of this persistence and need for a national approach to this problem is the failure to pass the Equal Rights Amendment. A number of papers have been written (Feldman et al., 1980) indicating that this amendment would not bring about the evils its opponents fear such as unisex toilets or mandated policies to place women in combat. On the other hand, it would not in itself cure all the problems that women and men face because of sexual stereotyping. Why then not pass it? Apparently there are strong forces at work to keep the sexual division of labor stereotyped at the conventional level either for profit or for political purposes. The problem of sex role stereotyping must be solved at the federal level because the issues are national in scope.

The major problem about the ERA is not so much what would happen if it is passed but the consequences of not passing it. What kind of world image does the United States have if it states to the world that it does not believe in equality for women? The analogy is not that it is like passing an amendment about equality for Black persons, but rather like saying that we could manage inequality at the local or state level and could trust everybody to act in a just way. We need to have a national statement about the equality of males and females in and out of the home to be a guide for behavior, a statement that either sex has no right to be violent toward the other. We need a national policy about equality as a background to changing sexist attitudes in interpersonal relationships. If we want to lower the amount of family violence, we must change the ideology about sexism.

It there were more democratic attitudes between partners in a marriage there is evidence that there would be less spousal violence. Strauss et al. (1980) report the result of a study on the relationship between the percentage of decisions that the couples reported as being made jointly and the extent of family violence. They found the more joint decisions the couple had, the less spousal violence. Stated in the opposite way, the more decisions were not made jointly, the greater the amount of conflict. We need more education about how to have more effective family relationships — not only in schools but also in programs such as an alternative-to-violence day celebrated across the nation.

Another finding of Strauss et al.'s study relates to the sources of spousal conflict. Conflict over children was the most significant area in predicting the extent of spousal violence. The greater the amount of conflict over children, the greater the percentage of husbands and wives who reported spousal violence. Less than 10 percent of couples who reported they had no conflict about children had spousal violence, while of those who said they always had conflict about children 70 percent reported that they had spousal violence during the year. There is still a good deal of pronatalism — pressuring women to be parents whether they want to or not. This pronatalism may have negative consequences on children who may be unwanted. Perhaps as a nation we should be less promiscuous about encouraging childbearing and not insist on parenthood for those who do not want to be parents.

We should provide more help to parents in child rearing. We do not allow teachers to deal with children until they know something about child development and have had some intership experiences with children. We do not allow potential parents who want to adopt children to do so without being sure of their motivation and their ability to care for children. Anyone, however, can be a natural parent — whether they want to or not. At least we can make it possible for only those who want to have children to have the opportunity to raise them. These findings suggest that there are important research findings that could be applied to national policy to alleviate violence in families. Shouldn't we pay as much attention to violence in families as we do to violence outside of the family?

Strauss (1971) suggests that there are three classes of theories to explain abuse. These theories are intraindividual, interpersonal, and societal. The intraindividual theories focus on the individual and her or his life experiences; the interpersonal are concerned primarily with the interactions between persons; while the societal theories focus on the macrosocietal factors. It may be that local agencies are more significant in dealing with the intraindividual and interpersonal causes of violence while and societal are best treated by larger governmental units. On the other hand, some findings about individual experiences leading to violence can generalize across single individuals. The research finding that having experienced violence as a child predisposes the adult to become violent has implications for governmental and other macrointerventions (e.g., disseminating this information across the country might act as a deterrent for some) National programs for early treatment of children shortly after they have experienced family violence might alleviate some of the problem. Knowing about the violence predisposing experiences of a person might be an aid in helping couples decide about parenthood.

THE FAMILY PROTECTION ACT

The Family Protection Act, H.R.-97, is a contradictory bill in regard to the relationship between the federal and state government and the family. On the one hand it is clearly opposed to any interference by the federal government in matters that it perceives as being within the jurisdiction of the state including state interference with the family. The child abuse section of the bill states, "No federal program, guideline, agency action, commission action, directive or grant shall be construed to abrogate, alter, broaden or supercede existing state statutory law relating to child abuse."

If this were not clear enough the bill continues in the next part (b) as follows: "No federal funds shall be expended for the operation of any child abuse program in any state unless such program has been specifically authorized and established by the state legislature of the state in which such program operates."

These two statements in the bill are clear evidence of a states-rights orientation that opposes federal control over matters within the family. At least the point of view is clear and unequivocal. However, this states-rights orientation is not so consistent within other aspects of the bill; for example, under Section 102(a) the bill states that no federal program, project or entity shall receive federal funds either directly or indirectly in regard to contraceptive or abortion services to an unmarried minor unless the parents or guardians are notified. There is no exception suggested in this section about whether or not a state has a law mandating or excluding notification of parents. At another place in this bill under Title III Education, Section 440C, dealing with courses of instruction and educational materials, the bill prohibits the expenditures of federal funds that relate to educational materials that do not reflect the American way of life as it has been historically understood (sex role stereotyped).

In other words, the federal government is to stay out of matters relating to the family in regard to abuse within the family, but it is to attempt to influence agencies, — federal, state and local, — to notify the family in case of sexual behavior of children and to influence schools to present only the conventional roles of family members. It seems to me that one can't have it both ways. The government can't be mandated to stay out of the family and also be influencing family matters. Either the family is a private institution protected from government interference or it is an institution that can be invaded by governments for the welfare of the families. It seems that there is another principle following the conservative line of approving stereotyped sex roles: It is all right for the father to be master of the minds and bodies of the other members of the family, and he is to be projected in this way by school textbooks. This is more like the real agenda than the purpose of maintaining states rights regardless of the issue.

In conclusion, the problem of family violence is widespread and more prevalent than violence outside of the family. Several kinds of state interventions were described and related to three theories about violence. If the orientation is that violence is primarily a personal or interpersonal matter, then different kinds of interventions may be desirable than if the orientation is societal. Finally, the Family Protection Act was examined and related to the questions about national policies or families. Nationwide policies are needed to help those who commit and those who are the victims of the family abuse. The decision to be made is not whether the federal government should have any part in dealing with family violence but rather which of many possibilities should be utilized by the federal government in dealing with these problems. Federal role is significant in most of these areas.

REFERENCES

FELDMAN, H. (1979) "Why we need a family policy." Journal of Marriage and the Family.
——— D. LOWELL, and J. ZIMBALIST (1980) "Women, men and the Equal Rights Amendment." Human Ecology Forum 11, 1: 3–12.
KINSEY, D., C. WARDELL B. POMOROY, and S. MARTIN (1948) Sexual Behavior in the Human Male. Philadelphia: W.B. Saunders.
MEISSELMAN, K. (1979) Incest. San Francisco: Jossey-Bass.
MULLIGAN, M. A. (1977) "An investigation of factors associated with violent modes of conflict resolution in the family." M.A. thesis, University of Rhode Island.
STRAUSS, M. (1971) "Some social antecedents of physical punishment: A linkage theory interpretation." Journal of Marriage and the Family 33: 658-663.
——— R. GELLES, and S. STEINMETZ (1980) Behind Closed Doors. Garden City, NY: Doubleday.

STATE CONTROL OF THE FAMILY

Questions

1. *What role should legislation play in regulating marital rape, incest, and homosexuality? Should marital rape be legally defined? How? What legislation is necessary for punishing people who commit incest?*

2. *Should two consenting adults be allowed to do anything they choose?*

3. *Is school the place to teach children morality?*

4. *Should a law enforcement agent be allowed to arrest a person for probable cause of marital abuse or rape?*

5. *Why do victims of incest, child abuse and marital abuse fail to report these crimes?*

6. *How much should the government be allowed to intervene in family matters?*

The Federal Government Should Promote Legislation Supporting the Traditional Family

TOM BETHELL

When a nation is strong and its government exercises a proper sense of restraint as to its role, demonstrating respect for the ability and independence of its citizenry, there is a natural harmony between the government and the family. A government that is diligent about defending the shores, preserving internal order, and issuing a stable currency is, at the same time, likely to understand the vital role that the family plays in promoting economic prosperity and in attending to the education and moral instruction of the young.

Each family, is, after all, ideally a minigovernment — with considerable authority being vested in the parents, the father in particular. In the past, wise governments have understood how destructive it would be to try to undermine parental authority or to arrogate parental roles to themselves.

Unfortunately, this is no longer the case. As Jean-Francois Revel points out in *The Totalitarian Temptation*, the unquestioned authority that used to be vested in the paterfamilias has now been transferred to the state. It would be considered an international outrage to interfere with the "internal affairs" of even the most evil regimes, such as those of Idi Amin and Pol Pot. In the same way, in Roman times the father's power of life or death over his children was not questioned by the state.

As the state has grown even larger, it has developed an increasingly hungry eye toward areas previously cordoned off from its dominion. What happens is that the enlarged, and therefore increasingly inefficient government bureaucracies begin to feel challenged by the multitude of minigovernments called families with their hitherto autonomous powers sealed off from the interference of the state.

Something like this is happening in the United States today. An expansionary, rapacious, bureaucratic state cannot stand the competition any longer and is today arrogating to itself the familial functions; the state wishes to reeducate us, remoralize us, and to relieve us of the burdens, pressures, and motivating forces of economic need.

It is interesting to note that, at the same time as it has moved into these new and inappropriate areas of responsibility, the state has also demonstrated a very relaxed view of its traditional functions: Defense spending is denigrated, even by the Secretary of Defense; criminals are held at best only partially responsible for their actions and often are regarded as rebels without a cause — bearing witness by their actions to the depraved state of society; while the currency is allowed to erode in value through an excessive use of the printing press.

This simultaneous dissolution and rampant expansion of the state is a most extraordinary thing. Sometimes I think that it is not simply a matter of bureaucratic expansion — bureaucrats trying to find more and more to do, promoting themselves by increasing the number of their subordinates, and related activities in harmony with Parkinson's Law. That undoubtedly has something to do with it. I fear, however, that there is a more directly negative force at work, an actual cancer, the mergence within the body politic of bureaucratic microbes whose primary impulse is to devour tissue.

I want to look now at one or two of the most important ways in which government action has had the effect of undermining traditional values. Such action falls into several categories — educational, legal, moral, and economic. I want to consider principally the economic undermining of the family. In my opinion this is one of the most serious assaults because it is the area last likely to trigger alarm bells with those admirable profamily counteractivists without whose efforts we would all be in far worse shape than we already are.

When the International Year of the Child began agitating on behalf of children's rights to sue their parents, almost everyone guessed that something monstrous was afoot. As long as public education is the lamentable thing that it is — and is placed above all egalitarian goals — then we know instinctively that all bureaucratic attempts to stifle private education are doomed to fail. And when the National Women's Conference in Houston and the White House Conference on Families start extolling lesbian rights, gay rights, and alternative life-styles, then we all know that the ideological battle lines have been drawn and that combat shall soon commence. But when someone at the Department of Health and Human Services (originally Health, Education and Welfare) says that we must all be a little more compassionate and do a little more for the underprivileged by expanding welfare benefits then he is very likely to receive no reply other than assent or perhaps, at worst, grudging acquiescence.

That is why I believe that the most serious assault on traditional family values today comes in the form of income transfer or welfare programs. We are not apt to realize how terribly destructive they have been. It is unfashionable to say it, but the truth of the matter is that it does not do people any good at all to give them money without their having to work for it. We have somehow lost sight of this simple truth, a truth that for thousands of years was enshrined in Judeo-Christian teachings but which in the twentieth century has been widely discarded — with disastrous results.

Let us look at this in a little more detail. In recent years, social welfare professionals eager to expand (they prefer to use the term "reform") welfare programs have pointed to an undoubted fact: There is a correlation between poverty and family breakup. Now what is the causal relationship here? The poverticians and welfare-rights organizations have immediately jumped to the conclusion that family breakup is caused by poverty. Think about that idea for a minute: Poverty causes family breakup. Notice how facilely it slanders — denies — the best qualities in men and women of faithfulness, love, and willingness to shelter and protect dependents? And notice also the blatant materialism on which it rests:

Marriages are made secure by plenty. The rich man is less likely to divorce than the poor man. A man stays with his wife only because he has provided for her, not in order to provide for her. We all know how false these propositions are. They are contrary to common sense about human nature and are contradicted by the statistical evidence that stares us in the face. In the United States in the 1930s, 1940s, and 1950s, there was far more proverty than there was in the 1960s and 1970s breakup but was far less likely.

The interesting point is that the Department of Health and Human Services (HHS) determined to set its view of human nature in concrete, as it were, by conducting academically approved welfare experiments. Accordingly, Stanford Research Institute and Mathematical Policy Research were funded to carry out the most extensive welfare experiments ever, costing the taxpayers many millions of dollars. They are now known as the Seattle and Denver Income Maintenance Experiments (SIME/DIME).

In effect, thousands of people in Seattle and Denver were given a guaranteed income at different levels of generosity and their subsequent work effort and family stability were compared with that of a control group that was not given any money. The experiments continued over 10 years, but you didn't read too much about them in the newspapers, because the results came out exactly contrary to the wishes of HHS and liberal opinion generally. Those being paid the guaranteed income reduced their work effort considerably, and their rate of family breakup turned out to be far higher than that of the control group.

Considered from the traditional point of view, these findings are not all surprising. Work is basically unpleasant, and if people are provided with an alternative to it they will be strongly inclined to take that alternative. Second, there is a tendency present in almost all married couples to fly apart at some stage, to behave irresponsibly — call it original sin, if you will. If men are assured that after they leave home the state will assume their responsibilities, they will be far more inclined to surrender to the temptation. The Seattle and Denver experiments confirmed this for those who needed proof.

Therefore, the correlation between proverty and family breakup is easily explained. Poor people become eligible for welfare, and the welfare destroys them. In short, those who would try to solve people's problems for them by giving them money (which in turn has been taken from other people) only succeed in making matters far worse. Ultimately, such reformers are combatting human nature. The realities of human nature have worked with a shattering effect upon those who have become part of our welfare culture. The great problem with welfare programs — and the problem is getting worse all the time — is that the benefits paid out are too high. They are comparable with, or even higher than, what welfare recipients can hope to obtain in the entry-level jobs for which they are qualified. In other words, when welfare recipients take a job, they frequently take a pay cut — and go off to work everyday at a what maybe an unpleasant job. Many of them quite rationally do not take these low-paying jobs and instead "demand" good jobs. It is important to realize that the fault here does not lie with those on welfare as much as it does with those in the government agencies who make the terrible mistake of imagining that, in their line or work, there can be no such thing as too much generosity.

I want to reassure you that this is not just the voice of a reactionary curmudgeon speaking. Dr. Jodie Allen, Deputy Assistant Secretary of Labor, has reported the following:

> As a result of humanitarian concerns, many states now provide welfare recipients with a package of benefits including cash assistance, food stamps, housing assistance, Medicaid, and other benefits which far exceed the value of their potential earnings. It is unreasonable to assume that welfare recipients will be willing to relinquish these benefits for a lower net income from work, particularly since working may be inconvenient, uncertain in duration, and expensive in itself [U.S. Congress, Senate, 1978: 38].

One might add, perhaps unpleasant.

My belief, then, is that welfare has been the most destructive of all the forces working against the family — more so, I think, than the transparently evil compaigns on behalf of abortion, homosexuality, pornography, and against religion. Welfare arrayed in the name of humanitarianism and compassion demoralizes families, deprives the father of his role as a provider and so, in the end, depraves him. In perceiving that he has no important role to perform, the recipient is likely to become embittered, an enemy of society, filled with hatred for the state that pays his wife (or the mother of his children) more money than he can earn, and inclined to turn toward a life of crime in response.

Welfare thus does not cure poverty, it creates it; and this is what is above all responsible for the ruined, dangerous condition of so many American inner cities. In the wake of the Miami destructive and rioting I do not believe that one commentator drew attention to the fearful degree of dependency on the state, with its accompanying loathing of the state, that our vast array of welfare programs has created. Black families in particular have been hit hard by the destructive effects of this dependency. Blacks are disproportionately on welfare (nearly half of all AFDC recipients are black) for two reasons. First, blacks were singled out for inclusion in welfare programs by welfare rights organizations hunting for clients in the 1960s. Second, many black leaders have made the serious mistake of viewing the conditions of blacks primarily in terms of retribution for the past, encouraging the notion that the "white establishment" should be made to atone for the sins of slavery by devising generous income-transfer programs. The "white establishment" was glad for the opportunity to do something about its guilt feelings. Unfortunately, the major victims of this leadership have been the dependent black families who are now in worse state than they were at the time of the "Moynihan Report" in the mid-1960s.

It might be unpopular to ascribe the eroded condition of many black families to well-intentioned government generosity. It calls into question the dominant liberal economic assumption of our time — to wit, that a shortage of money is the root of all evil. How much simpler to ascribe all such problems to racism and discrimination. The same thing is going to happen to Hispanics who are also disproportionately on welfare and who are beginning to experience disproportionate family breakup. Not, I submit, because of discrimination — what an incredibly facile slander on all Americans that is — but because of welfare itself.

Growing welfare payments and rising transfer programs mean higher taxes and inflation, and this is where we find the middle and upper-middle classes being hurt. The ever-increasing tax burden has had the effect of driving mothers out of the home, thus weakening families and increasing the demand for federally funded (of course) day-care centers. No doubt for these reasons, inflation and the tax burden are the most powerful forces aiding the women's liberation movement. Without wives' demands for new jobs to help pay the bills and taxes, it is likely that the movement currently would have little steam in it. President Carter boasted about the increase in the number of working women during his administration, without seeming to realize that this increase has undoubtedly come at the expense of the family.

The rapid growth of government at all levels during the 1970s means that almost everyone has to spend a good portion of his or her working day in an effort to pay the government's bills. Just as rising welfare payments increase the poor's dependence upon government, rising taxes diminish the independence of the middle class from government. There has been a tremendous loss of freedom, a surrender of our freedoms to the government, and a simultaneous undermining of the integrity of the family. If Mr. Carter really wanted to do something for the family — a dubious proposition, considering that everything in his record suggests that he was much more interested in further aggrandizing the state — by far the best thing he could have done would have been to recommend a large tax cut to Congress.

I said earlier that the attack on the family has taken various forms, I want to turn briefly to one of the most virulent — the legalistic. Particularly brazen is the thrust toward "children's rights," which I regard as the most undisguised assault on the traditional family yet seen. Let us think about the concept of children's rights for a moment. What do such rights imply? If a minor has rights equivalent to its parents, then it is implied that the violator of these newly won rights will be the parent. Children's rights are nothing but a novel mechanism for disrupting previously accepted levels of parental authority, and opening them up to scrutiny by the state. Joseph Sobran has written on this point:

> If children are citizens like their parents, then obviously the home can't be allowed any special exemption from that general policing power whereby the state protects citizens from each other. The more guidelines the state promulgates, the greater must be its power. And the more trivial the activities it claims to regulate, the closer and more minute must its supervision be.

Consider the following: If new laws "protecting" children make lawbreakers of their parents, who is going to advise the state of these violations of the law? Who is going to inform the state? Children's rights must in the end make informers of children. This was predicted by George Orwell's *1984,* and has of course been borne out in the totalitarian states such as the Soviet Union and Cuba. This, I think, is the most horrifying of all the aspects of life in the totalitarian societies; the realization that the family, formerly the center of love and trust, can thus be perverted by the state into an inescapable network of spies.

This may all seem rather far removed from our current situation, but we should be on our guard — 1984 is not that distant. The great fog of lies emanating from the Soviet Union sometimes makes it hard to tell exactly where we are. I notice that in the very interesting package of materials on the White House conference on families inserted into the Congressional Record by Senator Gordon J. Humphrey there was a quotation from IYC, a publication of the UN Secretariat of the International Year of the Child, stating that "the Soviet children enjoy in full the rights stipulated in the Declaration of the Rights of the Child proclaimed by the U.N. General Assembly." We are then told that the reason for this, the "decisive factor," is the socialist nature of the Soviet society (Congressional Record, 1980).

As far as I can tell, in our society in 1980 children's rights are confined to the areas of birth control, family planning information, and abortion — bad enough, of course. The Supreme Court has recently delivered itself of some odd rulings, denying that parents even have the right to be notified of judicial proceedings in which judges give abortion advice to minors. And the Social Security Act now prohibits a state from violating the rights to privacy and confidentiality of minors by notifying the parents that their children are obtaining family planning services.

I suspect, however, that the big change could come in the legal position of families if and when the liberal left ever succeeds in getting its way with regard to changing the definition of families. You will notice that this point is really one of the new hot items on the liberal agenda these days. Families in a pluralistic society must now be pluralized, evidently. White House Conference Chairman Jim Guy Tucker has been quoted as saying that "family" should be defined as "one or more adults living together with or without children" — a definition that could very well been written by gay activists.

The recently formed Office for Families within the Department of Health and Human Services notes in a "fact sheet" that one of its functions, ominously enough, will be to "bring greater recognition to the diversity and pluralism of American family life."

Why this eagerness to broaden the definition of families? The point is, I think, that the family constitutes a golden opportunity to implement the complete liberal agenda. Normally, this agenda-in-embryo must run the gauntlet of conservative scrutiny. But conservatives like the family, right? So they won't be against that, will they? Very well, then, quietly redefine the family so that it includes just about everyone except the most solitary of hermits. "Family policy" advocates within government thus perceive that they will be able to smuggle the full range of left/liberal programs — great income redistribution, full employment policies, minimum incomes, government-funded day-care, more widespread social services — in the virtuous guise of assistance to families and (here's the beauty of it) not require that the recipients of all these government goodies be members of anything so old-fashioned as a traditional family.

So be on your guard when you hear people talking about a new definition of a family. Be on your guard against any "assistance" to families that might come out of the Office for Families or the White House Conferences on Families. Be on your guard when you hear that the government is hunting for an appropriate "family policy."

Be on your guard, because I can assure that beneath the friendly rhetoric, the government in its present overgrown, voracious condition views the family in approximately the same "friendly" way the wolf regarded Little Red Riding Hood.

REFERENCES

Congressional Record (1980) May 9: S5029.
U.S. Congress, Senate (1978) Hearings before the Subcommittee on Public Assistance of the Senate Finance Committee, November 15–17. Washington, DC: U.S. Government Printing Office.

The Federal Government Should Not Foster Legislation Relating to the Family

EDWARD L. KAIN

This chapter argues that the federal government should promote free-choice legislation in family issues. The American promise of the right to life, liberty, and the pursuit of happiness can only be possible when individuals and families are free to make their own choices regarding the complex moral issues that face them in our rapidly changing society. Current legislation at the national level that purports to strengthen the "traditional family" reflects a naive understanding of the history of families in the United States. It oversimplifies a wide array of complex moral issues and threatens an unprecedented intrusion upon the rights of family members.

A wide variety of topics could be examined regarding government policies and families in the United States. This discussion concentrates on three issues that are particularly controversial as we enter the last two decades of the twentieth century: women's rights (specifically the Equal Rights Amendment), gay rights, and the abortion issue. This chapter begins with an overview of recent attempts to legislate the "traditional family" at the federal level. Current work in family history is used to illustrate some of the ways in which this legislation is based upon misconceptions of an idealized family in a mythic past. After this introductory discussion, each of the three issues on freedom of choice and families in the United States — women and equality, gay rights, and the abortion debate — are reviewed in turn.

Three general principles underlie the argument of this chapter. First, it is essential to place the discussion of the three issues within a historical context. We must understand the impact of social change upon families in the past century and question what is meant by the "traditional family." Second, we must be aware of the complexity of the moral issues being debated. Our thought must shift from simplistic categorical distinctions of right and wrong to a more sophisticated stance that recognizes the validity and integrity of a variety of moral positions. Finally, it remains clear that the social and natural sciences cannot resolve moral dilemmas. The data presented in this chapter illustrate how a sociologist would attempt to provide information about such controversial issues as ERA, gay rights, and abortion. These data, however, only illustrate the complexity of the issues, and cannot reveal which moral stance is correct. It is precisely for this reason that federal policy should promote free choice in family issues. Legislators are no more able to select the single correct moral position on family issues than are social and natural scientists. These questions can only be decided by individuals based upon their particular religious, political, and moral convictions.

ATTEMPTS TO LEGISLATE THE "TRADITIONAL FAMILY"

Before turning to each of the three issues to be examined in this chapter, it will be useful to review the historical context of the discussion. As we enter the decade of the 1980s, the "New Right" has mounted a campaign to save American society by shoring up what it regards as the traditional family. The centerpiece of the conservative moral agenda is an omnibus bill called the Family Protection Act. Senator Paul Laxalt of Nevada first introduced the bill to the Senate in September of 1979, and versions of the legislation were subsequently introduced to the House by Representative Hansen of Idaho (January, 1981) and Representative Smith of Alabama (June, 1981). In June of 1981 Senator Jepsen of Iowa introduced a revised version of the FPA (for himself and Mr. Laxalt), but Laxalt withdrew his support for this version in 1982.

The Family Protection Act is only one of several pieces of federal legislation introduced in the early 1980s which attempts to write into law what are described as traditional family values. Various versions of the Human Life amendment — an amendment to the Constitution stating that life begins at conception — also fall into this category. Because of the multiple versions of these bills and the way in which legislation evolves within the American political system, any discussion of a particular bill is outdated almost as soon as it is written. Rather than review all of the various pieces of legislation currently being considered, this discussion will use an early version of the Family Protection Act as an example to illustrate the types of misconceptions about family life which are built into these attempts to legislate traditional family values.

The Family Protection Act begins with the statement that it will act to "strengthen the American family and to promote the virtues of family life." It proposes amendments to such diverse pieces of legislation as the National Labor Relations Act, the Internal Revenue Code of 1954, the Higher Education Act of 1965, the Civil Rights Act of 1964, and the Food Stamp Act of 1977. The reader must ask, however, what is meant by the word "family" in this legislation? By treating the American family as a monolithic entity, the FPA ignores the diversity of contemporary families in this country and attempts to promote family structures for the future based upon a nostalgic image of an idealized past. The authors of this legislation would benefit from reading recent work in family history which attempts to dispel some of the myths about families in past time (see, for example, Gordon, 1978, and Rabb and Rotberg, 1973, for two collections of readings).

The new family history has only begun to reconstruct the details of family life in past time. Even though the evidence is not complete, the research during the last two decades on families in the preindustrial era has shattered a number of idealized conceptions about families before the industrial age. The first of these myths to fall was the idea that in the past most families were extended in structure and that the nuclear family is a product of the Industrial Revolution. Data from a wide array of countries and time periods suggests that nuclear family structures existed long before industrialization (Laslett, 1965; Laslett and Wall, 1972).

A second myth about families in the past is the idea that children were treated with more care and respect, in contrast to the modern world where familial values have declined. The reality of family life in the past is again quite different. In Colonial America, for example, childhood as we know it was barely recognized. Children were viewed as strong-willed selfish creatures whose wills must be "beaten down" or "broken" (Demos, 1975). Children began working in and outside of the home at an early age, often working hours that would shock most modern parents. Historian John Demos (1975) concludes in his overview of recent work in family history that "there is no golden age of the family gleaming at us from far back in the historical past. And there is no good reason to construe recent trends in terms of decline and decay."

Another important lesson to be learned from the new family history is the diversity of families in the past. Indeed it is incorrect to ask the question "What was *the* American family like in past time?" We must instead ask "What were American *families* like in the past?" In each historical period we find a variety of family structures and modes of everyday living. Farber (1972) suggests that social class has always been an important factor in determining how families are structured. Further, we cannot talk about a general pattern of social change and families — we must instead look at the different ways in which families have interacted with their changing environments depending upon their place within the broader social structure. Social class is only one point of variation. Race and ethnicity also have an influence upon family life. The work of McLaughlin (1971), for example, illustrates how Italian immigrant families in Buffalo, New York, at the turn of the century had work and family patterns that differed considerably from those of many other immigrant groups. Wives seldom worked outside of the home, as they did in many other immigrant families. Instead they did work that could be done in the home in addition to taking in boarders and lodgers.

As we turn to the Family Protection Act, it is important to keep in mind the diversity of family life in the past as well as in the contemporary United States. The Family Protection Act has many implications for individual and family rights. A few illustrations will be given here that relate directly to the three issues discussed in this chapter. The original version of the FPA began with a section of education. One of the provisions of this section denied federal funds for "purchase or preparation of any educational materials or studies relating to the preparation of educational materials, if such materials would tend to denigrate, diminish, or deny the role differences between the sexes as they have been understood historically in the United States."

The "historical understanding" of the family reflected in this legislation is a mythical family of peaceful bliss under patriarchal authority where the wife/mother is in the home raising children while the husband/father is a breadwinner in the marketplace. Such a conception is not an accurate portrayal of family life in either the past or present. Over half of the married women in this country work outside of the home. This is not a new phenomena. The percentage of married women working outside of the home has increased steadily since the late nineteenth century, and indeed projections are that two-worker husband/wife households will increase slightly through the end of the century while the percentage of one-worker households (including the "traditional" pattern) will decline (Masnick and Bane, 1980).

A number of tax exemptions later in the bill make laudable moves to ease the burdens of adoption for adoptees who are normally difficult to place — children who are handicapped, biracial, or over the age of 6. These exemptions, however, "shall not be allowed to an individual who is not a married individual . . . or to a married individual . . . who does not make a joint return of tax with his spouse for the taxable year." Most dual-earner couples choose to file separate returns. It is interesting that a "profamily" bill would deny such a tax break to this group, who would be most likely and able to adopt children such as the handicapped who would demand extra financial resources.

The Family Protection Act also has a number of provisions relating to the two other issues in this chapter, gay rights and abortion rights. Under the act, no federal funds will be available to programs that provide contraceptive devices or abortion services (including counseling) to an unmarried minor without notifying the parents or guardians of the minor. No funds under the Legal Services Corporation Act can be used to provide legal assistance in gay rights litigation or in abortion litigation. No federal funds would be available to any person or group who "presents homosexuality . . . as an acceptable alternative life style or suggests that it can be an acceptable life style." In addition, the FPA proposes that the Civil Rights Act of 1964 be amended so that the government shall not "seek to enforce nondiscrimination with respect to individuals who are homosexual or proclaim homosexual tendencies." Rather than being profamily, as its sponsors suggest, the Family Protection Act appears to be against women's rights, against gay rights, and antiabortion (as well as anticontraception and antiunion).

The Family Protection Act is not the only proposed legislation at the federal level that would directly affect individual and family decisions. It is simply the most comprehensive. A statute sponsored by Representative Henry Hyde and Senator Jesse Helms, for example, states that human life begins at the moment of conception. With the simple sweep of a pen upon a piece of legislation, they suggest that the complicated social, moral, legal, political, and medical issues surrounding the decision of when human life begins can be resolved.

This nation is based on fundamental principles involving freedom, individuality, and diversity. Many early settlers of our country came here to escape repressive governments and societies that did not allow them to live their lives according to their moral beliefs. The history of families in this country is on of diversity, and it is unfortunate that legislation like the Family Protection Act seeks to destroy that diversity by imposing one moral code upon people from a variety of religious, ethnic, and social backgrounds. Some of this diversity will be illustrated below as we move to a discussion of each of three issues: women's rights, gay rights, and abortion rights.

WOMEN AND EQUALITY

A conservative position on the role and rights of women unually involves two facets. First is the assumption that men and women are inherently different (usually a biological explanation is used). Second is the assumption that these differences have been and should continue to be reflected in separate roles for males and females. As a result, the traditional view asserts that changes in the roles occupied by men and women (but particularly women) are a threat to human nature and the natural order. The threat is precipitated by unwarranted intervention, with the accusing finger pointed at big government, "women's libbers," or the liberal left.

The anthropological and historical records, however, indicate that "human nature" in relation to the sexes is extremely pliable. Margaret Mead's classic work on sex and temperament (1935) in three societies clearly illustrated that what is defined as masculine and feminine is a *social* construction and not solely dictated by biology. Looking at three societies in New Guinea, Mead found that among the Mundugumor both male and female roles would be defined as masculine using our Western standards; among the Arapesh both were essentially "feminine;" and the Tchambuli reversed the distinctions we tend to make in our country. There are undeniable biological differences between the sexes, but social and cultural pressures are central in shaping, limiting, and directing behaviors in ways that are defined as appropriately male or female.

Certainly there has always been a sexual division of labor in this country, but the different role expectations and definitions for men and women have not always taken their current form. In an agricultural era when production was in the home or on the land nearby, the everyday activities of men and women had much more in common. Conceptions of the so-called traditional family where women's place is in the home were not solidified until the late eighteenth and early nineteenth century when the factory system moved production out of the home. It was at this point historically that womanhood and domesticity became linked, particularly in the middle class (Welter, 1966). The development of physically separate spheres was thus accompanied by an ideology that defined the proper sphere of woman as in the home, away from the world of work. This ideology of separate spheres still affects the way we define men and women today.

Decade by decade, since 1890, more women have crossed the boundary into the world of men and obtained jobs outside of the home. At first they were largely unmarried women, but slowly more and more married women entered the labor force; and since 1950, increasing numbers of women with small children have been working outside of the home. (See Kain, 1981, for a discussion of these changes.) The transformation of women's roles has not been the simple result of some subversive force such as big government or the women's movement attacking the traditional family. Rather, the work of a number of historians indicates that the entry of women into the industrial and professional labor force involved what Brumberg and Tomes (1981) have called a "complex interaction of economic, structural and cultural forces."

Current attitudes about women's rights and roles are similarly complex. Analysis of sample surveys show that women's attitudes in this country have moved toward more equalitarian role definitions. These attitudes vary in different social groups. In particular, higher education and employment both predict more equalitarian attitudes (Mason et al., 1976). Women who believe that maternal employment is harmful to children are much more likely to support a traditional division of labor (Mason et al., 1976: 593). Change over time is clear in attitudes toward women working. In 1970, 42 percent of respondents in a national Harris poll favored "efforts to strengthen and change women's status in society." By 1975, 63 percent of a Harris sample said they favored such change. A survey question asked in 1936, 1969, and 1976 shows even more striking changes. Only 19 percent of respondents in a 1936 survey approved when asked, "Do you approve of a married woman earning money in business or industry if she has a husband capable of supporting her?" By 1969, 55 percent of respondents indicated approval. In 1976, the same question found 70 percent approval among women and 65 percent approval among men (deBoer, 1977).

Turning to attitudes toward the Equal Rights Amendment one finds similar variation in attitudes by a variety of background factors. Region, for example, is closely related to attitudes about the ERA. The states that had not ratified the amendment by the beginning of the 1980s were all in or contiguous to the South or Southwestern United States (Christian Science Monitor, 1981). Overall, however, the American population supports the ERA. In 1977, 66.4 percent of the people in a national sample who had heard or read about the ERA said that they either strongly or somewhat favored the amendment. Only 24.1 percent stated that they strongly or somewhat apposed to the ERA (NORC, 1980).

The Equal Rights Amendment simply states that discrimination shall not occur in this country on the basis of sex. The ERA does not demand that women leave the home for the workplace nor does it suggest that they should. It would simply ensure, among other things, that if women choose to work they would not be treated differently on the job than would men. Opposition to equal rights for women is firmly based in the assumptions of natural differences between the sexes. These assumptions are so rooted in our cultural heritage that they are seldom questioned. We would never assume, for example, that because a person is born Italian their proper role in life is to be a priest, or that because a person is born black they should become a bus driver, janitor, or domestic worker. Many of us assume, however, that because a person is born a woman, they should prepare for a life of domesticity and child rearing — or at least take care of most household responsibilities in a dual worker family. These assumptions are powerful because they are often so implicitly accepted and form what has been called a non conscious ideology (Bem and Bem, 1970).

Like the ERA and women's rights, issues surrounding the rights of homosexuals have been very controversial in recent decades. Again, an understanding of both the historical context and the complexity of the moral issues points out that free choice legislation should be supported at the national level.

GAY RIGHTS: MORAL AGREEMENT VERSUS FREEDOM

The tolerance of homosexuality has varied widely in different historical and cultural settings (Bullough, 1976; Ford and Beach, 1951). In ancient Greece, for example, homosexuality was widespread. Homosexual relationships were institutionalized in both the educational and military institutions (Bullough, 1976). The United States, in contrast, has a particularly repressive history in relation to gay rights. Indeed seventeenth-century America denied homosexuals the right to life itself. The death penalty for homosexual behavior was still universal in the colonies in 1776 (although there is no evidence of its ever having been enforced). In 1786 Pennsylvania dropped the death penalty, and slowly these laws were repealed with South Carolina's statute being the last to change in 1873 (Crompton, 1976).

Homosexuality and gay rights cannot be adequately addressed in terms of a dichotomous model. We cannot think of sexual behavior as an either/or decision — gay versus straight. Starting with the early work of Kinsey et al., researchers have suggested that sexual preference instead falls along a continuum (Kinsey et al., 1949; Blumstein and Schwartz, 1977; Bell and Weinberg, 1978).

Similarly, it is unrealistic to think of the gay rights issue as pro- versus anti-gay positions. In particular, moral opposition to homosexuality does *not* mean support of discrimination against homosexuality. It is certainly true that most Americans disapprove of homosexuals relations, and these attitudes vary by factors such as age, region, and education (Nyberg and Alston, 1977). Studies examining attitudes toward the rights of homosexuals (including freedom of speech, the press, and jobs) also indicate that urban residence, higher amounts of education, Jewish or nonreligious states, youth, and residence in Northeast or Pacific states all predict more liberal attitudes regarding gay rights (Irwin and Thompson, 1978).

Despite the wide variation in attitudes about gay rights by social grouping, the striking fact remains that moral opposition to homosexuality does *not* mean opposition to the civil rights of homosexuals. A 1979 Roper survey, with a sample representative of the United States population, asked a question concerning job and housing discrimination against homosexuals. Table IX–B.1 illustrates how the single variable of education affects attitudes on this aspect of gay rights. As education increases both the support for equality increases and the percentage of respondents indicating uncertainty decreases (Virginia Slims, 1980).

Note that even in the group least likely to support gay rights, a much larger percentage feels that legal discrimination is unjust

TABLE IX–B.1
Respondents Supporting Equality or Discrimination toward Homosexuals as a Function of Education
(in percentages)

Position on Discrimination	Amount of Education			
	0–11 Grade	High School Graduate	College	Postgraduate
Support legal equality	49	59	68	74
Legal discrimination is okay	31	27	21	18
Don't know	20	14	11	8

than supports unequal treatment of homosexuals. Clearly a much more complex analysis is necessary to understand the many determinants of gay rights' attitudes. This example simply illustrates how variation in a single factor such as education results in wide variation in the support of gay rights.

Questions from another sample surveys illustrate that the issue is even more complex. A 1970 poll conducted by the Institute for Sex Research found that attitudes about job discrimination varied by profession. Less than 25 percent of the respondents felt that homosexual men should be allowed to be court judges, schoolteachers, or ministers, while approximately 85 percent felt that male homosexuals *should* be allowed to be artists, musicians, or florists. A 1977 Harris poll found similar variation by occupation. Acceptance of homosexuals in jobs varied from 27 percent of gay counselors in a camp for young people through 86 percent approval of gay artists (deBoer, 1978: 272).

As with women's rights, social data and research cannot adjudicate the issue of gay rights. They can, however, point to wide variation in moral positions and attitudes by social groupings and illustrate the complexity of the decisions that are involved. Rather than a choice between right and wrong, gay rights questions involve a number of complicated issues. The debate over abortion in this country involves even more complexity.

PRO-LIFE VERSUS PRO-CHOICE: ANOTHER FALSE DICHOTOMY

There were no abortion statutes in the United States at the beginning of the nineteenth century. Abortions were performed, and few forms of abortion were illegal. In contrast, almost all of the United States had strict antiabortion laws by the year 1900 (Mohr, 1978). The fascinating story of this transition in national policy involves a number of interacting historical forces. Among other things, the rise in the incidence of abortion, the increased publicity afforded abortion, and changes in the types of women having abortions all had an impact upon public opinion and legal doctrine in this country. Public attitudes toward abortion grew more negative in the late nineteenth century as more married, native born, white, Protestant, middle and upper class women began to turn to abortion to control fertility. In addition, the medical profession launched a massive lobbying effort to outlaw abortion, which ultimately proved successful (Mohr, 1978; see also Šauer, 1974). The nineteenth-century American family does not provide us with a golden age of the traditional family in which abortion was unknown. Rather, as with the previous issues an array of historical forces and changes have shaped the ways in which abortion has been socially defined in our country.

A large number of researchers have examined contemporary abortion attitudes. Again, a picture of diversity, complexity, and change emerges. Individual positions on abortion are strongly influenced by a wide variety of social characteristics including region, religious affiliation, race, sex, education, age, religiosity, and occupation (Blake, 1971; Rosen et al., 1974; Blasi et al., 1975; Arney and Trescher, 1976; deBoer, 1978; Tedrow and Mahoney, 1979). Any explanation of why and how a particular individual chooses his or her stance on abortion would involve some combination of these and other factors, but variation by one single social characteristic — education — will again illustrate the diversity of abortion attitudes in this country.

As with the data on homosexual rights presented in Table IX–B.1, we find increased amounts of education increases the percentage of people supporting abortion rights and decreases the percentage who are unsure about their position on abortion legislation. When a national sample is asked whether or not the law making abortion legal should be repealed, 43 percent of those with less than a high school education support repeal, while only 28 percent of those with at least some post-graduate education agree that the law should be repealed. Of the people in the first group 17 percent — contrasted with only 7 percent in the second group — are undecided on the issue. (Data are from a 1979 Roper survey sponsored by Virginia Slims.)

There is clear variation in attitudes between people, but there is also intraindividual variability on the abortion issue. An individual's position on whether or not abortion should be legal depends upon the situation surrounding the pregnancy. There is overwhelming support in this country for legal abortion if there is a strong chance of a serious defect in the baby (80.3 percent), if the mother's health is seriously endangered by the pregnancy (87.7 percent) or if the pregnancy is a result of rape (80.2 percent). Even those persons who are more likely to hold strong moral convictions about abortion, such as Catholics, favor legal abortion in these cases. There is less support for legal abortions in cases where the woman does not want more children, cannot afford to have more children, or is unwed and does not want to marry the man (rates of approval range from 45–50 percent in these cases. (These figures all refer to a 1980 national survey conducted by NORC, the National Opinion Research Center.)

In the section on gay rights it was noted that there is a difference between morally supporting a behavior and legally supporting a behavior. An individual could easily feel that homosexuality is morally wrong yet support free legal choice on the rights of homosexuals. The same is true regarding abortion. One does not need to be pro-abortion (or condone it morally) to be pro-choice. This distinction is made very clear by a survey conducted by the Yankelovich organization for Life Magazine. Of the women surveyed 56 percent believed that having an abortion was morally wrong, yet 67 percent agreed that "those who feel that any woman who wants an abortion should be permitted to obtain it legally" (Life, 1981: 46–47). Only 41 percent of these same women believed that abortion is morally wrong for an unmarried teenager, and 72 percent supported legal abortion in that case (Life, 1981: 49–50). The issue is clearly not a simple case of right and wrong.

The false dichotomy is further intensified in the abortion debate by the use of such terms as pro-life versus pro-choice. The term pro-life is a naive simplification of a number of factors. First of all, abortion opponents are not consistently in favor of life in their attitude structure. Using the 1980 NORC General Social Survey, if we look only at those people who oppose abortion we find that in *all* circumstances they are more likely to favor the death penalty in cases of murder than they are to oppose the death penalty (see Table IX–B.2). This is particularly true in the "soft" cases where there is no threat to the life of the mother or child. (Please note that the population of the United States in general is more in favor of capital punishment in murder cases than it is against. The point here is that pro-life is a misnomer for the group of people who oppose abortion.)

A second way in which a pro- versus anti-life dichotomy oversimplifies the abortion controversy involves the determination of when life actually begins. Any number of points can be chosen to distinguish life from nonlife, including the point of conception

TABLE IX–B.2
Support and Opposition to Capital Punishment in Murder Cases among Those Opposed to Legal Abortion, United States, 1980 (in percentages)

Respondents Are Opposed to Legal Abortions in the Case where	Position on Capital Punishment in Cases of Murder	
	Favor	Oppose
there is a strong chance of defect in the baby	54.3	45.7
the woman's own health is seriously endangered by the pregnancy	56.2	43.8
she became pregnant as a result of rape	57.9	42.1
the family has a low income and cannot afford any children	67	33
she is not married and does not want to marry the man	68.2	31.8
she is married and does not want any more children	68.2	31.1
the woman wants it for any reason	70.4	29.6

(as in the Hyde-Helms bill), the point at which fetal movement is perceived (the quickening doctrine of English common law which was the position taken in early nineteenth century America), and viability outside of the mother's body (as in the Supreme Court decision of 1973). Any of these decisions is relatively arbitrary as even before fertilization the individual sperm and egg cells are living. The decision remains one of moral conviction, and that morality must remain the choice of individuals and families in a country whose social fabric is woven of diverse groups who hold different moral beliefs regarding the conception and inception of human life.

AMERICAN FAMILIES AND FREEDOM OF CHOICE

This brief discussion leaves many questions unanswered and unexplored. There has been no mention, for example, of women and the draft, adoption and parenthood rights by homosexuals, or differential access to abortion services based on income level. Space limitations do not allow adequate coverage of all the problems involved in the three issues.

The coverage here does, however, illustrate the three central points expressed at the outset: (1) A historical understanding of family diversity and variation in attitudes dispels any myth of a peaceful, monolithic, happy, traditional family in the past; (2) wide variation in attitudes on family issues in this country makes impossible the notion that complex issues like women's rights, gay rights, or abortion rights are simple questions of right and wrong which can be legislated for all people at the national level; and (3) data from the social sciences cannot solve our moral dilemmas. These data do increase our understanding of the complexity of social reality, and moral choices, however. All three of these points suggest that attempts to legislate what has been viewed as the traditional family are misdirected. This mythical family does not and never has existed. When the federal government becomes involved in family issues, it should support free choice legislation so that individuals and families can make their own choices on the complex moral issues that they face. The United States is a country of diversity. We must pass on to future generations a culture whose laws, norms, and values cherish and support that diversity in a world of rapid social change.

REFERENCES

ARNEY, W. R. and W. H. TRESCHER (1976) "Trends in attitudes toward abortion, 1972-1975." Family Planning Perspectives 8, 3: 117-124.

BELL, A. P. and M. S. WEINBERG (1978) Homosexualities. New York: Simon & Schuster.

BEM, S. and D. BEM (1970) "Case study of a nonconscious ideology: Training the woman to know her place," in D. Bem [ed.] Beliefs, Attitudes, and Human Affairs. Belmont, CA: Wadsworth Publishing Company.

BLAKE, J. (1971) "Abortion and public opinion: The 1960-1970 decade." Science 171: 540-549.

BLASI, A. J., P. J. MacNEIL and R. O'NEILL "The relationship between abortion attitudes and Catholic religiosity." Social Science 50, 1: 34-39.

BLUMSTEIN, P. W. and P. SCHWARTZ (1977) "Bisexuality: Some social psychological issues." Journal of Social Issues 32, 2: 30-45.

BRUMBERG, J. J. and N. TOMES (forthcoming) Reviews in American History.
BULLOUGH, V. L. (1976) Sexual Variance in Society and History. Chicago: University of Chicago Press.
Christian Science Monitor "Women's Rights Amendment: The days dwindle." July 1: 4.
CROMPTON, L. "Homosexuals and the death penalty in colonial America." Journal of Homosexuality 1, 3: 277–293.
deBOER, C. (1978) "The polls: Attitude toward homosexuality." Public Opinion Quarterly 42, 2: 256–276.
——— (1977a) "The polls: Abortion." Public Opinion Quarterly 4: 553–564.
——— (1977b) "The polls: Women at work." Public Opinion Quarterly 4: 553–564.
DEMOS, J. "Myths and realities in the history of American family life," in H. Gruenbaum and J. Christ [eds.] Contemporary Marriage. Boston: Little, Brown.
The Family Protection Act bill H.R. 311. 1981.
The Family Protection Act bill H.R. 3955. 1981.
The Family Protection Act bill S. 1378. 1981.
The Family Protection Act bill S. 1808. 1979.
FARBER, B. (1972) Guardians of Virtue: Salem Families in 1800. New York: Basic Books.
FORD, C. S. and F. O. BEACH (1951) Patterns of Sexual Behavior. New York: Harper & Row.
GORDON, M. [ed.] (1978) The American Family in Social-Historical Perspective. New York: St. Martin's.
IRWIN, P. and N. L. THOMPSON (1978) "Acceptance of the rights of homosexuals: A social profile." Journal of Homosexuality 3, 2: 107–121.
KAIN, E. L. (1981) "Historical perspectives on women: Work, and marital status in the United States." Presented at the 1981 meetings of the National Council on Family Relations.
KINSEY, A. C., W. B. POMEROY, and C. E. MARTIN, Sexual Behavior in the Human Male. Philadelphia: W.B. Saunders.
LASLETT, P. (1971) The World We Have Lost. New York: Scribner's.
——— and R. WALL [eds.] (1972) Family and Household in Past Time. Cambridge, MA: Cambridge University Press.
Life Magazine (1981) "Abortion: Women speak out, an exclusive poll." November: 45–54.
MASNICK, G. and M. BANE (1980) The Nation's Families: 1960–1990. Boston: Auburn House.
MASON, K. O., J. L. CZAJKE, and S. ARBER (1976) "Change in women's sex-role attitudes, 1964–1974." American Sociological Review 41, 4: 573–596.
McLAUGHLIN, V. (1971) "Patterns of work and family organization: Buffalo's Italian." Journal of Interdisciplinary History II: 299–314.
MEAD, M. (1935) Sex and Temperament in Three Primitive Societies. New York: Morrow.
MOHR, J. C. (1978) Abortion in America. New York: Oxford University Press.
NORC (1980) General Social Surveys, 1972–1980: Calculative Codebook. Chicago: NORC, University of Chicago.
NYBERG, K. L. and J. P. ALSTON (1977) "Analysis of public attitudes toward homosexual behavior." Journal of Homosexuality 2, 2: 99–107.

RABB, T. K. and R. I. ROTBERG [eds.] (1973) The Family in History. New York: Harper & Row.

ROSEN, R. A. H., H. H. WESLEY, J. W. AGE, and F. P. SHEA (1974) "Health professionals' attitudes toward abortion." Public Opinion Quarterly 38, 2: 159–173.

SAUER, R. (1974) "Attitudes to abortion in America, 1800–1973." Population Studies 28, 1: 53–67.

TEDROW, L. M. and E. R. MAHONEY (1979) "Trends in attitudes toward abortion: 1972–1976." Public Opinion Quarterly 43, 2: 181–189.

Virginia Slims (1980) The 1980 Virginia Slims American Women's Opinion Poll, Study 678. The Roper Center.

GOVERNMENTAL CONTROL

Questions

1. *Historically, have Americans favored central government intervention in matters considered private? Do most Americans favor laws that protect the family? What groups are demanding government regulation of sexual and family matters?*

   What role does the separation of church and state play in this controversy?

   Is there such a thing as legislation of morality; or is legislation of family matters simply an interpretation of existing laws within the framework of the U.S. Constitution?

   Are there laws and regulations that clearly contradict each other?

2. *Do welfare policies that guarantee income promote or prevent the stability of poverty families?*

3. *How would you define the "traditional family?" What alternative life-styles have emerged that do not fit this definition? Does the "traditional family" exist?*

4. *What is the Family Protection Act, and what does it hope to accomplish with respect to women's rights, gay rights, and abortion rights?*

5. *What are the objections to the Equal Rights Amendment that are preventing its passage?*

6. *What is the difference between moral opposition to homosexuality and discrimination against homosexuals?*

7. *What is the difference between being "pro-abortion" and "pro-choice"?*

THE LAW AND SEXUALITY

X–A

Certain Forms of Sexuality Should Be Illegal to Protect Individuals and Society

JERRY FALWELL

The legality and illegality of specific sexual acts is currently a very controversial topic. In every era there have been conservative people who held traditional beliefs about the dignity of the family. Based upon the heritage of the Judeo-Christian ethic, they have believed that forms of sexual activity that violate the monogamous male/female relationship are injurious to the health of society and, therefore, should be declared unlawful.

Whereas adultery is now looked upon by many as an "unfortunate disloyalty," it is called an act of sin in the Bible (I Corinthians 6:18). Homosexuality is equally condemned in both the Old and New Testaments (Deuteronomy 23:17; Romans 1:26–28). Incest was prohibited by the Law of Moses (Leviticus 20:11–17) and denounced by the apostle Paul (I Corinthians 5:1–5).

294

BIBLICAL ETHICS VERSUS NATURAL ETHICS

To biblically committed people the ultimate issue in ethics is that of revealed ethics as opposed to natural ethics. Thus, Catholics, Protestants, and Jews acknowledge a common ethic based upon theism (belief in God). The Judeo-Christian theistic ethic finds its basis in the Old and New Testament Scriptures. Cornelius Van Til clarifies this matter stating, "What we mean is that the Old and the New Testaments together contain the special revelation of God to the sinner, without which we could have no true ethical interpretation of life at all" (1974:15).

Likewise, the theist's view of the function of law is based upon the legal-ethical commands of God as revealed to the writers of scripture. Russell Kirk notes that even Plato argued that the achievement of justice could not be gained by following nature (as some sophists had declared); rather, it could be found only by obeying the *nomos* (law).[2] The question is, whose law? Are we to acknowledge the laws of God as revealed in scripture or the general consensus of society?

The maintenance of any society depends upon the conscious commitment to and enforcement of some form of law. The function of law is essential to any society's stability and perpetuity. Jewish and Christian concepts of law go back to the self-revelation of God to man. "Thou shalt not" is the basis of divine law from the opening chapters of the Bible. It is reinforced in the commands of Moses which governed every aspect of Jewish life, and in the teachings of Jesus who urged his followers to "Go ye therefore, and teach all nations, baptizing them . . . teaching them to observe all things whatsoever I have commanded you" (Matthew 28:19–20). Thus, human consent to any matter is irrelevant if it does not bear the sanction of God's approval.

THE LAW OF LOVE

Any discussion of ethics must include an understanding of the relationship of love to the law. The word "ethics" derives from the Greek *ethos,* meaning custom or practice prescribed by law. In

Christian usage it relates to the term *anastrophe,* "manner of life."[3] Thus, Christian ethics go beyond mere outward conduct or behavior to the inner attitudes of men. Jesus, therefore, dealt with lust as the basis of adultery and hatred as the basis of murder (Matthew 5:21–28).

The ethical theologian John Murray observed that "ethics must take into account the dispositional complex of which the overt act is the expression. This is to say, biblical ethics has paramount concern with the heart out of which are the issues of life."[4]

Biblical ethics views not only the actions of individuals as individuals, but individuals in their corporate relationships. Believers are commanded to love (1) God, (2) themselves (3) their spouses, (4) their neighbors, (5) their enemies. Their love is to be expressed beyond the limits of normal human love because they have become the recipients of the love of God.

Human love is distinguished in the Greek language between *eros* (passion or physical/emotional love) and *phileo* (brotherly love). Both of these are limited by the natural responses of others (i.e., we "love" those who love us). By contrast, the New Testament speaks of *agape* as unlimited divine love. It is this love that is the "fruit of the Spirit" (Galatians 5:22) and that springs out of "a pure heart, a clear conscience and genuine faith" (I Timothy 1:5). It is this love that is described in the well-known passage in I Corinthians 13.

Without question love is the fulfillment of the law in biblical teaching (see Romans 13:8–10). However, we must also remember that loving God and our neighbor are themselves commandments. Unfortunately, our contemporary society often overlooks this basic fact. Today we tend to negate biblical commands in the name of "love." Popular expression says: "How can it be wrong, when it feels so good?" Modern ethicists argue that the mutual agreement of consenting adults makes any relationship "right."[5] The vague concept becomes "love makes all things right." Unfortunately, that same mentality is now arguing that incest can be "positive" and even "beneficial" (DeMott, 1980). Recently, the Sex Information and Educational Council of the United States (SIECUS) circulated a paper expressing skepticism regarding "moral and religious pronouncements with respect to incest" (DeMott, 1980).

The opposition that is often assumed to exist between love and commandment overlooks the basic fact the love itself is exercised in obedience to a commandment: "Thou shalt love." Thus, love is neither ultimate nor original. It is dictated by a consideration that is prior to itself. Love is obedience to the commandment of God. Jesus went so far as to say, "If ye love me, keep my commandments" (John 14:15).

LIBERTY AND LIMITS

The Bible clearly teaches the value and significance of sexual fulfilment. Solomon advised young men to be "ravished always with the love of their wives" (Proverbs 5:19), and the Book of Hebrews states "marriage is honorable in all, and the bed undefiled" (Hebrews 13:4). The apostle Paul commands married couples not to "defraud" each other by unnatural abstinence and recommends a healthy and regular sexual relationship to avoid the temptation of adultery (I Corinthians 7:3–5).

At the same time, however, the scripture just as clearly teaches the importance of sexual responsibility. Paul also said, "For this is the will of God, even your sanctification, that ye should abstain from fornication" (I Thessalonians 4:3). Here the English word "fornication" translates the Greek word *porneia* meaning, in classical usage, "sexual sins" (premarital, extramarital and homosexual).[6] The biblical commands against sexual sins are intended to protect the individual from being "defrauded," not merely to prohibit his sexual expression (I Thessalonians 4:6).

That the Bible prescribes limits to the free expression of sex has long been recognized by Catholic, Protestant and Jewish scholars alike.[7] This prohibition is based upon the biblical view of marriage as a permanent covenant by a man and woman who pledge themselves before God to live together as husband and wife (Malachi 2:14). Thus marriage results in the union of two persons into a companionship of oneness (Genesis 2:24). Adultery, by contrast, is the interruption of a "stranger" who violates that covenant (Proverbs 2:17).

Marriage involves two people in a life union. Sex alone is a life-uniting act and does not in and of itself constitute "marriage." Thus the New Testament clearly condemns prostitution because it reduces the dignity of marital unity to selfish physical indulgence. The two people involved may not view their relationship as anything more than an impersonal transaction. Lewis Smedes observes, "There is nothing casual about sex, no matter how casual people are about it" (1976:129). When a couple uses each other in such a manner and attempt to put each other away afterwards, they have in reality done something that was meant to inseparably join them (I Corinithians 6:12–20).

TWO SHALL BECOME ONE

The scripture certainly allows for the single life (Matthew 19:12), but it also emphasizes that "man" (generically) is only complete as male and female. In Genesis 2:24 we are told that in marriage "a man shall leave his father and his mother, and shall cleave to his wife, and they shall become one flesh." They are two and yet they are one. They are two unique and distinct individuals, but they are also a team with a deep commitment to each other.

The three verbs used in Genesis 2:24 indicate the purpose of marriage: leaving, cleaving, becoming one flesh. "Leaving" involves a departure from one's parents and the establishment of the legal union of marriage.[8] "Cleaving" comes from a Hebrew word which means to stick together or glue together. It is a permanent bond between man and woman. "Becoming one flesh" involves a sexual relationship, but it is also a reality which transcends the physical. It is the shared experience of two persons who have experienced the leaving-cleaving-weaving dynamic.

The purpose of sexual relationships within marriage is three-fold: unification, recreation, and procreation. Thus, all of these roles demonstrate the need for marital fidelity in order to build a spiritually and emotionally secure family.[9]

CAN WE LEGISLATE MORALITY?

The penetrating question that is always asked by promoral and antimoral people alike is, Can we legislate morality? I believe the answer is a resounding yes: We have, we are, we can, and we must legislate morality. We have laws against murder, rape, incest, stealing, and disturbing the peace. These laws represent a legislated morality. Someone determined these issues to be moral concerns and made laws to enforce them for the protection of others.

The real issue is *what* morality should we legislate? We all agree that deliberate premeditated murder is wrong. But we do not all agree that abortion is murder. Most of us are absolutely opposed to forcible rape. Why? What if there were a pro-rapist lobby? Should we legalize only that which two adults commonly consent to do together? Does "common consent" make a practice moral?

These are tough questions. Every society must face these kind of issues and determine and answer. Before you answer, ask yourself: what is the *basis* of my moral principles? Do I decide moral issues based on my own personal preference, on the common good of society, or on the absolute statements of inspired scripture?

Those of us who believe that the Bible is in fact the Word of God accept it as authoritative in all matters of morality. For those who accept the Judeo-Christian heritage, adultery, incest and homosexuality are wrong because the Bible says they are wrong. To legalize immorality is to invite the judgment of God. Therefore, these forms of sexuality should be illegal to protect both people themselves and society in general.

NOTES

1. Van Til discusses at length the epistomological presuppositions of theistic ethics arguing that the "objective" morality of the idealist is at bottom as subjective as the "subjective" morality of the pragmatist.

2. See the discussion of Russell Kirk, *The Roots of American Order* (1974: chap. 1). He traces the origin of all American ethical law to the concept of ultimate truth, without which, he argues, there can be no consistent legal system.

3. *Ethos* occurs twelve times in the New Testament and the verb *etho* appears four times. *Anastrophe* is used 13 times and refers to the blessing of the manner of life which is compatible with godliness (*easebeiais*).

4. See this excellent study of the various aspects of biblical ethics by John Murray, *Principles of Conduct* (1964: 13). He observes that the proper study of biblical ethics is not merely an empirical survey of Christian behavior but rather the delineation of an ethical manner of life based upon biblical revelation.

5. Some trace this attitude back to Sigmund Freud's concepts as expressed in his "Three Essays on the Theory of Sexuality," in the *Standard Edition of the Complete Works of Sigmund Freud* (1953 vols. IV and V). For other discussions M. Keeling, *Morals in a Free Society* (1967); E. M. Schur, *Crimes Without Victims* (1965); M. Hunt, *The Natural History of Love* (1959); E. Kennedy, *The New Sexuality* (1972); F.A. Beach, (ed) *Sex and Behavior* (1965).

6. On the Biblical usage of *porneia* and its Hebrew antecedent *zahnah* refering to all types of sexual sins, see the extended discussion in Jay Adams, *Marriage, Divorce and Remarriage* (1980), pp. 51–59. See also πορνια in W.F. Arndt and F.W. Gingrich, *A Greek-English Lexicon of the New Testament* (1951:699).

7. See the extensive verification in Norman Geister, *Ethics: Alternatives and Issues* (1971:196–210); Helmut Thielicke, *The Ethics of Sex* (1960); and Roland Bainton, *What Christianity Says about Sex, Home and Marriage* (1957).

8. See the excellent discussion of the importance of legal marriage in Walter Trobisch, *I Married You* (1971). He especially emphasizes that an unmarried couple may have love and sex, but they lack the security of a legally responsible relationship.

9. See the insightful comments of Paul Vitz, in *Psychology as Religion: the Cult of Self-Worship* (1977: 83–90). He notes the popularity of television programs about large, successful families (*Little House on the Prarie, The Waltons, Eight is Enough,* etc.) as meeting a basic societal need for effective groups and family relations in contrast to a decade of overt selfism.

REFERENCES

ADAMS. J. (1980) Marriage, Divorce and Remarriage. Philadelphia: Presbyterian and Reformed Publishing Co.

ARNDT, W. F. and F. W. Gingrich (1951) A Greek-English Lexicon of the New Testament. Chicago: University of Chicago Press.

BAHNSEN, G. (1978) Homosexuality: A Biblical View. Grand Rapids, MI: Baker Book House.

BAINTON, R. (1957) What Christianity Says about Sex, Home, and Marriage. New York: Association Press.

BEACH, F. A. [ed.] (1965) Sex and Behavior. New York: John Wiley.

DEMOTT, B. (1980) "The pro-incest lobby." Psychology Today (March): 11–16.

FREUD, S. (1953) Standard Edition of the Complete Works of Sigmund Freud. London: Hogarth Press.

GEISTER, N. (1971) Ethics: Alternatives and Issues. Grand Rapids, MI: Zondervan.

HUNT, M. (1959) The Natural History of Love. New York: Knopf.

KEELING, M. (1967) Morals in a Free Society. London: SCM Press.

KENNEDY, E. (1972) The New Sexuality. Garden City, NY: Doubleday.

KIRK, R. (1974) The Roots of American Order. La Salle: Open Court.

LAHAYE, T. (1978) The Unhappy Gays. Wheaton: Tyndale House.

LOVELACE, R. (1978) Homosexuality and the Church. Old Tappan, NJ: Revell.

MURRAY, J. (1964) Principles of Conduct. Grand Rapids, MI: Eerdmans.

SCHAEFFER, F. and C. E. KOOP (1979) Whatever Happened to the Human Race? Old Tappan, NJ: Revell, 1979.

SCHUR. E. M. (1965) Crimes Without Victims. Englewood Cliffs, NJ: Prentice-Hall.

SMEDES, L. (1976) Sex for Christians: The Limits and Liberties of Sexual Living. Grand Rapids, MI: Eerdmans.

THIELICKE. H. (1964) The Ethics of Sex. New York: Harper & Row.

TROTISCH, W. (1971) I Married You. New York: Harper & Row.

VAN TIL, C. (1974) Christian Theistic Ethics. Philadelphia: Presbyterian and Reformed Publishing Co.

VITZ, P. (1977) Psychology as Religion: the Cult of Self-Worship. Grand Rapids, MI: Eerdmans.

WHITE, J. (1978) Eros Defiled: The Christian and Sexual Sin. Downers Grove, IL: Inter-Varsity Press.

Any Form of Sexuality between Consenting Adults Should Be Acceptable and Not the Concern of the Legal System

RUSTUM ROY

MONIST GROUPS IN A PLURALIST AMERICAN SOCIETY

The relationship between the ethical values of a culture and its law is somewhat less problematic in a monist culture (Iran today is an example). It is in pluralist cultures that the tension between the relationship of the culture's most deeply held religious and ethical values and the legal framework within which its citizens must be constrained arises most acutely. What the Moral Majority has

Author's Note: I am greatly indebted to my wife, Della, and our several friends in the Sycamore Community and the Company at Kirkridge who have made these ideas come alive.

recently attempted is to reverse the flow of history and return America to a hitherto unpracticed monism. I will show that this position is thoroughly anti-American and equally anti-Christian. This by itself does not, of course, mean that its position is incorrect; but the stringent monism — "only my view is true, correct, good, or legal" — of the Moral Majority flies in the face of the quintessence of the American experiment.

THE FOCUS ON SEXUAL BEHAVIOR

I will confine my attention to the Moral Majority's positions on sexual laws and sexual ethics not only because I believe that many of the same attitudes may be generalized to other fields, but because it is principally in this area that they have chosen to make their stand. The opening paragraphs of a fund raising letter I received signed by Mr. Jerry Falwell in August, 1981, as evidence the choice of the sex-marriage area as the principal battleground:

Is Our Grand Old Flag Going Down The Drain?

Dear Friend,

I have bad news for you:

The answer to the question above is "YES!"

Our grand old flag is going down the drain. Don't kid yourself. You may wake up some morning and discover that Old Glory is no longer waving freely.

Just look at what's happening here in America:

- Known practicing homosexual teachers have invaded the class-rooms, and the pulpits of our churches.

- Smut pedlars sell their pornographic books — under the protection of the courts!

- And X-rated movies are allowed in almost every community because there is no legal definition of obscenity.

- Meanwhile, right in our own homes the television sreen is full of R-rated movies and sex and violence.

- Believe it or not, we are the first civilized nation in history to legalize abortion — in the late months of pregnancy! Murder!

How long can all this go on?

I repeat: Our grand old flag is going down the drain.

THE ORIGINS OF ETHICS AND CIVIL LAWS

Let us begin by first taking a look at the origin of the human institutions of laws and their relationship to a society or culture's most deeply held religious values. These relationships are represented in a schematic form in Figure X-B.1. This figure shows that all laws originate from a survival value of a tribe, a society, a culture or a nation. Such values are determined or discovered by sheer trial and error. From such experience, it is found that certain behavior patterns are functional and others are dysfunctional.

Now the task before the leadership within an ancient culture (and indeed of the total culture itself) was to support these values with the maximum authority and maximum mechanism of enforcement that would ensure their observance. How this enforcement of behavior patterns is achieved is the story of the iteration between ethics and the law and of the evolution of human societies. More recently it is the story of modern society where such evolution has been drastically affected by the rise of human autonomy fueled by the science and technology revolution.

What the left hand information loop expresses is that in the earliest times the simplest way to achieve the sanction of force and power behind a value was to show its derivation from "divine law." At a time when the power of the transcendent over the daily affairs of human beings was profound — and this was true for the first several millenia of human society right up until the last several hundred years — it was obvious that any desired behavior pattern had to have the force of divine oracular revelation behind it. Observe also that such enforcement patterns prevailed only over relatively small populations in relatively confined geographic areas (e.g., Semitic tribes in the eastern Mediterranean). The first iteration begins within this loop. Even divine laws must be tested against the rock of human experience. Within Western tradition the step function discontinuity occurs with Jesus. Jesus in a magisterial set of oppositions of both precept ("the law says . . . but I say . . . ") and example (healing on the sabbath, eating with unwashed hands, etc.) replaces the Jewish "divine law" by "fulfilling" or "completing" it with the new universal Christian "divine-human law" which in abbreviated form is the imperative of other-centered love.

But the focus of this chapter is the second loop of the diagram. How does one enforce behavior outside the set or monist group

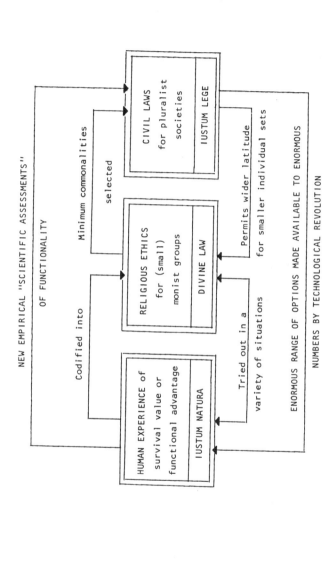

NEW EMPIRICAL "SCIENTIFIC ASSESSMENTS"
OF FUNCTIONALITY

Minimum commonalities
selected

Codified into

CIVIL LAWS
for pluralist
societies

IUSTUM LEGE

RELIGIOUS ETHICS
for (small)
monist groups

DIVINE LAW

HUMAN EXPERIENCE of
survival value or
functional advantage

IUSTUM NATURA

Permits wider latitude
for smaller individual sets

Tried out in a
variety of situations

ENORMOUS RANGE OF OPTIONS MADE AVAILABLE TO ENORMOUS

NUMBERS BY TECHNOLOGICAL REVOLUTION

Figure X-B.1   The Interconnection between Civil Laws, Human Experience Codified as Empirical Science, and Religious Ethics

(tribe) that pays allegiance to one particular religious view? A society that contains more than one tribe then selects a set of behaviors, presumably more or less the common denominator of most of its members, and codifies these into civil laws. Civil law and religious ethics in general have no more complicated a relation than this: The former is the pluralist common denominator of the different monist subunits within the group. Both law and ethics are intended to achieve behaviors that achieve survival and well-being. But Figure X-B.1 makes a most basic point in the arrows that complete the loops from right to left. The ultimate test of all ethical and legal puddings still lies in the eating: in how well they work in human experience. This is not some radically new idea. Martin Luther typifies a long tradition in his comments on these relations; and in the titles to the three boxes I have used two from Luther: instum natura (right by nature) and instum lege (right by law). A commentary by H. Bornkamm on Luther reads as follows

"The state is the natural sphere for the realization of both of these sections of the natural law. . . . "

We must distinguish between this natural law and what Luther calls natural justice (Recht). The latter is not a system of rules or of an established jurisprudence, nor is it even patent to all; but it is the sum total of the vital rights *that have developed from human intercourse and associations.* . . . For this reason Luther translates the ancient antithesis instum natura and instum lege (that which is right by nature and that which is right by law), with sound and ailing law. "For what is done *in conformity with nature* proceeds well even without all laws, perhaps even in violation of all laws." By natural justice Luther, therefore, means the unwritten measures *demanded and suggested by a given situation* [1958: 248; emphasis added].

For Luther the middle box, the new (Christian) law of God, was straight out of the Gospel "Love God, and your neighbor as yourself," as well as "Therefore all things whatsoever you would that men should do to you, do ye even so to them." What is enormously significant in this context is the use of human experience (intercourse and associations) and explicitly including the *situational determinism* in deciding not only legality but goodness. For this latitudinarism is essential not only in a pluralist American society, but even more so now in an increasingly heterogeneous "one world" being realized by the technological revolution.

TECHNOLOGY: CREATOR OF
THE SUPERPLURALIST DILEMMA

The moralistic right wing has misidentified its enemy. Tim LaHaye in "The Battle for the Mind" laid the groundwork for defining the enemy as "secular humanists." He is wrong simply because they have been around a long time — American history simply reeks of the stuff. It is the *technological revolution* that has given two new dimensions to pluralism which has caused the mild cultural panic on which the moralistic right has successfully capitalized. Science-based technology (SbT) has no inherent values. This is a theme I have developed extensively in my Hibbert Lectures, "Experimenting with Truth" (Roy, 1980). But by making "social intercourse" possible on an undreamed of scale of extent and depth, SbT has forced an intermixing of monist societies. Hence, it has widened the range of units which must for some purposes be governed by the same civil laws (e.g., Hindu and Buddhist minorities in the United States). Second, it has made new opportunities (new situations) available on a radically new scale. Take as the statistically most important example in our present context the availability of contraceptive devices. Or consider some others: When *Fanny Hill* was first published 300 years ago, it was available literally to only hundreds of the elite of society. When it was republished in the sixties and seventies, it probably sold in the tens of millions. X-rated movies swamp all other kinds in Rome's deregulated TV world, literally invading the monist Vatican.

These factors in the creation of superpluralist one world — shown in the bottom of the large loop closure — have in fact given rise to the dominance of the latter over the smaller loops. In a universal sense we will need the broadest set of civil laws that are self-consistent with human experience. Hardly does this relegate the role of religion to a lesser role. In "Experimenting with Truth" I have, indeed, made the opposite point: In that the best and broadest religious values (first small loop) already express the best of human experience (i.e., they embody the results of social-scientific experiments), it will be those that will provide the most important guidelines for human behavior. Our science-based technology needs the hegemony of a religious (holistic in time and space) worldview, but one which in Luther's terms "conforms with nature."

SCIENCE-BASED THEORETICAL CRITIQUE OF LEGALISM

The scientific revolution also has exposed a fundamental defect in all legalisms. All nonstatistical laws have this serious defect: The very fact of their codification flies in the face of the inherent nature of the universe. This nature, much to the discomfiture of all legalists, now has the sanction of modern science and technology as its basic support. The statistical nature of truth, the noncausal fundament of reality at the subatomic level, the basic element of chance which is the warp of life as much as human collective and social will is its woof, is the cause of the mismatch of any legal system and its manifestation or observance in society. What I am saying is that all laws are designed for a mythical average person, and the very existence of a precise written law violates to some extent the very desired canon of behaviors it seeks to enforce for the simple and fundamental reason that human beings are not identical. Hence what is right for one may be to a greater or lesser degree wrong for the other.

Let us return to the figure. The feedback established between rigid laws and a permitted range of behavior slowly leads to the modification of those laws, but the laws are connected in a loose sort of way to particular ethics. Now while laws may be changed by legislatures and other societal devices, it is not quite as simple to get the self-appointed committees and religious presidential commissions to act with the same speed and in the same direction in issuing revised creeds or manifestos or whatever. Moreover, biblical literalists among Jews and Christians would appear to be stuck with biblical text. As will be seen however, as there is little that is relevant or consistent in biblical sexual ethics this need not prove to be a limitation. Yet it is the source of the problem for all religious groups where it is assumed that the canon is closed, that all truth has been revealed once and for all. An inevitable clash is therefore established between the *evolutionary nature of reality* and human society (especially under the push of SbT) and the *fixed nature* of the once-and-for-all *"divine laws."* In terms of our figure the information loop is broken. Such a situation is not rare; in fact, the too-rapid growth of SbT has made it a commonplace.

For the vast majority of the cultures existing in the world today, this unresolved tension between behavior of the masses and traditional religious ethics is a description of the real situation. Such cultures have an ethical pattern deriving from religious values and which has in the past formed the only direct connection with the real forces achieving behavior control through the society's civil laws. Now behavior has changed and with it certain civil laws. Therefore the conflict that now exists between the laws of the state and the religious ethical values has simply been swept under the rug or ignored. Such a situation is often intolerable, and occasionally bursts of cultural disintegration occur as a result of this intrinsic tension. By far the most dramatic of these is, of course, the situation in Iran today. Iran, however, is perhaps only the most extreme version of the tension being felt in many parts of the Islamic world where a highly legalistic culture is being forced to come to terms with the rapid evolution of a technologically dominated world culture. The Moral "Majority" and its religious and political efforts can therefore be seen as America's own attempt to resolve this internal conflict by the *minority* attempting to continue making simplistic connections between Bible and behavior.

THE AMERICAN EXPERIMENT: UNIQUE ANOMALY OR WORLD PARADIGM?

It could well be argued that the United States stands as an example of a country or a nation without a theoretical basis in deeper values. If a culture is defined by its unique set of religious beliefs, its language, its food, its clothing, and above all by its highest values, then the very existence of a plural set of values would lead to a contradiction in terms. How can one culture affirm simultaneously not only differences in food and clothing and language but also differences in the highest values in its religious and ethical traditions? This fundamental contradiction is at the heart of the American experiment. This is, of course, well known. But is was the very basis on which the United States, with its federal structure, attempted to reconcile a plurality of values[1] within a singular political framework. When William Penn and his

Quakers escaped the monism of the Church of England or Roger Williams came with his Baptists for the same reason, or Lord Baltimore set up a Catholic enclave, it was all in the effort to get away from the conflict between their religious values and the monist values of the religious clash from which they had come. In the United States the federal structure permitted a certain latitude of viewpoints with respect to peripheral societal and legal values but it avoided the fundamental question as to *how wide a latitude* of conflicting values could be protected and given rights within the political structure. Yet the evolution of the new worldwide culture dominated by the impact of science and technology as a homogenizing force has proven that the basic question inherent in the American experiment was merely the harbinger of what was to come on a world scale. Its resolution is essential for the survival of the new one-world culture. In the *"ancien regime"* it was possible for different cultures to maintain their distinct value structures mainly because of the lack of interaction, commerce, and contact among them. Today the technological monster has put us in a melting pot with such an intense degree of communication — instantaneous 3-D and color transmission of television signals from any point on the globe to any other, of such an intermixture of food and dress so that the number of foreign restaurants in any American city has grown explosively and Indian fabrics and dress styles are adopted by American youth, and so on. The world today has become a macroscopic version of the America of the late eighteenth century. What sexual laws will be adequate and appropriate for such a world culture, recognizing that subsets along national or sectarian lines may choose more stringent restrictions consistent with the larger whole?

SEXUAL VALUES, ETHICS, AND THE LAW

In the above section we have attempted to set into context the more general framework within which our question regarding sexual values and the law should be asked. With respect to the derivation of sexual laws made by the state, we will first show that these have only in the vaguest way been derived from the Judeo-Christian ethic made explicit in the biblical record. Let us first look at a short summary of the kind of categories of sexual laws or values that may be found in the Bible: (1) laws regarding marriage, and (2) laws regarding sexual behavior. I will treat each of these in turn.

BIBLICAL LAWS REGARDING MARRIAGE AND DIVORCE

Mainstream Christian (and Jewish) societies have derived their behavior codes by the complex iterative processes described in the preceding sections by a combination of nonliteral interpretations of the Bible, the experience of the Church through the ages, and the experience of the community. But all those who look for their values in the Bible alone with even a modicum of honesty and objectivity must end up terribly confused by the literal record of the Bible on marriage and divorce. The confusion is so profound that only those who wish to use the Bible as a single source of laws need really come to terms with it. Let us address the question of monogamy or, more accurately, monogyny which became the apparent cultural norm of American society *allegedly* based on the Bible. What does the biblical record say about monogamy? The Old Testament, of course, is not committed to monogamy in any way whatsoever. There are no explicit laws on monogamy; and surely the great lawmakers, the detailed lawmakers of Judaism, would not have left such a major issue open had they been concerned with the enforcement of monogamy. From the polygamous record of the founders of Judaism: — Abraham and Moses to Solomon and David, — we can hardly conclude that monogamy is either the only way or even the best way for the structure of sexual relations or family life. The New Testament clearly contains no injunctions for monogamy or against polygamy. In Titus 1:6, the very fact that Paul says one should search out people who have been married only once to serve as elders implies that many others had been married more than once within the Christian fold and by no means are these latter either criticized or cut off from the community.

At one stroke, therefore, we have demolished the belief that American marriage laws 3000 years later have been based on biblical values. Indeed, the conflict of the United States with the Mormons over polygamy arose precisely on this point. Should the biblically *permitted* polygamy and polyandry be allowed within the

American legal system? The answer arrived at in the case of the Mormon issue was "No!" Here is a strange turnabout indeed, where the Bible is more permissive than law. It is in my view one of the greatest errors made in social arrangements in the entire American cultural revolution. I am convinced that a healthy family structure and the very institution of marriage itself will be enormously strengthened by permitting at least oligogamy and oligoandry. (These two terms are meant to imply a subset of polygamy and polyandry where the numbers of spouses are small, presumably a number between two and four or five spouses or contractually related intimate partners.) Such expanded families being permitted and affirmed by culture would, in my view, be much more suitable as a societal development today than the rigid enforcement and affirmation of monogamy as the only way. The empirical record of the postwar years in the United States shows that monogamy as the only way is only with the greatest difficulty compatible with a culture so deeply committed to mobility, freedom, preservation of individual growth, and so on.

But the troubles for the biblical literalists looking for guidance on marriage have hardly begun. Just as much as the fundamental teaching of the Old Testament permissiveness with regard to number of spouses is violated by the American law, on the other side of the coin its basic permission of divorce flies in the face of explicit New Testament teachings.[2] Here the conflict is between the New and the Old Testament: The Old Testament permits divorce under certain boundary conditions whereas Jesus explicitly denies the need for divorce and remarriage. Of all the rubbish that has been written by religious apologists and hack theologians not one has faced up to the simple facts of this iteration between human experience and what is called religious ethics. As society demanded divorce in the great ethical-legal battle of the last century, religious ethics has quietly evolved to the position where no church (with a minor exception of the minority group of powerful Catholic *leadership*) any longer opposes the ethical sanction of divorce for incompatibility. Thus wisdom is brought to our highest values partly from the human experience. The Moral Majority will have to stand firmly against divorce and remarriage basing it on *New* Testament injunctions if it has to maintain a consistent position.

BIBLICAL LAW REGARDING INDIVIDUAL
SEXUAL BEHAVIOR

The Bible says not one word anywhere about masturbation: not one word. It is universally conceded that the so-called sin of Onan, caught spilling his semen on the ground, was misread as an injunction against masturbation. Interestingly enough this "sin" which so exercised the Church and continues to keep confessional booths filled is not receiving any attention from the Catholic or Protestant right today.

The troubles for literalists multiply as we move to a second category — sexual behavior for and among consenting adults. The biblical record is very explicit in the Old Testament and very divided in the New. Explicit injunctions against certain kinds of sexual activities exist only in the Old Testament (Leviticus 18, Deuteronomy 14, etc.). For instance, intercourse between certain blood relations and intercourse with animals is forbidden. Not only is homosexuality forbidden but it (along with adultery) is punishable by death. No one in the Moral Majority has, too my knowledge, advocated a biblical standard on these matters!! In the New Testament, *Jesus it totally silent on such matters.* The *gospels* contain not a single word of advice or sexual behavior. If anything Jesus, the great situational ethicist, is often regarded as overly permissive. Not only did he break with Jewish tradition at every point in his personal, free, friendly relationships with women but by extending this friendship to persons such as Mary Magdalene and the "wine bibbers and tax collectors" he put himself in a radical stance vis-à-vis Jewish law on relational and sexual matters. Jesus never said one word about homosexuality or abortion. His only comment on adultery was to violate Old Testament law (by not consenting to the stoning) thus being vastly more permissive than the legalists of his day.

But it is not only in Jesus that we see human experience as allowed — in a situational way — to modify the law. The story of Onan is, in fact, a very important one for a view of Old Testament marital-sexual ethics. The sin committed by Onan was, of course, not masturbation as noted above. Onan's sin was that he did not obey the Jewish law which demanded that he "commit adultery" with his deceased brother's wife. The Jewish law demands that if a man dies childless that the next youngest brother should have intercourse with the deceased man's wife, in order that his blood line may continue. Is not this a situational violation of one of the Ten Commandments? It is not spelled out for how long this should continue and for how many children. But it is certainly true that in many such expanded-family societies this practice was widely prevalent. In Hindu society as well as in early Jewish society such widows were more or less incorporated into a joint family and their sexual and childbearing needs met by the husband's brothers.

It is precisely within this humane, experiential, and situation-responsive context that we can set a later Christian interpretation of marriage and sexual patterns. In a striking passage reprinted below, Luther, writing on the "Estate of Marriage" (1962: 13), provides the most extraordinarily specific advice—*advising* regular "adultery" within a marriage and placing the preservation of marriage above the proscription of "adultery."[3]

> I once wrote down some advice concerning such persons for those who hear confession.[2] It related to those cases where a husband or wife comes and wants to learn what he should do: his spouse is unable to fulfil the conjugal duty, yet he cannot get along without it because he finds that God's ordinance to multiply is still in force within him.

> What I said was this: if a woman who is fit for marriage has a husband who is not, and she is unable openly to take unto herself another-and unwilling, too, to do anything dishonorable-since the pope in such a case demands without cause abundant testimony and evidence, she should say to her husband, "Look, my dear husband, you are unable to fulfil your conjugal duty toward me; you have cheated me out of my maidenhood and even imperiled my honor and my soul's salvation; in the sight of God there is no real marriage between us. Grant me the privilege of contracting a secret marriage with your brother or closest relative, and you retain the title of husband so that your property will not fall to strangers. Consent to being betrayed voluntarily by me, as you have betrayed me without my consent."

> I stated further that the husband is obligated to consent to such an arrangement and thus to provide for her the conjugal duty and children, and that if he refuses to do so she should secretly flee from him to some other country and there contract a marriage. I gave this advice at a time when I was still timid.

ORIGINS OF THE NEW MORALISTIC
RIGHT POSITIONS

We are therefore left with a quandary. We have shown beyond argumentation that the Bible is not the source of the Moral Majority's alleged marital and sexual values. Where, then, did they come from? In order to answer that question, we must first take a quick look at the kinds of sexual values the Moral Majority espouses.

The letter quoted at the beginning of the article clearly identifies the following major areas of concern:

(1)   Nudity, sexual stimulation, sexual pleasure (in part, pornography);
(2)   homosexuality;
(3)   abortion.

Obviously this set has no connection with biblical specifics which are, as we have seen, a very uncertain trumpet on sexual and marital ethics. The origin of this mixed bag must lie elsewhere.

NATIONALISM, NOT MORALITY, AS THE
ENERGIZING FORCE

The clue to the origin was present in the letterhead of the stationery that had been used for the letter quoted at the beginning. Prominently displayed was the U.S. flag: Note that the appeal starts with the question "Is the *flag* (*not* the gospel) going down the drain?" Martin Marty writing recently on "Ethics and the new Christian Right" spots this but fails to emphasize it:

> Moralism, labeled "Puritanism" in North America and dismissed by H.L. Mencken and his followers as the haunting fear that someone somewhere might be having a good time, was enhanced when Americans separated church and state. No longer "established," the churches nevertheless remained tax-exempt; and they needed to defend the largesse they received by demonstrating their value to the republic. *They had to proclaim their moral contribution to the good society because they could not appeal to the rightness of their doctrine* [1981; emphasis added].

The appeal of the New American Right draws its strength from the perception of the general U.S. population that something is very wrong in America. The accident of history by which the United States had a uniquely powerful position after WWII has devolved to the rapidly worsening economic and political situation of the 1980s. The downward readjustment relative to the USSR, Western Europe, and Japan in power and economic privilege has never been interpreted to the American public as a desirable, unavoidable, and necessary good. Martin Marty missed the boat in the analysis of his own data. This group can surely not be labelled accurately as the New *Christian* Right for it is the New *American* Right (NAR). Here again compare Marty's analysis of what the NAR stands for and what it stands against.

> As moderates and liberals came to advocate the social gospel or other systemic approaches, the conservatives retreated advocating "virtues" against "vices." No matter what society did, an individual citizen or believer had control over his or her own good actions. The individual could "take the pledge," *stop using profane language, refrain from gambling, stay away from prostitutes*. The church, however, dared not work for peace. Seeing history as a series of cosmic battles with the militant church at their center, the New Christian Right has disdained pacifists and looked suspiciously at peacemakers. *Descended from a long line of hawks, in any tendency toward national crisis it chooses the military way.* [1981; emphasis added].

The result is now evident. The driving force which creates and sustains the NAR is the national military crisis it perceives for its beloved America. To proclaim and prove its value to society in its desire to regain Military preeminence and economic superiority, the NAR now tries to enlist "appropriate morals and ethics." Observe how downright laughable they are: stop swearing, gambling, and womanizing. Unwilling to indict the social failures of a beloved America, they turn to find the scapegoat within the nation and purify themselves not by genuine repentance but by ritual washing. When railing against the failure of their nation, the Jewish prophets talked exclusively about the great social problems: "Let justice role down like waters," not "Don't visit prostitutes."

But the focus on sexual morality as the cognate of military failure has some deeper psychological root. Dr. Strangelove and his concern for his "vital juices" before nuclear bombing is not so strange. Barbara Tuchman, commenting some years ago in a newspaper interview on the possible connection of maleness to war-making made the point that male sexuality as always a "test" of erection, of penetration, of arousing the woman, of inseminating her. It therefore becomes the personal analogue of the archetypal struggle in the world for dominance. This, I think, is the correct analysis of the interest in sexual morality by the New American Right. America's power will be "restored" again only if we preserve our "vital juices" which are threatened by the new aberrant permissive sexual behavior, especially by nudity, pornography, homosexuality, and legalized abortion. These were not permitted when America was strong. They are all leaking away America's "vital juices." Ergo, eliminate them and America will be strong again.

There you have it. The sexual morality of the New American Right comes not from the Bible but from Strangelove. In terms of Figure X-13.1 it is in fact an attempt to define the divine law by the civil law. (It is reversing the bottom arrow of the right hand loop, narrowing the range of permitted behaviors.) That the entire NAR phenonemon has its origins in the military posture and in violence has been dealt with in detail by Prescott to whose work I now turn.

VIOLENCE AND SEXUAL PATTERNS

The brilliant work by James W. Prescott (1975, 1976, 1978) has made all the connections I allude to and has discussed them in great detail. Prescott, a neurophysiologist of the National Institute of Child Health and Human Development and one of the pioneers in the rocking treatment of autistic children, has written extensively on his research which makes several valuable points:

(1)   Frequent bodily touch, and fondling and especially rocking of children by parents is very important in healthy psychic and emotional development. There is extensive clinical but also biological evidence for these effects.

(2)   Some (much!) violence in personality development in our society is as a result of deprivation of physical pleasure: touch, massage, rocking.

(3)   The antipleasure (especially sexual pleasure) syndrome of social and political responses is the label or cover that hides the

proviolence, pro-death-penalty, promilitary aggrandizement of certain political subgroups.

Prescott's studies which range from the most sophisticated brain biology to anthropology of ancient cultures (correlating their toleration of abortion with other traits) to political analysis of federal and Pennsylvania legislatures form a landmark in the field. His analysis of the social practices of abortion-practicing tribal cultures against those that do not permit abortion clearly showed a strong correlation between the cultures that forbid it and those that (1) kill, torture, and multilate enemies captured in war; (2) practice slavery; and (3) are patrilineal. His analysis of the voting patterns in 1974 in the U.S. Senate showed "highly significant statistical relationships between voting against abortion and voting to continue supporting the war in Vietnam, supporting no-knock laws and opposing handgun control legislation." Mencken was right at a profounder level than he knew. There is a substantial minority of persons in the United States *who have never figured out the place of pleasure in their own lives and cannot tolerate others having much of it.*[4]

The parallels Prescott draws of correlation between behaviors in primitive societies and in the U.S. Senate strongly support my earlier point that we are dealing in the New American Right phenomenon with *a political group (civil law) trying to change "religious laws"* (in Figure X-13.1) and not vice versa. Jerry Falwell is a political creation of Ronald Reagan's ascendancy and not vice versa. Both are the result of the climate of America's last hurrah for the entrepreneurial capitalist resistance to a much more egalistarian division of wealth and power.

CAN CHRISTIANS HELP FORMULATE LAWS AND MORALS FOR AMERICA'S NEED?

In a recent article R. H. Bube, editor of the Journal of the American Scientific Affiliation, a journal serving conservative Christians with scientific backgrounds, wrote directly on the topic at hand. Typical of his sound scholarship and measured approach Bube put it thus:

There are two types of question that might be asked: (1) If Christians were in the majority, should they impose their moral values upon minority non-Christians through the legal system? (2) Since Christians are in the minority, what specific approaches does life in a pluralistic society require?

Even if Christians were in the majority, it would clearly be inappropriate to attempt to legislate in matters of personal belief. It is just as inappropriate for non-Christians in the majority to attempt to legislate in matters of personal belief. *Acceptance of beliefs*, if they are to have any value, *must not be coerced*. For Christians in the minority to attempt to legislate beliefs is not only inappropriate but also foolhardy, for it gives approval to all other conflicting minorities to proceed in the same way

In establishing legal requirements in a pluralistic society, no group can be allowed to make its beliefs into law, so that dissent becomes crime. *Laws must be guided by the consensus on the effect of actions on society*, and not on particular belief or religious systems. *Such laws must be permissive and not restrictive in form*; those things that are not allowed to certain individuals because of their belief system must not be arbitrarily imposed upon them by law. Such conclusions, however, do not contradict the basic conviction that Christians will have insights in those requirement that should be incorporated into human law because of the needs of society, since it is exactly these needs which are the concern of divine law [1981; emphasis added].

I believe that just in these times of utter confusion in societal values, the formation of good civil laws needs the inspired insight and the wisdom of human experience present in the Christian (and other religious) weltanschauung. I have discussed above how the new physics has illuminated our understanding of the statistical nature of much reality and truth. This forms a new theoretical base for situation ethics.

In earlier paragraphs, I stated that Jesus was the great situation ethicist. In a classic work by Prof. Paul Ramsey called "Basic Christian Ethics" he makes the detailed case of how Jesus explicitly and purposively broke the Jewish laws with regard to eating of the show bread, with regard to his disciples plucking corn off the fields, with regard to healing on the Sabbath, and so on. He obviously did this for a purpose to illustrate a higher good; namely, that human need transcends the legal framework and when the two conflict then human need must be our guide. This argument has never been refuted since presented by Ramsey in 1956. But the conflict between the Moral Majority and Jesus is much deeper than that. It is, of course, a conflict in attitude of not only rendering not unto Caesar but of elevating trivial issues to a central position — this is, of course, the great heresy. Jesus' single ethical value was "operationalized love" (which translates into actively seeking to know what is good for the other and actively expending time, energy, and money to bring out or work for that good for the other). That is my modern translation of the commandment "to love God and your neighbor as yourself."[5]

What, then, have I been able to establish so far? That there is absolutely not the slightest vestige of connection between the positions on sexual ethics taken by the Moral Majority and any self-consistent sexual marital ethic that could be derived from the Bible. I have shown further indeed that there is no such thing as a Christian sexual ethic. I repeat that. In our book "Honest Sex," my wife and I went to some pains to show that no single sexual behavior pattern could be found as the value structure that is advocated for all Christians. While this may be at first rather surprising, a moment's reflection by analogy will show that indeed it is true. Let us take the analogy of the dietary laws. In Judaism the dietary laws were strict. In Christianity such biblically explicit laws were explicitly voided. How come? A radical "permissiveness" was introduced into the Christian dietary habits with Paul saying that *all things* are edible[6] (although adding with Paul also that not necessarily do all things edify). The identical radical permissiveness extends to sexual behavior among consenting adults. Everything is allowed that other-centered love allows: Everything is forbidden that other-centered love forbids.

Dietary laws have been gradually rendered unnecessary as a requirement for human health since it is not necessary to be quite as careful about shellfish or about pork and the trichinosis it may carry. The autonomy of individuals in society has been increased. Just so, some of the sexual laws that at one time were written largely to protect the property issue via unwanted children have also become unnecessary. Observe the great deal of energy that was expended over the last few hundred years on the proscription of masturbation. All of this is now seen as unnecessary, as it was totally falsely ascribed to scripture. In a very similar way the twisting of scripture now being undertaken on behalf of the new positions regarding abortion and homosexuality will prove to be unrelated to Biblical ethics. Abortion is not mentioned in the Bible; and were it so potent an evil as the New American Right makes out, the indictment of the stupidity of the Church would be complete. How is it that dozens of Popes said nary a word on it? How is it that possibly the greatest theologian, Thomas Aquinas, explicitly said it was all right roughly in the first trimester? No, as I have been at pains to point out, these are not ethical concerns with political impact but rather a religious veneer on a political issue. They are, however, minor perturbations on the dangerous human road to autonomy. That great myth of the Garden of Eden — which always exists, even if it never actually happened — has told us of our human peril, increased freedom through knowledge without increased guidance from love.

So sexual ethics stands today on the very edge of a truly Augustinian release from rule. "Love God and then do as you please," Augustine said. The details of sexual behavior are by now surely autonomous from Christian ethics. This does not mean that Christian insight has nothing to offer to guide human behavior. First, violence (coercion of another) is the great universal proscription. (That is, of course, why rape is so vile; why sexual intercourse between a victimized younger person by another older one can be a sin; likewise the presence of coercion in homosexuality would make it wrong.) Second, genuine concern (love) for *all* others requires an attention and possible self-restraint rarely achieved. Third, an honesty and integrity in all contractual relations is necessary to the fabric of society and personality.

But a truly Christian sexual ethic in America today would be more pro-active and less re-active. It would stand for actively discussing the fresh incorporation of body into the newly made-holy whole of body-mind-spirit. These are some ethics and laws that could be worked on:

(1)   Affirming the healthy role for nudity (after all the nudist movement in England a century ago was led by clerics) in a culture totally schizophrenic about its own bodies — using partial-nudity in every possible venue to sell products, yet wanting to attach fig leaves to nude statues! Affirming the value — found in many Eastern cultures — of touch and massage.

(2) Affirming the finding that human experience (and the biblical record) supports the idea that alternatives to the *nuclear family could be very valuable in reconstituting healthy family life and a healthy environment for rearing children. This would require both moral and legal support for polyandry and polygamy of a kind.*

(3) Affirming the possibility that sexual pleasure under specific controled conditions could be the vehicle for deep mystical religious experiences (which up to now only minor Eastern sects have dared to say). This again would support the permission of such "experimentation with truth."

The difficulty that exists for Christians in making a contribution to future-oriented sexual *laws*, is that there has been so little writing of future-oriented Christian *ethics* on sex and marriage. The New American Right presents nostalgic eightieth- to ninetieth-century views. The mainstream church is standing pat, increasingly becoming part of the problem rather than the solution. Since our book *Honest Sex* appeared in 1968, only one other — James B. Nelson's *Embodiment*— can be called a Christian theology of sex for the present and future. This is clearly the place for Christians to begin. Do they have anything to add to a *contemporary* understanding of sex *ethics* in our world; if so, they can help with sex laws.

NOTES

1. However, it must be noted that this pluralism only encompassed *by today's standards* a very narrow "bandwidth." America's manifest destiny was to be a Protestant (hence plural) Christian country. When I came to the United States in 1945, I experienced it exactly as that — a fervently religious but pluralistically protestant and hence highly tolerant culture.

2. The case of Anita Bryant is a poignant reminder that explicit flagrant violation of a biblical injunction can be conducted in public, all the while proclaiming the supremacy of peripheral biblical values for others!

3. One of the most important tasks is to remove the stigma of the word "adultery" from relations between loving consenting adults where no other contracts are violated. We coined the term "co-maritial" sexuality in our earlier book (1968).

4. That this is not ancient history is evident in the fact that on April 3, 1973, Representative Mullen in the Pennslyvania House of Representatives, introduced as an amendment to a bill on cave-protection (!) a measure to make adultery and fornication (including *all* premarital sex) illegal because "it is against the law of

God. I think all of us believe in God." Many bills in the federal and state legislature in the 1981 sessions echo these sentiments.

5. In his concern for the neighbor throughout the New Testament Jesus neglects sexual matters and focuses on the poor and down-trodden, showing that his main ethical concern is for the eradication of poverty and the institution of justice wherever possible. His parables, his actions, his own life-style all bear witness to an identification with the poor and a deep and abiding concern for justice. It is therefore possible to examine whether, in fact, the Moral Majority takes its ethics and value structure from Jesus. We find virtually no injunction in any literature of the Moral Majority suggesting a simple life-style, a minimization of the cupidity that characterizes the American society supporting the Moral Majority. We find virtually no references to money except "send money to support us." We find no references to the poor while Jesus continually speaks of the poor. We find in life-style that its leaders do not live the simple life-style of the Jesuit priests in Nicaragua or of Dorothy Day in New York City or the great Protestant missionary enterprise in many parts of this country and the world. So here again we find that a virtual 100 percent anti-Jesus, anti-Christian position is taken by the moral majority.

6. The Cornelius story in Acts X is explicitly there to void the dietary laws. The Pauline statement about freely choosing to not eat meat "if meat caused my brother to stumble" is the operation of Christian love in the presence of a community of people of different values.

REFERENCES

BUBE, R. H. (1981) "Crime, punishment and responsibility." Journal of the American Scientific Affiliation 33, 105.
BORNKAMM, H. (1958) Luther's World of Though. St. Louis, MO: Concordia.
LUTHER, M. (1962) Luther's Works, vol. 45 (W. I. Brandt, ed.). Philadelphia: Muhlenberg Press.
MARTY, M (1981) "Ethics and the New Christian Right." Hastings Report 11, 14.
PRESCOTT, J. W. (1978) "Abortion and the 'right to life': Facts, fallacies and fraud — parts 1 and 2." The Humanist 18 (July/August).
——— (1976) "Violence, pleasure and religion." Bulletin of Atomic Scientists 32, 62.
——— (1975) "Body pleasure and the origins of violence." The Futurist 9, 64.
RAMSEY, P. (1953) Basic Christian Ethics. New York: Scribner.
ROY, R. (1980) Experimenting with Truth. Elmsford, NY: Pergamon
——— and D. M. ROY (1968) Honest Sex. New York: New American Library.

THE LAW AND SEXUALITY

Questions

1. *Why are nonmonogamous acts viewed as harmful to the health of society?*
2. *Should the general consensus of society dominate or form the basis of civil law?*
3. *Does or should the mutual consent of adults make any form of relationship or act right?*
4. *Can morality be legislated? Whose morality should dominate?*
5. *Does technology cause the development of sexual laws that do not reflect the evolutionary nature of reality and divine laws?*
6. *Is American civil law more restrictive than biblical law?*
7. *Should federal law prohibit adultery and premarital sex because it is against the "will of God"?*
8. *Is the Moral Majority a religious group trying to change civil law or a political group trying to change biblical law?*
9. *Were original religious laws regarding monogomy primarily designed as a method of protecting inheritance rights?*

ABOUT THE AUTHORS

TOM BETHELL, a graduate of Oxford University, has had a varied and distinguished career in journalism. After having worked as a reporter for the *Vieux Carré Courier* In New Orleans, he became Editor of *New Orleans Magazine*. The following year he moved to Washington, D.C., and joined the staff of the *Washington Monthly* as an editor. In 1977 he was made Washington Editor of *Harper's* magazine, for which he has continued to write. He also became Washington Editor for the *American Spectator*. Some of his articles have won national awards, notably a 1979 article in *Harper's* about the federal budget that won first prize in the John Hancock Awards and an honorable mention in the Gerald Loeb Award. In the same year he won first prize in the Amos Tuck Award for an article on the energy crisis. In 1981 Bethell held the position of writer-in-residence at the *Los Angeles Herald Examiner*, and later that year was appointed to the DeWitt Wallace Chair of Communications at the American Enterprise Institute in Washington, D.C. In 1984, he continues with *Harper's* as a contributing editor and as Washington Editor of the *American Spectator*. Bethell, a Roman Catholic, was born and raised in England.

W. PETER BLITCHINGTON received his Ph.D. in psychology from Georgia State University in 1975. From 1976 to 1982 he was an Assistant, then Associate, Professor of Educational and Counseling Psychology at Andrews University. In 1982, he accepted the position of Assistant Director of Behavioral Sciences for the Family Practice Residency at Florida Hospital in Orlando, Florida. Dr. Blitchington has written several books and has published articles in such journals as the *Journal of Clinical Psychology*, *Educational and Psychological Measurements*, *Personnel Psychology*, *Phi Delta Kappan*, and the *Journal of Creative Behavior*.

MICHAEL A. CAMPION, completed his undergraduate work at the University of Minnesota. He received his master's degree from St. Thomas College, and his Ph.D. in counseling psychology from the University of Illinois. He is the author of several books and numerous magazine articles, and also writes a weekly newspaper column. Campion is a psychologist in private practice, and his firm has offices in Illinois and Indiana.

CATHERINE S. CHILMAN, Professor at the School of Social Welfare, University of Wisconsin — Milwaukee, has her M.A. in social work from the University of Chicago, and Ph.D. in psychology from Syracuse University. A widow, she has three daughters and six grandchildren. Her work experience includes teaching and research in the field of the family at various universities plus family-related research and publication within the federal government during the 1960s. Her books include *Growing Up Poor, Your Child from 6–12*, and *Adolescent Sexuality in a Changing American Society: Social and Psychological Perspectives for the Human Services Professions*. She has also published chapters in many other scholarly books and journals and has served as a consultant to numerous government agencies and universities.

JERRY FALWELL currently serves as founder and Chancellor of Liberty Baptist Schools. His awards include a 1981 Food for the Hungry International and Christian Humanitarian of the Year. In 1979 he was elected Clergyman of the Year by the Religious Heritage of America. He received his degree of theology at the Baptist Bible College in Springfield, Missouri. He also received degrees at the California Graduate School of Theology and Central University of Seoul, Korea. He is the father of three children: Jerry Jr., Jeannie, and Jonathan.

HAROLD FELDMAN is currently Professor Emeritus at Cornell University in the Department of Human Development and Family Studies. Feldman has a master's degree in social work from the University of Minnesota and a Ph.D. in clinical and social psychology from the University of Michigan. He has been Principal Investigator of many research projects including studies on the development of the husband-wife relationship, the welfare woman's employment and her family, the filial obligation, and parents' rights. His major research focus has been on people who've "made it," and Feldman has summarized this research in a monograph.

Feldman has taught courses in the family, human sexuality, personal counseling, and on the human male, among many others. He has taught in the Women's Studies Program at Cornell University since the program's beginning. Currently he is teaching a new course called "The Development of the Adult Filial Relationship."

Feldman has also served on many committees and councils. He has worked with the White House Conference on Aging, the U.S. Select Committee on Aging, and the National Council on Aging. He has been President, Program Chairman, and Member of the Board of Directors of the Groves Conference on Marriage and the Family. He has been on the Board and Executive Committee of the National Council on Family Relations, and was Chairman of a committee called the Post Meeting Implementation Conference. He has just been elected as Secretary of the National Council.

JEANNINE GRAMICK has been a Roman Catholic nun of the Congregation of the School Sisters of Notre Dame since 1960. A Ph.D. in Education from the University of Pennsylvania, she has taught in junior and senior high schools and was an Assistant Professor of Mathematics at the College of Notre Dame of Maryland, the University of Maryland, and the University of California at Los Angeles. In 1977 she became a Cofounder and Codirector of New Ways Ministry, a social justice center working for reconciliation for sexual minorities and the churches. Her recent book is entitled *Homosexuality and the Catholic Church* (Thomas More Press, 1983). As a member of the national board and executive committee of the National Assembly of Religious Women, Jeannine Gramick is strongly committed to social justice and the issues affecting women in church and society.

VIRGINIA A. HEFFERNAN received her M.A. in sociology from Catholic University of America in 1972. For the past few years, she has conducted sexuality education workshops in Catholic parishes in the Washington, D.C., area and other parts of the U.S. and Canada. Immediately prior to this work, she was Program Director for the National Council of Catholic Women. For over 20 years, Mrs. Heffernan has been engaged in Catholic marriage work, both as a volunteer and as a professional. Her writing has appeared in Catholic publications such as *America*, *Marriage Encounter*, and

Communio. She was a member of the National Council on Family Relations and of the Groves Conference on Marriage and the Family. Currently, she is a theology student at the Washington Theological Union, a Roman Catholic seminary. The procreative principle is operative — the Heffernans have five children and two grandchildren.

EDWARD L. KAIN is an Assistant Professor in the Department of Human Development and Family Studies at Cornell University. He received his B.A. in sociology and religion from Alma College, Michigan, in 1976. His Ph.D. in sociology was completed in 1980 at the University of North Carolina at Chapel Hill. Social change and families forms the core of his research interests. His previous work has included examinations of the never-married in the United States, changing images of men and women in advertising, and attitudes of rural women toward changing work and family roles. Currently he is working on two projects. The first examines marital status and mental health in New York State; and the second uses national survey data to look at changes in attitudes over the past decade about a variety of family issues, including abortion, homosexuality, and interracial marriage.

NOEL P. KEANE received his B.S. from Eastern Michigan University and his J.D. from University of Detroit Law School. He is the author of *The Surrogate Mother* (Everest House), as well as "Legal Problems of Surrogate Motherhood" *(Southern Illinois University Law Journal)*, "Surrogate Motherhood: Past, Present and Future" (prepared for the Committee on Ethics, Humanism and Medicine), and "The Surrogate Parenting Contract" (presented at the annual conference of the Association of Family and Conciliation Courts, Toronto, 1983). He has been involved in surrogate parenting since 1975, with clients in Chile, Australia, Italy, England, Germany, Greece, Canada, and the United States. Noel is an Irish Catholic. He and his wife Kathryn have two children: Christopher, age 16, and Douglas, age 12.

GRACE KETTERMAN was born in 1926 in Central Kansas near Newton. One of seven children, she spent most of her childhood on a Kansas farm. In 1948 she finished pre-med at the University of Kansas and finished medical school there in 1952. She served as a pediatrician for many years and then began study in child psychiatry. This interest led to her acceptance of the directorship of a Florence Crittenton Maternity Home in 1967. Four years later, feeling the pressure of the needs from her own children and family, she left the home and began to invest her time and efforts into the local agency to help it extend its services from help for the unwed mother to a remarkably effective psychiatric treatment center for children and adolescents. She serves as Medical Director today with services being provided for 130 young people. She has authored several books and is currently working on two more. She lectures quite extensively and has a five-minute radio program called "You and Your Child" that is now aired on over 140 stations.

JOHN A. W. KIRSCH is currently Associate Professor of Biology, Department of Biology, and Associate Curator in Mammalogy, Museum of Comparative Zoology, Harvard University. He was born in Oswego, in 1941. He received his B.S. in biology at Wagner College, Staten Island; his Ph.D. in zoology, at the University of Western Australia; and completed two years of postdoctoral work at the University of Kansas. He has done extensive work in research with tobacco and bean genetics, ecology of insular and mainland marsupial populations, physicological ecology of marsupials, and fieldwork in Nicaragua, South America, Chile, and Argentina. He is a member of numerous societies including the AAAS, American Society of Mammalogists, American Society of Plant Taxonomists, and Society of Systematic Zoology. He has been active in teaching at Yale and Harvard from 1973 to 1979. Dr. Kirsch is author of many articles and is currently working on a number of books: *The Natural History of Marsupials* (coauthored with M. Renfree); *Taxonomic Theory and Practice* (coauthored with J. E. Rodman); and *Handguide to the Mammals of Australia* (coauthored with F. Knight).

JUDY LONG is an Associate Professor of Sociology at Syracuse University. She received her education at the University of Michigan in Ann Arbor and her undergraduate work in Radcliffe College in Massachusetts. She has taught as an Assistant Professor of Sociology at Cornell University as well as an Assistant Professor of

Psychology at Cornell. Dr. Long has done consulting for General Motors, the National Institute for the Aging, and the United States Commission on Civil Rights. She has coauthored with Pepper Schwartz *Sexual Scripts: The Social Construction of Female Sexuality* (Dryden Press, 1977) and is the author of *The Second X: Sex Role and Social Role* (Elsevier, 1979). She has been published in several books and has written a series of articles on topics of psychology and the dimension of women's work force participation.

JO ANN M. MAGDOFF received her Ph.D. from Princeton University in 1977 in anthropology. From 1977 to 1979 she was a Special Candidate at the Columbia University's Center for Psychoanalytic Training and Research, studying psychoanalytic theory and technique. While at Columbia, she was an editor of the Columbia Psychoanalytic Bulletin. After several years of university teaching and research, Dr. Magdoff decided to devote herself full-time to a private practice in psychotherapy. She completed further training in marriage and family therapy, and has been elected to the board of the New York Association of Marriage and Family Therapists. She is also a contributor to the New York Association's Newsletter. Dr. Magdoff is currently engaged in research on the parent-child dyad and on theory and practice in treating depression. In addition to writing on aspects of psychotherapy, she has published papers on symbolic analysis.

DAVID MARCOTTE was born in 1936 in Bloomfield, New Jersey. He is married and the father of five. His internship was completed at Mary Hitchcock Memorial Hospital in New Hampshire, and his residence at Chapel Hill, North Carolina. From 1970 to 1973 he was involved in the study of psychoanalysis at Medical University of Southern Carolina, Charleston. Currently he is Staff Psychiatrist at Dorthea Dix Hospital. Dr. Marcotte has published numerous articles in several medical journals, ranging in subject from "Sexuality in the 80's" to "Physicians' Identification and Treatment of Victims of Physical Abuse." His presentation topics include "Heterosexuality in Our Culture," "Sex Education in Medical Education: Impact and Implications," and "Sexual History Taking and Sensitivity."

JOSH McDOWELL is an author and traveling lecturer. A graduate of Wheaton College, a magna cum laude graduate of Talbot Theological Seminary, and a member of two national honor societies, he has authored seven best-selling books. He has lectured at more than 580 universities in 58 countries. Some of his most popular lectures present a biblical perspective on human sexuality. He also serves on the faculty of the International School of Theology.

ANDREA PARROT is a lecturer in the Department of Human Service Studies in the College of Human Ecology at Cornell University. Courses she teaches include Human Sexuality, The Ecology and Epidemiology of Health, Health Care and the Consumer, Teaching Human Sexuality in Community and School Settings, and Sexual Concerns and Health Problems of the Adolescent. Andrea received her B.S. from SUNY, Plattsburgh, her M.S. from SUNY, Albany, and her Ph.D. from Cornell University. She has taught at Cornell for three years; she has been a secondary school teacher, director of a teenage mother program, and a consultant to Wadsworth and John Wiley publishing companies and Sunburst Corporation. She has published in the areas of teenage pregnancy, sex role stereotyping, human sexuality, and techniques for teaching human sexuality. She is also involved in research on acquaintance rape and sexual assault among college students.

BRUCE RAU was born in 1947 in St. Louis, Missouri. He completed his education in Purdue University, University of Missouri Medical School, and his residence in Psychiatry, Vanderbilt University, Tennessee. He is currently Medical Director of Mandala Center, Inc. in Winston-Salem, N. C. He has served as Chief of Staff, and Staff Psychiatist in the years 1978 to date. He has published an article entitled, "Voodoo in the General Hospital: A Case of Hexing and Regional Enteritis" in the *Journal of the American Medical Association* (1975). He chairs several professional committees including Professional Activities Committee, Nursing Care, Library Sub-committee, Executive Committee of Medical Staff.

GEORGE A. REKERS is presently Professor and previously Head of the Department of Family and Child Development at Kansas State University. He serves as Chairman of the Family Research Council of America. He received his Ph.D. in psychology from UCLA and was previously a Visiting Scholar at Harvard University and Chief Psychologist and Associate Professor in Psychiatry at the University of Florida. He is the author of *Shaping Your Child's Sexual Identity* (Baker, 1982), and *Growing Up Straight* (Moody, 1982), and coauthor of *The Christian in an Age of Sexual Eclipse* (Tyndale, 1981) and over 50 journal articles and book chapters.

RUSTUM ROY is currently a faculty person at the Pennsylvania State University. He serves as Chairman of the Science, Technology and Society Program at the same university. He has been significantly involved in numerous committee reports across the world: Characterization of Materials in Washington, D.C.; Ceramics Processing in Washington, D.C.; Science, Technology and the Church in New York; Mineral Science and Technology: Needs, Challenges and Opportunities in Washington, D.C.; and Equilibria and Kinetics in Modern Ceramic Processing in Tokyo, Japan. Roy has published articles in *Chemical and Engineering News, Science*, the *Hindustan Times*, and the *AAAS Science Education News*. He has also written numerous articles on theology, ethics, and values.

WALTER R. SCHUMM is Assistant Professor of Family and Child Development at Kansas State University. He received his Ph.D. in family studies in 1979 from Purdue University and has since published over 30 articles and book chapters.

LAURA J. SINGER is President and founder of "SAM" — Save a Marriage, Inc. — and Interpersonal Development Institute, Inc. A practicing psychotherapist her special interests are in marital and family therapy. She is a Fellow and Past President of the American Association For Marriage and Family Therapy. Formerly an Adjunct Associate Professor at Columbia University's Teacher's College, Dr. Singer has been a visiting faculty member at the New School and is a fellow and faculty member of the American Institute for Psychotherapy and Psychoanalysis. She is a Consulting Editor for the *Journal of Sex and Marital Therapy,* and is the coauthor of "Sex Education on Film," and *Stages — The Crises That Shape Your Marriage.* Dr. Singer was the host of *Living Together,* a television series on marital therapy, and has been a guest panelist on radio and television news and public affairs programs. Her current research is on marital relationships between therapists and their spouses.

JOHN STEINBACHER was from 1967 to 1977 one of America's best known newsmen. In 1972 and 1973 he won the Journalist of the Year award from We the People, and his biography appears in such notable publications as *Who's Who in the West, Notable Americans,* and *Men of Distinction.* His undergraduate studies were at Pacific University in Oregon; he has done graduate work at UCLA, Sacramento State, San Francisco Theological Seminary, Long Beach State, and USC. Steinbacher has served as a social worker and has taught in both public and private schools. He was a special investigator for the Congressional Investigation of the Aid to Children program. He is the author of a number of books, including *Bitter Harvest, The Child Seducers, Wayfarers of Fate, An Inward Stillness,* and *An Inward Healing.* He is the founder and Executive Director of the Cancer Federation, located in Riverside, California.

ED WHEAT is a family physician and surgeon in Springdale, Arkansas, and is a recognized authority on premarriage and marriage counseling. As a certified sex therapist, he sees patients from all parts of the United States. He has authored two books: *Intended for Pleasure* (Revell, 1981)—considered the standard reference manual on sex from the Christian perspective—and *Love-Life: For Every Married Couple* (Zondervan, 1980), named one of the five best contemporary Christian books of the year. His books and counseling cassette albums have been translated into Chinese, Japanese, Spanish, Dutch, and German, and are used by counselors worldwide. Dr. Wheat presents seminars at large churches and colleges and has appeared on numerous television and radio programs in this country and Canada. He has served as Guest Lecturer in the Department of Psychiatry at the University of Arkansas School of Medicine and at Dallas Theological Seminary. He is founder of Bible Believers Cassettes, Inc., which makes thousands of counseling cassettes on marriage and the family available to the public on free loan. He and his wife, Gaye, have three married daughters and four grandchildren.

Some questions posed in **Human Sexuality:**

Should couples test their sexual compatability before they decide to get married? Is procreation the primary purpose of intercourse? Has the women's movement produced a "male crisis"? Why are nonmonogamous acts viewed as harmful to the health of society? To protect individuals and society, should certain forms of sexual expression be outlawed? Should there be laws to govern who should have children? Is homosexuality or bisexuality more biologically natural than heterosexuality? Can morality be legislated? Could the media play a responsible role in sex education? If both therapist and client are consenting adults, is intercourse between them wrong? What rights should a surrogate mother have with respect to the child after it is born? What is the "Ken and Barbie" syndrome? Should marital rape be legally defined? What are the pros and cons of sexual relationships that involve neither affection nor commitment?

SAGE PUBLICATIONS
The Publishers of Professional Social Science
Beverly Hills London New Delhi